Metaphor & Memory

Metaphor & Memory

ESSAYS

Cynthia Ozick

1 9 89

Alfred A. Knopf   New York

THIS IS A BORZOI BOOK
PUBLISHED BY ALFRED A. KNOPF, INC.

Copyright © 1980, 1983, 1984, 1985, 1986, 1987, 1988, 1989 by Cynthia Ozick

All rights reserved under International and Pan-American Copyright Conventions.
Published in the United States by Alfred A. Knopf, Inc., New York,
and simultaneously in Canada by Random House of Canada Limited, Toronto.
Distributed by Random House, Inc., New York.

Owing to limitations of space, all acknowledgments for permission to reprint
previously published material can be found on page 285.

Library of Congress Cataloging-in-Publication Data
Ozick, Cynthia.
Metaphor & memory.
I. Title.   II. Title: Metaphor and memory.
PS3565.Z5M44   1989   809   88-45769
ISBN 0-394-54701-2

Manufactured in the United States of America
First Edition

FOR

YUDEL AND GNESHA

Contents

Forewarning

Here is a late learning: a fiction writer who also writes essays is looking for trouble. While stories and novels under the eye of a good reader are permitted to bask in the light of the free imagination, essays are held to a sterner standard. No good reader of fiction will suppose that a character's ideas and emotions are consistently, necessarily, inevitably, the writer's ideas and emotions; but most good readers of essays unfailingly trust the veracity of non-narrative prose. A story is known to reflect in its "attitudes" the concrete particularities of its invention; every story is its own idiosyncratic occasion, and each occasion governs tone, point of view, conclusion. A story, in brief, is regarded as an ad hoc contrivance, and if it is called as witness, it is in the court of the conditional, the subjective, the provisional, even the lyrical.

An essay, by contrast, is almost always hauled before the most sobersided court of all, presided over by judges who will scrutinize the evidence for true belief: absolute and permanent congruence of the writer and what is on the page. An essay is rarely seen to be a bewitched contraption in the way of a story. An essayist is generally assumed to be a reliable witness, sermonizer, lecturer, polemicist, persuader, historian, advocate: a committed intelligence, a single-minded truth-speaker.

But when a writer writes both stories and essays, something else can happen: the essays will too often be forced into a tailoring job for which they were never intended. The essays, like chalk marks, are used to take the measure of the stories. The essays become the stories' interpreters: their clues, or cues, or concordances, as if the premises of the essays were incontrovertibly the premises of the stories as well. As if the stories were "illustrations" of the essays; as if the essays expressed the ideational (or even at times the ideological) matrix of the stories.

All these notions are, I am afraid, plain foolishness. They imagine that there is a commanding difference between essays and stories, and that the difference is pure: essays are "honest" and stories are made up. The reality is otherwise: all good stories are honest and most good essays are not. Stories, when they succeed *as* stories, tend to be honest even when they concern themselves with fraudulence, or especially then (Tolstoy's *The Death of Ivan Ilych* comes instantly to mind); stories are moods—illuminations—that last in their original form. A new story will hardly contradict a prior one: each has worked for, and argued, its own embodiment, its own consummation. Stories are understood to represent desire, or conviction, at its most mercurial. Originality, in fiction, *means* mercurial. Nobody wants all the stories a writer produces to resemble one another, to conform to a predictable line. The truth of one story is not implicated in the truth of the next.

But essays are expected to take a "position," to show a consistency of temperament, a stability of viewpoint. Essays are expected to make the writer's case. Sometimes, of course, they do; I feel fairly sure the book reviews in this volume incorporate judgments that time and temper will not seriously alter. Yet most essays, like stories, are not designed to stand still in this way. A story is a hypothesis, a tryout of human nature under the impingement of certain given materials; so is an essay. After which, the mind moves on. Nearly every essay, like every story, is an experiment, not a credo.

Or, to put it more stringently: an essay, like a story or a novel, is a fiction. A fiction, by definition, is that which is made up in response to an excited imagination. What is fictitious about the essay is that it is pretending not to be made up—so that reading an essay may be more dangerous than reading a story. This very foreword, for instance, may count as a little essay: ought it to be trusted? (Remember the Cretan captured by Greeks. Questioned, he replied: "All Cretans are liars." Was this a truthful confession, or only another sample of a Cretan lying? After all, even Tolstoy, whom we think of as the quintessential novelist, was a kind of Cretan. First he wrote *Anna Karenina*; then he wrote "What Is Art?"—condemning the writing of novels. Which Tolstoy should we believe?)

The point is not that essays are untrustworthy. Obviously, an essay will fail if it is not intellectually coherent, if it does not strike you as authentic (ideas must be earned, not merely learned), if it is not felt to be reliably truth-telling. An essay must show all these indispensable signs of consonance and conscience—but only for the duration of its reading, or a bit longer. If its "authenticity" is compelled to last much beyond that, the reader will be tying the writer down by small stakes and long strings, like Gulliver; and no essayist (except maybe a Gibbon or a Montaigne—certainly no contemporary essayist) is as big as that. In other words, if a writer of stories is also a writer of essays, the essays ought not to be seized as a rod to beat the writer's stories with; or as a frame into which to squeeze the writer's stories; or, collectively, as a "philosophy" into which to pen the writer's outlook.

Does all this mean that virtually no essay can have an enduring probity? Well, if a story can be empowered with constancy and incorruptibility, so can an essay; but only in the same way, contingent on its immanent logic or marrow-song. No story, and no essay, has the practical capacity to act itself out in the world; or ought to. All the same, if it seems that I am denying plausible truth-telling to the essays in this book, or that I don't want them to represent me, it isn't so: each, little or long, was pressed out in a mania of (ad hoc, occasional, circumstantial) conviction: the juncture—as in any fiction—of predicament and nerve. The essays herein do represent me: didn't I tackle them, shouldn't I "take responsibility" for them, whatever unease (or even alienation) they may cause me afterward? What I *am* repudiating, though, is the inference that a handful of essays is equal to a *Weltanschauung*; that an essay is generally anything more than simply another fiction—a short story told in the form of an argument, or a history, or even (once in a very great while) an illumination. But never a tenet.

C.O.

April 17, 1988

Metaphor & Memory

Cyril Connolly and the Groans of Success

I first came on a paperback reprint of Cyril Connolly's *Enemies of Promise* when I was already in my despairing middle thirties. Though I had been writing steadily and obsessively since the age of twenty-two, I was still mainly unpublished: a handful of poems, a couple of short stories, a single essay, and all in quirky little magazines printed, it seemed, in invisible ink. Connolly's stringent dissertation on the anatomy of failure had a morbid attraction for me: it was like looking up one's disease in the *Merck Manual*—I knew the symptoms, and it was a wound I was interested in. One day I urgently pressed my copy of Connolly on another failed writer a whole decade younger than myself; we were both teaching freshman composition at the time. He promised to read it; instead he hurried off into analysis and gay pride. I never saw the book again. My ex-colleague has, so far, never published. *Enemies of Promise* went out of print.

After that, I remembered it chiefly as a dictionary of low spirits; even as a secret autobiography. Over the years one of its interior

Published in *The New Criterion*, March 1984

3

titles—"The Charlock's Shade"—stayed with me, a mysterious phrase giving off old mournful fumes: the marsh gas writers inhale when they are not getting published, when they begin to accept themselves as having been passed by, when envy's pinch is constant and certain, when the lurch of humiliation learns to precede the predictable rebuff. Writers who publish early and regularly not only are spared these hollow desolations, but acquire habits of strength and self-confidence. Henry James, George Sand, Balzac, Mann: these amazingly prolific presences achieved as much as they did not simply because they began young, but because they were permitted to begin young. James in America started off with book reviews; so, in London, did Virginia Woolf.

But in my despairing thirties it was hardly these colossi of literary history I was fixed on. All around me writers five years older and five years younger were having their second and third novels published, establishing their idiosyncratic and intractable voices, and flourishing, sometimes with the left hand, this and that indomitable essay: Mailer's "The White Negro," Sontag's "Notes on Camp," Roth's "Writing American Fiction," Baldwin's "The Fire Next Time," Styron's reply to the critics of *Nat Turner*, and so on. John Updike, the paramount American instance of early publication, conquered *The New Yorker* in his twenties, undertaking even then the body of reviewing that nowadays rivals the amplitude and weight and attentiveness of Edmund Wilson's. At about the same time, in the New Rochelle Public Library, I pulled down from a high shelf of the New Books section a first volume of stories called *By the North Gate*. The author was an unknown writer ten years my junior; not long afterward, the name Joyce Carol Oates accelerated into a ubiquitous force. A good while before that, in college, I had known someone who knew Truman Capote; and Capote had published in magazines before he was twenty.

In short, these were the Famous of my generation, and could be read, and read about, and mulled over, and discussed. They were—or anyhow they embodied, they were shot through with —the Issues; and meanwhile I was a suffering onlooker, shut out. I could not even say that I was being ignored—to be ignored you have first to be published. A hundred periodicals, both renowned and "little," sent me packing. An editor who later went to Hollywood to write *Superman* led me into his *Esquire* cubicle to turn back a piece of fiction with the hard-hearted charm of indifference; he looked like someone's baby brother. Another day I stood on the threshold of the office of the *New York Review of Books*, a diffident inquirer of thirty-five, and was shooed away by a word thrown out from a distant desk; I had come to ask for a review to write. *Partisan, Kenyon, Sewanee, American Scholar, Quarterly Review, Furioso*, dozens of others, declined my submissions. An editor of a small Michigan periodical, a poet, wrote to remark that I "had yet to find a voice." In New York, a respected reader at a well-known publishing house, having in hand three quarters of my novel, said it wouldn't do, and rocked me into a paralysis of hopelessness lasting nearly a year. And all the while I was getting older and older. Envy of the published ate at me; so did the shame of so much nibbling defeat. Twenty years of print-lust, muscular ambition, driving inquisitiveness, and all the rest, were lost in the hurt crawl away from the locked door. I wrote, and read, and filled volumes of Woolworth diaries with the outcry of failure— the failure to enter the gates of one's own literary generation, the anguish of exclusion from its argument and tone, its experience and evolution. It wasn't that I altogether doubted my "powers" (though often enough I did, profoundly, stung by disgrace); I saw them, whatever they were, scorned, disparaged, set outside the pale of welcome. I was ashamed of my life, and I lived only to read and write. I lived for nothing else; I had no other "goals," "motivations," "interests"—these shallownesses pointing to what the babblers of the hour call psychological health. Nor was it raw Fame I was after; I was not deluded that publishing a first novel at twenty-five, as Mann had done, would guarantee a *Buddenbrooks*.

What I wanted was access to the narrowest possibilities of my own time and prime; I wanted to bore a chink. I wanted a sliver of the apron of a literary platform. I wanted to use what I was, to be what I was born to be—not to have a "career," but to be that straightforward obvious unmistakable animal, a writer. I was a haunted punctuator, possessed stylist, sorter of ideas, burrower into history, philosophy, criticism; I wrote midnight poetry into the morning light; I burnished the sentences of my prose so that each might stand, I said (with the arrogance of the desperately humiliated), for twenty years. And no one would publish me.

For this predicament, it was clear, I needed not an anodyne, but salt—merciless salt. Connolly not only supplied the salt, he opened the wounds, gave names to their mouths, and rubbed in the salt. He analyzed—or so it appeared—all the venoms of failure. He spoke, in a kind of metaphoric delirium borrowed from Crabbe, of "the blighted rye," "the slimy mallow," "the wither'd ears"— all those hideous signs of poison and decomposition from which the suffocated writer, kept from the oxygen of the age, deprived of print, slowly dies. There was no victory crow to be had from reading Connolly. If he provoked any sound at all, it was the dry cough that comes with panic at the dawn's early light.

This, at least, is how, all these years, I have kept *Enemies of Promise* in my head: as a mop and sop for the long, long bleeding, the intellectual slights, the disgraced imagination, the locked doors, the enervating growths of the literary swamp, the dry cough of abandonment. The rest I seem to have forgotten, or never to have noticed at all, and now that the book is once again on the scene, and again in paperback, I observe that it is a tripartite volume, and that, distracted by what I believed to be its diagnostic powers, I missed two thirds of its substance. What I once saw as a pillar of salt turns out to be, in fact, a puff of spun sugar. And this is not because I have "gotten over" the pounding of denigration and rejection; I have never properly recuperated from them, and on their account resent the white hairs of middle age with a spite-fulness and absurdity appropriate only to the hungry young.

"*Enemies of Promise* was first published in 1938," Cyril Connolly's 1948 Introduction begins, "as a didactic enquiry into the problem of how to write a book which lasts ten years." Yet the question of literary longevity is raised and almost instantly dropped; that this particular book has now "lasted" more than four decades is hardly the answer. And I am not sure it *has* lasted, at least in the form it claims, i.e., as an essay about certain ideas. It hangs on instead as a curiosity, which does not mean it is wholly obsolete; it is only peculiar. Even in organization there is peculiarity: a trinity that does not immediately cohere. The first section divides prose style into Mandarin (a term Connolly takes credit for coining in this context) and vernacular; surely this issue is with us as bemusedly as ever. The second section—"The Charlock's Shade," which so fed my gripes and twinges—now looks to be not so much about failure as about success and its distractions. The third part, finally, is a memoir of Connolly's childhood in a boarding school for the rich called St. Wulfric's, and afterward at Eton. In my zealously partial reading long ago, though I was attracted by Connolly's definitions of Mandarin and vernacular diction, it appears I never took in the autobiographical segment at all; and what drew me to "The Charlock's Shade" (or so it now strikes me) was three lone sentences, as follows:

> Promise is like the mediaeval hangman who after settling the noose, pushed his victim off the platform and jumped on his back, his weight acting as a drop while his jockeying arms prevented the unfortunate from loosening the rope.

> Sloth in writers is always a symptom of an acute inner conflict, especially that laziness which renders them incapable of doing the thing which they are most looking forward to.

> Perfectionists are notoriously lazy and all true artistic indolence is deeply neurotic; a pain not a pleasure.

Here, and only here, was the poisonous wisdom that served my travail. All the rest supposed a sophistication and advancement that meant nothing to a writer who had barely begun, and Connolly's classifications of dangers hardly applied. To succeed as a writer, he admonished, beware of journalism, politics, "escapism," sex, and success itself. Journalism: never write "a review that cannot be reprinted, i.e. that is not of some length and on a subject

of permanent value." Politics: once the writer "has a moment of
conviction that his future is bound up with the working classes
. . . his behaviour will inevitably alter"—in other words, he will
be much improved. "Escapism": drink, drugs, talk, daydreaming,
religion, sloth. Sex: hazards of homosexuality, domesticity, babies,
wives. And, aha, success: here the peril lies in getting taken up
by the upper crust, according to E. M. Forster's dictum as cited
by Connolly: "To be aristocratic in Art one must avoid polite
society." But how could any of these cautionary alarms have mattered to a writer who had for years gone altogether unnoticed?
Speaking for myself: I never thought about politics. Journalism
was something less than a snare, since no one would offer me so
much as a five-hundred-word review. I was in no danger of becoming a fad or a celebrity. I didn't drink or shoot up. I confined
religion to philosophical reading, and daydreaming to a diary. I
had no baby and no wife. (Connolly, though he mentions Virginia
Woolf among the Mandarins, has an ineradicable difficulty in pos-
iting a writer who is not male. This is a pity, because the writer's
husband is a worthy, perplexing, and often tragic subject.) Even
talk was no drain; what went up into air for others, I mainly put
down in letters to literary friends—letters, those vessels of calculated permanence. Then what in Connolly could possibly appeal
to the untried and the buried? In his infinite catalogues of "promise" and its risks, only the terrors of perfectionism and the pain of
sure decline had the least psychological concurrence. For the sake
of this pins-in-the-ribs pair, Connolly stuck.

He begins now to unstick. "It was Edmund Wilson who remarked that [*Enemies of Promise*] was not a very well-written book,"
Connolly confesses. Wilson was right. Connolly is a ragged writer,
unraveling his rags behind him as he goes, and capable of awful
sentences. If Wilson recoiled from some of them, it might have
been in part on account of Connolly's description of Wilson's own
Axel's Castle, which, we are reminded, "includes essays on Yeats,
Valéry, Eliot, Proust, Joyce and Gertrude Stein. His summing
up," Connolly continues in a typically unpunctuated long breath,
"is against them, in so far as it is against their cult of the individual

which he feels they have carried to such lengths as to exhaust it for a long time to come but it is a summing up which also states everything that can be said in their favour when allowance for what I have termed 'inflation' is made." (Observe that the style is neither Mandarin nor vernacular, but Rattling Boxcars.)

Patches of this sort might unglue any essayist, but there is something beyond mere prose at stake. Did Connolly notice that his so-called enemies of promise were in reality the appurtenances of certain already-achieved successes? The warning that journalism threatens art applies, after all, only to fairly established writers long familiar with the practice of getting paid for writing. "He is apt to have a private income, he renews himself by travel," Connolly says of the homosexual writer, assuming long-standing privilege and money. A successful wife, he remarks, not only is "intelligent and unselfish enough to understand and respect the working of the unfriendly cycle of the creative imagination," but "will recognize that there is no more sombre enemy of good art than the pram in the hall." And of course: "Of all the enemies of literature, success is the most insidious."

Does failure ever appear at all in *Enemies of Promise*—the word or the idea? Once. "Failure is a poison like success. Where a choice is offered, prefer the alkaline," and that is all. Such sentiments burn rather than salve. And even while cautioning against the "especial intimacies" of the fashionable, Connolly has a good word for them: "It must be remembered that in fashionable society can be found warmhearted people of delicate sensibility who form permanent friendships with artists which afford them ease and encouragement for the rest of their lives and provide them with sanctuary." And in defense of the seductions of wealth not one's own: "It is because we envy [social success] more than other success that we denounce it so often," Connolly explains. He himself does not denounce the ingratiation of writers with the rich so much as their ingratiation with one another:

> There is a kind of behaviour which is particularly dangerous on the
> moving staircase—the attempt to ascend it in groups of four or five

who lend a hand to each other and dislodge other climbers from the steps. It is natural that writers should make friends with their contemporaries of talent and express a mutual admiration but it leads inevitably to a succession of services rendered and however much the writers who help each other may deserve it, if they too frequently proclaim their gratitude they will arouse the envy of those who stand on their own feet, who succeed without collaboration. Words like "log-rolling" and "back-scratching" are soon whispered and the death-watch ticks the louder.

The death-watch? If there is any warning being rattled in all this, surely it must compete with the complicit wink of the sound counselor. A denunciation, one might say, that has the look of a paragraph in a handbook on the wherewithal of success. And a wherewithal that, at a particular rung of society, is affable enough: the comfortable network of class and school associations.

It is the moment for bluntness. *Enemies of Promise* is an essay—according to the usual English conventions of the early part of the twentieth century—about class and modishness. It has almost no other subject important to Connolly. There are digressions on, say, age, that are nearly worthwhile—more worthwhile when the aperçu is not Connolly's own (though the syntax is): "Butler said an author should write only for people between twenty and thirty as nobody read or changed their opinions after that." There is much recognizable humanity in this, whereas Connolly, attempting to generalize in his own voice, manages mainly a self-indulgent turn: "The shock, for an intelligent writer, of discovering for the first time that there are people younger than himself who think him stupid is severe." Or: "It would seem that genius is of two kinds, one of which blazes up in youth and dies down, while the other matures, like Milton's or Goethe's. . . . The artist has to decide on the nature of his own or he may find himself exhausted by the sprint of youth and unfitted for the marathon of middle age." As if one could choose to be Milton or Goethe merely by deciding, as Connolly advises, to "become a stayer." Modishness dominates: the notion of likely styles in will, the short-length will and the longer-range.

Modishness rules especially in the politics. Writing in 1948 (the famous year of Orwell's *Nineteen Eighty-Four*), Connolly suggests that he has "retained all the engagingly simple left-wing militancy [of 1938] since it breathes the air of the period." True enough: ten years after its composition, Connolly is offering us *Enemies of Promise* frankly as a period piece. But the point of the exercise, we are bound to remember, is that ten years after its composition he is also offering it as a successful instance of "how to write a book which lasts ten years." Are we to conclude, then, that the more a book is dated, the longer its chances of survival? A remarkable hypothesis. No, it won't wash, this period-piece candor: Connolly had no wish to revise or update or tone down the "left-wing militancy" (less "engaging," forty-five years later, and in an age of left-linked terrorism, than he might have supposed); perhaps it was only "artistic indolence." Or perhaps it was because of an intuition about his own character and its style: a certain seamlessness, the absence of self-contradiction. Connolly is always on the side of his own class, never more so than in his expression of "left-wing militancy." It is not that Connolly, in 1938, is mistaken when he declares that "today the forces of life and progress are ranging on one side, those of reaction and death on the other," or that "fascism is the enemy of art," or that "we are not dealing with an Augustus who will discover his Horace and his Virgil, but with Attila or Hulaku, destroyers of European culture whose poets can contribute only battle-cries and sentimental drinking songs." He means Hitler: but the very next year, in 1939, the year of the Hitler-Stalin pact, would he have been willing to mean Stalin too? "The poet is a chemist and there is more pure revolutionary propaganda in a line of Blake than in all *The Rights of Man*," he asserts: a sophistry that can only be the flower of an elitist education. In 1938 what literary intellectual was not moved by the word "revolutionary"?

Nothing, in fact, is less dated than the combination of Connolly's elitism and his attraction to revolutionary militancy. Any superficial excursion into universities in Western Europe and the United States currently bears this out, nowhere more vividly than in

American elitist departments, history, literature, and political science especially. All this is a cliché of our predicament as it was of Connolly's. "The atmosphere of orthodoxy is always damaging to prose," Orwell wrote in *Inside the Whale*, and here is Connolly as prooftext: "Often [solidarity with the working classes] will be recognized only by external symptoms, a disinclination to wear a hat or a stiff collar, an inability to be rude to waiters or taxi-drivers or to be polite to young men of his own age with rolled umbrellas, bowler hats and 'Mayfair men' moustaches or to tolerate the repressive measures of his class." This wizened sentence may be worth the belly laugh due anachronism, but its undigested spirit lingers on. For "disinclination to wear a hat" substitute an earnest inclination to wear Che boots. And "the repressive measures of his class" is as bruisingly trite and vacuous as any bright young Ivy graduate's assault on the American bourgeoisie, of which he or she is the consummate product.

The consummate product of his class. Should Connolly be blamed for this? Probably. Orwell went to the same schools at the same time, Eton preceded by St. Cyprian's (St. Wulfric's in Connolly's genial account, Crossgates in Orwell's lugubrious one), and saw straight through what Connolly thrived on. Orwell despised the tyrant-goddess who ruled over St. Cyprian's; Connolly maneuvered to get on her good side. And of Eton Connolly writes (in the ardently arrested parochial tone of one of the "bloody-minded people at the top"), "My last two years of Eton . . . were among the most interesting and rewarding of my whole life and I do not believe they could have been so at any other public school or in any other house than College." The allusion is to school elections; Connolly was, we learn, an ecstatic member of the exclusive "Pop," which he counts, along with romantic homoerotic adolescence, among those "experiences undergone by boys at the great public schools . . . so intense as to dominate their lives." Orwell, reviewing *Enemies of Promise* soon after its appearance, hoots: "He means it!" And sums up the politics of those cosseted few who, between 1910 and 1920, after "five years in a lukewarm bath of snobbery," have fabricated sympathies they have no way of feeling: "Hunger, hardship, solitude, exile, war, prison, persecution, manual labor—hardly even words. No wonder," Orwell charges, "that the huge tribe known as 'the right left people' found it so easy to condone the purge-and-Ogpu side of the Russian régime and the horrors of the First Five Year Plan. They were so gloriously incapable of understanding what it all meant."

Nothing in his brief 1948 introductory note to *Enemies of Promise* tells us whether Connolly did or did not remain one of the right left people a decade later. "We grow up among theories and illusions common to our class, our race, our time," Connolly opens his schooldays memoir, but only as a frame for the apology that follows: "I have to refer to something which I find intolerable, the early aura of large houses, fallen fortunes and county families common to so many English autobiographies." He ends by fretting over whether "the reader can stomach this." What is even harder to stomach is a self-repudiation that is indistinguishable from self-congratulation. The memoir itself, with its luxuriant pleasure in "our class, our race, our time," its prideful delight in British Platonism, "popping up in sermons and Sunday questions . . . at the headmaster's dinner-parties or in my tutor's pupil-room," its insurmountable glorying in the stringent achievements of an English classical education—the memoir itself repudiates nothing, least of all the narrator's background, character, or capacities. To preface such an account of high social and intellectual privilege with the hope that it can be "stomached," and then to proceed with so much lip-smacking delectation, is, as Orwell saw, to understand nothing, and to stop at words.

Words, it turns out, are what deserve to last in *Enemies of Promise*—not Connolly's own sentences, which puff and gasp and occasionally strangle themselves, but the subject of his observations about styles of prose. Critical currencies have altered in the extreme since Connolly first set down his categories of Mandarin and vernacular, and unless one reminds oneself that these terms once had some originality of perspective (they are not so facile as they sound), they drop into the hackneyed posture they now permanently evoke. It is true that the New Criticism, which had the assurance of looking both omnipotent and immortal, has come and gone, and that the universal semiotics shock even now hints at softening, if not receding (though only slightly, and then out of factionalism). And other volumes of this kind, siblings or perhaps descendants of *Enemies of Promise*, have ventured to record the politics and history of the writer's predicament—among them critical summaries by Malcolm Cowley, Van Wyck Brooks, John Aldridge, Alfred Kazin, Tony Tanner, Tillie Olsen. The post-Connolly landscape is cluttered with new literary structures of every variety. All the same, Connolly's report on the increasing ascendancy of journalistic style over the life of contemporary fiction—language stripped of interpretive complexity, language stripped even of "language," i.e., of the resources of the lyrical or intellectual imagination—remains urgent. The Mandarin "dialect," as Connolly intelligently calls it (and he is wary in his praise of it, especially when it decays into dandyism, "the ability to spin cocoons of language out of nothing"), has now given way to a sort of telegraphic data-prose, mainly in the present tense, in which sympathies and deductive acuities are altogether eliminated. In poetry, the minimalists (whether in all their determined phalanxes they know it or not) are by now played out, moribund, ready for a turning; only the other day I heard a leading subjectivist, a lineal heir of William Carlos Williams, yearn aloud to sink into a long Miltonic sequence. But among fiction writers, the fossilized Hemingway legacy hangs on, after all this time, strangely and uselessly prestigious. (I attribute this not to the devoted reading of Hemingway, but to the decline of reading in general.)

Connolly's distinctions and his exposition of them, however, address the adherents of both "dialects." "From the Mandarins," he exhorts, the writer

> must borrow art and patience, the striving for perfection, the horror of clichés, the creative delight in the material [a phrase that itself arouses horror], in the possibilities of the long sentence and the splendour and subtlety of the composed phrase. From the Mandarins, on the other hand, the new writer will take warning not to

burden a sober and delicate language with exhibitionism. There will
be no false hesitation and woolly profundities, no mystifying, no
Proustian onanism.

From the "talkie-novelists," he continues—i.e., from the laconic
anti-stylists influenced by film—the new writer can acquire the
"cursive style, the agreeable manners, the precise and poetical
impact of Forster's diction, the lucidity of Maugham, last of the
great professional writers, the timing of Hemingway, the smooth
cutting edge of Isherwood, the indignation of Lawrence, the honesty of Orwell," as well as the gift of construction. (It is notable
that in nearly fifty years not one of these names, not excluding
Maugham and Isherwood, has lost its high familiarity, and Orwell,
in fact, has increased in prestige.) The defects of realist or colloquial
style Connolly lists as the consequence of "flatness"—"the hom-
ogeneity of outlook, the fear of eccentricity, the reporter's horror
of distinction, the distrust of beauty, the cult of violence and
starkness that is masochistic." Nowadays we might add the conviction of existential nihilism. "It is no more a question of taking
sides about one way or another of writing, but a question of
timing," Connolly sensibly concludes. All these are good and salubrious particulars—though it is worth recalling that, in prose at
least, and wherever we find ourselves in the cycle of reaction, there
are no stripped-down Conrads or Joyces; and that modernism never
turned its back on plenitude.

As for my own disappointment in encountering *Enemies of Promise*
after so long a hiatus: it was never Connolly's fault that I made
up a book that wasn't there. I wanted to brood over failure. Connolly presides over the groans of success. He knows no real
enemies—unless you count the threat to revolution ambushed in
Mayfair moustaches.

William Gaddis and the Scion of Darkness

Carpenter's Gothic is William Gaddis's third work of fiction in thirty years. That sounds like a sparse stream, and misrepresents absolutely. Gaddis is a deluge. *The Recognitions*, his first novel, published in 1955, matches in plain bulk four or five ordinary contemporary novels. His second, *JR*, a burlesquing supplementary footnote appearing two decades later, is easily equivalent to another three or four. Gaddis has not been "prolific" (that spendthrift coin); instead he has been prodigious, gargantuan, exhaustive, subsuming fates and conditions under a hungry logic. His two huge early novels are great vaults or storehouses of crafty encyclopedic scandal—omniscience thrown into the hottest furnaces of metaphor. Gaddis knows almost everything: not only how the world works—the pragmatic cynical business-machine that we call worldliness—but also how myth flies into being out of the primeval clouds of art and death and money.

To call this mammoth reach "ambition" is again to misrepresent. When *The Recognitions* arrived on the scene, it was already too late for those large acts of literary power ambition used to be good for.

Published as "Fakery and Stony Truths," *The New York Times Book Review*, July 7, 1985

Joyce had come and gone, leaving footprints both shallow and deep everywhere in Gaddis's ground—the opening dash, for instance, as a substitute for quotation marks: a brilliantly significant smudge that allows no closure and dissolves voices into narrative, turning the clearest verisimilitude into something spectral. Gaddis, imperially equipped for masterliness in range, language, and ironic penetration, born to wrest out a Modernist masterpiece but born untimely, nonetheless took a long draught of Joyce's advice and responded with surge after surge of virtuoso cunning. *The Recognitions* is a mocking recognition of the implausibility of originality: a vast fiction about fabrication and forgery, about the thousand faces of the counterfeit, and therefore, ineluctably, about art and religion. In the desert years of long ago, when I was a deluded young would-be writer tangled up in my own crapulous ambition, *The Recognitions* landed on my grim table (and on the grim tables of how many other aspirants to the holy cloak of Art?) and stayed there, month after month, as a last burnished talisman of—well, of Greatness, of a refusal to relinquish the latter-day possibilities of Joyce, Mann, James, Woolf, Proust, the whole sacral crew of those old solar boats. That, I think now, was a misreading of Gaddis's chosen ground. He knew what monuments had gathered behind him, but—seizing Joyce's dialogue-dash as staff—he willingly moved on. He was not imitating a received literature; he was not a facsimile Joyce.

Gaddis was, in fact—and is—new coinage: an American original. To claim this is to fall into Gaddis's own comedy of "enamored parodies weighed down with testimonial ruins." Originality is exactly what Gaddis has made absurd; unrecognizable. Yet if it is obligatory to recapitulate Gaddis's mockery through the impact— the dazzling irruption—of his three-decades-old first novel, it is because *The Recognitions* is always spoken of as the most overlooked important work of the last several literary generations. Tony Tanner: "The critical neglect of this book is really extraordinary." David Madden: "An underground reputation has kept it on the brink of oblivion." Through the famous obscurity of *The Recognitions*, Gaddis has become famous for not being famous enough. *Carpenter's Gothic*—a short novel, but as mazily and mercilessly adroit as the others—should mark a turning: it should disclose Gaddis's terrifying artfulness, once and for all, to those whom tonnage has kept away. *Carpenter's Gothic* may be Gaddis-in-little, but it is Gaddis to the brim.

The title itself, the name of an architectural vogue, is a dangerous joke. It alludes to a style of charm that dissembles—that resplendent carved-wood fakery seductively laid out along the Hudson a century ago, "built to be seen from the outside," its unplanned insides crammed to fit in any which way—"a patchwork of conceits, borrowings, deceptions," according to McCandless, the owner of one of these "grandiose visions . . . foolish inventions . . . towering heights and cupolas." McCandless is a geologist, a novelist, a heavy smoker with a confusing past. He has locked up one room containing his papers, reserving the right to visit it, and rented the house to a young married couple, Paul and Elizabeth Booth. Paul, like the house, has grandiose visions. He works as a public relations man for the Reverend Ude's evangelical operations, which reach as far as Africa; when Ude drowns a boy while baptizing him, Paul in his inventive fecundity—he is a desperately hollow promoter—twists this into a usable miracle. Liz, Paul's wife—wistful, abused, hopeful, humble, herself quietly deceitful—is, along with her ne'er-do-well brother Billy, heir to a mining combine intent on scheming itself back into a business empire's version of African colonialism. Paul, a combat veteran, was formerly bagman for the company under the chairmanship of Liz's father, a suicide; the company is now in the hands of Adolph, the trustee. Adolph keeps Liz, Billy, and Paul on short rations. Obedient to Paul's several scams, Liz goes from doctor to doctor, patiently pursuing an insurance fraud. McCandless reveals himself as the discoverer of the African gold the company is after, and seduces Liz. But there is no gold; McCandless is a lunatic impostor. In the end, brother and sister die of too much imposture.

All this crammed-in conspiring, told bare, is pointless soap-opera recounting. We have run into these fictional scalawags before, rotted-out families, rotted-out corporations, seedy greedy preachers and poachers, either in cahoots with or victims of one another, and sometimes both. They are American staples; but "plot" is Gaddis's prey, and also his play. Triteness is his trap and toy. He has light-fingered all the detritus that pours through the news machines and the storytelling machines—the fake claims, fake Bible schools, fake holy water out of the Pee Dee River spreading typhus, a bought-and-paid-for senator, an armed "Christian survival camp," fake identities (Paul, pretending to be a WASP Southerner, is probably a Jew), the mugger Paul kills. Plot is what Gaddis travesties and teases and two-times and swindles.

Yet these stereotypical illusions, these familiar dumping grounds of chicanery, turn to stony truths under Gaddis's eye—or, rather, his ear. Gaddis is a possessed receiver of voices, a maniacal eavesdropper, a secret prophet and moralizer. His method is pure voice, relentless dialogue, preceded by the serenely poised Joycean dash and melting off into the panning of a camera in the speaker's head. Speech is fragmented, piecemeal, halting and stunted, finally headlong—into telephones continually, out of radio and television. Through all these throats and machines the foul world spills. The radio is a perpetual chorus of mishap and mayhem, pumping out its impassive dooms while the human voice lamenting in the kitchen moans on:

> —Problem Liz you just don't grasp how serious the whole God damn thing is . . . the bottle trembled against the rim of the glass, —after him they're after me they're after all of us. . . . He'd slumped back against word of two tractor trailer trucks overturned and on fire at an entrance to the George Washington bridge, —fit the pieces together you see how all the God damn pieces fit together, SEC comes in claims some little irregularity on a Bible school bond issue next thing you've got the IRS in there right behind with misappropriation of church funds for openers, problem's their new computer down there's just geared to their mailing list if they don't build their mailing list there won't be any funds what the whole God damn thing is all about, you get these Bible students they're smart enough digging up Ephusians but they count on their fingers nobody knows where in hell the last nickel went,

and on and on: fire, death, fraud, money, voice voice voice. The voices are humanity seeping out, drop by drop, a gradual blood-letting. It isn't "theme" Gaddis deals in (his themes are plain) so much as a theory of organism and disease. In *Carpenter's Gothic* the world is a poisonous organism, humankind dying of itself. The process is gargoylish: a vaudeville turn. Paul's scribbled diagram of a promotion scheme, with all its arrows pointing cause-and-consequence, is mistaken for a map of the fourteenth-century Battle of Crécy. The "big ore find on the mission tract," a lie, is designed to lure American military imperialism into Africa. Liz, roused against McCandless, cries out (quoting Paul muddying it up: Ephusians for Ephesians, now Clausnitz for Clausewitz), "Clausnitz was wrong, it's not that war is politics carried on by other means it's the family carried on by other means," and McCandless, sneering at tribe against tribe, nation against nation, replies: "Well good God! They've been doing that for two thousand years haven't they?"

McCandless is Gaddis's strong seer, a philosophical trader in scourging tirades: ". . . talk about a dark continent I'll tell you something, revelation's the last refuge ignorance finds from reason. Revealed truth is the one weapon stupidity's got against intelligence and that's what the whole damned thing is about. . . . you've got enough sects slaughtering each other from Londonderry to Chandigarh to wipe out the whole damned thing. . . . just try the Children's Crusade for a sideshow, thousands of kids led into slavery and death by a twelve year old with a letter from Jesus. . . .—all four horsemen riding across the hills of Africa with every damned kind of war you could ask for. . . . seven hundred languages they've all been at each other's throats since the creation war, famine, pestilence, death, they ask for food and water somebody hands them an AK47 . . ." Paul, meanwhile, is Gaddis's weak seer, discloser of the shoddy morning news: "Draw the line, run a carrier group off Mombasa and a couple of destroyers down the Mozambique channel, bring in the RDF and put the SAC on red alert. They've got what they want."

Is *Carpenter's Gothic* a "political" novel? An "apocalyptic" novel? A novel of original sin without the illusion of salvation? It is tempting to judge Gaddis as Liz finally judges McCandless: "Because you're the one who wants it," she accuses him, "to see them all go up like that smoke in the furnace all the stupid, ignorant, blown up in the clouds and there's nobody there, there's no rapture or anything just to see them wiped away for good it's really you, isn't it. That you're the one who wants Apocalypse, Armageddon all the sun going out and the sea turned to blood you can't wait no, you're the one who can't wait! . . . because you despise their, not their stupidity no, their hopes because you haven't any, because you haven't any left." But not long after this outburst Liz learns from McCandless's wife—who appears out of nowhere like a clarifying messenger—that McCandless was once in a mental hospital. Another clue hints at a frontal lobotomy. A world saturated in wild despair, and only in despair, turns out to be a madman's image.

Even while he is handing over this straw of hope—that the evangelist of darkest calamity is deranged—Gaddis the trickster may be leading us more deeply into hopelessness. If McCandless, the god of the novel and its intellectual sovereign, the owner of that false-front house of disaster, whose pitiless portrait of our soiled planet we can recognize as exactly congruent with truth-telling—if McCandless is not to be trusted, then where are we? Does Gaddis mean us to conclude that whoever sees things-as-they-are in their fullest tragic illumination will never be credible except under the badge of lunacy? Or does he mean McCandless—whose name, after all, suggests he is the scion of darkness—to speak for the devil? And if so, is Gaddis on the devil's side, if only because the devil is the most eloquent moralist of all? And a novelist to boot, whose papers are irredeemably scrambled in that secret messy room he is forever cleaning up, that room "like Dachau," choked with smoke, where the Bible is stored upside down?

The true god of the novel—god of invention, commerce, and cunning—is of course mercurial Gaddis himself. He is a preternatural technician and engineer: whatever turns, turns out to turn again; things recur, allusions multiply, pretexts accrete, duplicities merge, greed proliferates, nuances breed and repeat. The center holds horribly: "you see how all the God damn pieces fit together." No one in *Carpenter's Gothic* is innocent or uninjured or unheard. It is an unholy landmark of a novel; an extra turret, so to speak, added on to the ample, ingenious, audacious Gothic mansion William Gaddis has slowly been building in American letters.

Italo Calvino:
Bringing Stories to Their Senses

Not long before his death in 1985, Italo Calvino undertook to write
five stories on the five senses. He completed three—on the powers
of tongue, ear, nostrils—gathered now in a nervous, narrow, daz-
ing volume; a cerebral accident swept him away before he could
arrive at the fingertips and the eye.

The trio of tales in *Under the Jaguar Sun* are not "experimental."
Calvino, an authentic postmodernist (despite the clamor, there are
not so many of these), does not experiment: the self-conscious
postmodernist is also a devil-may-care post-experimenter. No one
has understood the gleeful and raucous fix—or tragedy—of the
latter-day artist more penetratingly than Italo Calvino. The writer's quest has traditionally been to figure out the right human
questions to ask, and if we still love the novels of, say, George
Eliot, it is because we are nostalgic for the sobriety of a time when
the right questions could be divined. In the disorderly aftermath
of Joyce, Kafka, Agnon, Borges, all the questions appear to be
used up, repetitive, irrelevant; and their answers—which only

Published as "Mouth, Ear, Nose," *The New York Times Book Review*, October 23,
1988

recently *did* take on experimental form—have been marred by struggle, stoicism, and a studied "playfulness" more plucky than antic. After Kafka, after Borges, what is there to do but mope?

Calvino sets aside both questions and answers for the sake of brilliant clues and riddling intuitions. He gives up narrative destination for destiny, clarification for clairvoyance. He invents a new laughter suitable to the contemporary disbelief in story. In short, Calvino re-addresses—and magisterially re-enters—the idea of myth, of "the tale." In earlier works, he imagined Marco Polo as Scheherazade, mesmerizing Kublai Khan with jewellike accounts of walls, images, weather, names, humors, fates; or he noted that "the objects of reading and writing are placed among rocks, grass, lizards, having become products of the mineral-vegetable-animal continuum." He even invoked—in the exhilarating pages of *If On A Winter's Night A Traveler*—a Father of Stories, "the universal source of narrative material, the primordial magma." A learned, daring, ingeniously gifted magus, Calvino has in our own time turned himself into the Italian Grimm: his *Italian Folktales*, a masterwork of culling and retelling, is devoted precisely to the lure of the primordial magma—myth spawned by the body of the organic and inorganic world.

The three tales of *Under the Jaguar Sun* are, accordingly, engendered by the human nervous system—the body as a cornucopia of sensation, or as an echoing palace with manifold windows, each a shifting kaleidoscope. The Modernists have already hinted at how the fundamental story-clay, the myth-magma, can spring out of taste—remember Proust's madeleine; or smell—Mann's diseased Venice; or sound—Forster's *ou-boum* in the Marabar Caves. Yet these merely metaphorical resonances will not content Calvino. He slides back behind them to the primary ground of perception: ganglia and synapse. He fuses fable with neuron. By driving story right down to its biological root, to cell and stimulus, he nearly annihilates metaphor. Calvino's postmodernism is a literalism so absolute that it transports myth to its organic source, confining story to the limits of the mouth, the ear, the nose.

But what seems to be confinement and limitation—the mouth,

after all, is only a little chamber—widens to rite and mystery. The title story opens with a scrupulous recounting of Mexican cuisine (the reader is likely to salivate), and winds up in a dazzlement of wit and horror. The narrator and Olivia, a tourist couple who are vaguely estranged, are in Mexico on a holiday. They are diligent about seeing the sights and obsessive about trying every exotic dish. The husband is somewhat apathetic ("insipid," Olivia calls him, as if he needed seasoning) while Olivia is intense, inquisitive, perilously inspired. Her passion for food is sacerdotal, almost creedal. Studying her "voluptuous mastication," the narrator is overcome by a revelation of his own: "I realized my gaze was resting not on her eyes but on her teeth . . . which I happened to be seeing for the first time not as the radiant glow of a smile but as the instruments most suited to their purpose: to be dug into flesh, to sever it, tear it."

Husband and wife investigate the "gastronomical lexicon" of various localities, including *chiles en nogada*, "wrinkled little peppers, swimming in a walnut sauce whose harshness and bitter aftertaste were drowned in a creamy, sweetish surrender," and *gorditas pellizcadas con manteca*, "plump girls pinched with butter." The very name of the latter returns them to their hotel room in a rare state of sexual arousal. And meanwhile their days are given over to exploring the ruins of ancient Aztec and Olmec civilizations—temples where human sacrifice was practiced, with the complicity of willing victims, by priests who afterward consumed a certain "ritual meal." Olivia presses their guide to speculate on the possible flavors of that unspecified dish—following which, during a supper of shrimp soup and goat kid, the husband fantasizes that "I could feel my tongue lift me against the roof of her mouth, enfold me in saliva, then thrust me under the tips of the canines. . . . The situation was not entirely passive," he reflects, "since while I was being chewed by her I felt also that I was acting on her, transmitting sensations that spread from the taste buds through her whole body." Without such reciprocity, "human sacrifice would be unthinkable."

Of course this is also a comic immersion in the psychology of that "universal cannibalism," as the well-chewed narrator terms it, that "erases the lines between our bodies and . . . *enchiladas.*" And incidentally makes marriages work.

If the mouth can both smile and devour, the ear is all petrified anxiety. To listen acutely is to be powerless, even if you sit on a throne. In "The King Listens"—the crown of this extraordinary collection—the suspected eavesdropping of spies, unidentifiable movements and whispers, signals of usurpation, mysterious knockings, the very noise of the universe, imply terror and imprisonment. The ear turns out to be the most imagining organ, because it is the most accomplished at deciphering; still, on its own, it cannot be confident of any one interpretation, and wheels frenetically from conjecture to conjecture. In the end, the monarch around whom the life of the palace stirs does not know whether he is a king or a caged prisoner in the palace's secret dungeon.

Transposition of ruler and ruled—the theme, to be sure, of Chekhov's "Ward No. Six," and even (more frivolously) of J. M. Barrie's *The Admirable Crichton.* But Calvino's mythopoetics has no theme; the primordial magma is beyond, and below, what story is "about." And the palace itself, we soon recognize, is a maze leading to a tunnel: the configuration of the human ear.

The last and shortest tale—"The Name, the Nose"—is not, I think, a success, though here as in the others the brilliance of language never falters. Calvino's aim is to juxtapose the primitive and the rococo, the coarse and the highly mannered, in order to reveal their congenital olfactory unity. To emphasize the bond of nose with nose, he constructs a somewhat blurry triptych. A decadent French gentleman visits Madame Odile's *parfumerie* in search of the scent of the vanished lady he waltzed with at a masked ball. A neanderthal man-beast runs with the herd in pursuit of females, lured by the explicit odor of a single escaped female. After a bleary night of beer, marijuana, and sex, the drummer of a London rock band wakes up in a cold and filthy rooming house fixed on the smell of the girl he slept with, though she has long since cleared out. In brief, the nose, no matter who is wearing it, is an aboriginal hunter. It is all too artful, too archetypal, too anthropological—

and especially too programmed and thematic. No use sniffing here after the primeval mythos. The sophisticated aroma is of Calvino, writing.

James Whistler—acclaimed a master painter in his own time, if not in ours—once declared that "the master stands in no relation to the moment at which he occurs." Possibly. But it is also a sign of the masterly imagination that it will respond lavishly to the moment's appetite—and appetite is elemental, the opposite of fashion. Calvino occurring in any span of decades other than those vouchsafed him is inconceivable. He was meant to flourish on the heels of Kafka. That he flourishes in an English prose equal in brio and originality to Nabokov's is owed to his noteworthy translator, William Weaver, who brings to Calvino's voice the ear, the savor, and the quizzical nostrils of a fellow poet.

The Sister Melons of
J. M. Coetzee

The literature of conscience is ultimately about the bewilderment of the naive. Why do men carry guns and build prison camps, when the nurturing earth is made for freedom? To the outcast, the stray, the simpleton, the unsuspecting—to the innocent—the ideologies that order society are inane, incomprehensible. Comprehension comes unaccoutered, stripped, uninstructed—like Huck Finn on the loose, who merely knows what he knows. And what the pariah Huck knows, against the weight and law and common logic of his slaveholding "sivilization," is that the black man is whole, the rightful owner of his life and times.

In *Life & Times of Michael K*, J. M. Coetzee, a South African born in 1940, has rewritten the travail of Huck's insight, but from the black man's point of view, and set in a country more terrible —because it is a living bitter hardhearted contemporary place, the parable-world of an unregenerate soon-after-now, with little pity and no comedy. Conscience, insight, innocence: Michael K cannot aspire to such high recognitions—he is "dull," his mind is "not

Published as "A Tale of Heroic Anonymity," *The New York Times Book Review*, December 11, 1983

quick." He was born fatherless and with a disfigurement: a harelip that prevented him from being nourished at his mother's breast. When he needs some tools to make a cart to transport his dying mother, he breaks into a locked shed and takes them. The smallest transgression, undetected and unpunished, the single offense of his life; yet nearly every moment of his life is judged as if he were guilty of some huge and undisclosed crime—not for nothing is his surname resonant with the Kafkan "K." His crime is his birth. When as a schoolchild he is perplexed by long division, he is "committed to the protection" of a state-run orphanage for the "variously afflicted." From then on he is consistently protected—subject to curfews, police permits, patrols, convoys, sentries, guns, a work camp with wire fences, a semi-benevolent prison hospital: tyranny, like his school, "at the expense of the state."

Though a mote in the dustheap of society, he is no derelict. From the age of fifteen he has worked as a gardener in a public park in Cape Town. His worn and profoundly scrupulous mother also lives honorably; she is a domestic servant for a decent enough elderly couple in a posh seaside apartment house. They have gone to the trouble of keeping a room for her—an unused basement storage closet without electricity or ventilation. Her duties end at eight o'clock at night six days a week. When she falls ill, she is dependent on the charity of her employers. The building is attacked, vandalized, the residents driven out. Michael K is laid off. The country is at war.

The purpose of the war, from one standpoint—that of a reasonable-minded prison-master—is "so that minorities will have a say in their destinies." This is indisputably the language of democratic idealism. In a South African context such a creed unexpectedly turns Orwellian: it means repression of the black majority by the white minority. Yet in Coetzee's tale we are not told who is black and who is white, who is in power and who is not. Except for the reference to Cape Town and to place names that are recognizably Afrikaans, we are not even told that this is the physical and moral landscape of South Africa. We remain largely uninstructed because we are privy solely to Michael K's heart, an organ that does not deal in color or power, a territory foreign to abstractions and doctrines; it knows only what is obvious and elemental. Another way of putting this is to say that—though there is little mention anywhere of piety or faith, and though it is the prison-masters alone who speak sympathetically and conscientiously of rights and of freedom—Michael K responds only to what appears to be divinely ordered, despite every implacable decree and man-made restraint. He names no tyranny and no ideal. He cares for his mother; he cares for the earth; he will learn how they come to the same in the end.

With laborious tenderness, with intelligent laboriousness—how intelligent he is!—Michael K builds a crude hand-drawn vehicle to restore his mother to a lost place that has become the frail ephemeral text of her illness, no more substantial than a vision: a bit of soil with a chicken run, where she remembers having once been happy in childhood. The town nearest this patch is only five hours away, but without a permit they may not go by train. No permit arrives. They set out clandestinely, the young man heaving the weight of his old mother in the cart, dodging military convoys, hiding, the two of them repeatedly assaulted by cold and bad weather and thugs with knives. To Michael K at the start of the journey, brutality and danger and stiffness of limb and rain seem all the same; tyranny feels as natural an ordeal as the harshness of the road.

On the road his mother deteriorates so piteously that Michael K must surrender her to a hospital. There he is shunted aside and she dies. Without consultation her body is cremated and given back to him, a small bundle of ashes in a plastic bag. He holds his mother's dust and imagines the burning halo of her hair. Then, still without permission, he returns her to the place of her illumination and buries her ashes. It is a grassy nowhere, a guess, the cloudrack of a dream of peace, the long-abandoned farm of a de-parted Afrikaaner family, a forgotten and unrecorded spot fallen through the brute mesh of totalitarian surveillance.

And here begins the parable of Michael K's freedom and re-sourcefulness; here begins Michael K's brief bliss. He is Robinson

Crusoe, he is the lord of his life. It is his mother's own earth; it is his motherland; he lives in a womblike burrow; he tills the fruitful soil. Miracles sprout from a handful of discovered seeds: "Now two pale green melons were growing on the far side of the field. It seemed to him that he loved these two, which he thought of as two sisters, even more than the pumpkins, which he thought of as a band of brothers. Under the melons he placed pads of grass so that their skins should not bruise." He eats with deep relish, in the fulfillment of what is ordained: the work of his hands, a newfound sovereignty over his own hands and the blessing of fertility in his own scrap of ground. "I am becoming a different kind of man," he reflects. For the first time he is unprotected. When he has grown almost unafraid, civilization intrudes.

A whining boy who is a runaway soldier takes over the farm-house and declares himself in need of a servant. A group of guerrillas and their donkeys pass through by night and trample the seedlings. Michael K flees; he is picked up as a "parasite" and confined to a work camp. But because he has lived in the field as a free man—in the field "he was not a prisoner or a castaway . . . he was himself"—he has learned how to think and judge. "What if the hosts were far outnumbered by the parasites, the parasites of idleness and the other secret parasites in the army and the police force and the schools and the factories and offices, the parasites of the heart? Could the parasites then be called parasites? Parasites too had flesh and substance; parasites too could be preyed upon."

From the seed of freedom Michael K has raised up a meta-physics. It is not the coarse dogma of a killer-rebel or a terrorist; he does not join the guerrillas. He sees vulnerable children on all sides—the runaway who wants to be taken care of, the careless insurgents who are like "young men come off the field after a hard game," even the young camp guard with diabetes, callous and threatening, yet willing to share his food, who will end up as a prisoner himself. "How many people are there left who are neither locked up nor standing guard at the gate?"

But behind the gate Michael K cannot eat, cannot swallow, cannot get nourishment, and now Coetzee turns his parable to one of starvation. Repression wastes. Tyranny makes skeletons. Injustice will be vomited up. "Maybe he only eats the bread of freedom," says a doctor in the camp for "rehabilitation," where Michael K is next incarcerated. His body is "crying to be fed its own food, and only that." Behind the wire fences of a politics organized by curfew and restriction, where essence is smothered by law, and law is lie, Michael K is set aside as a rough mindless lost unfit creature, a simpleton or an idiot, a savage. It is a wonder, the doctor observes, that he has been able to keep himself alive. He is "the runt of the cat's litter," "the obscurest of the obscure." Thus the judgment of benevolent arrogance—or compassion indistinguishable from arrogance—on the ingenious farmer and visionary free man of his mother's field.

Coetzee is a writer of clarifying inventiveness and translucent conviction. Both are given voice gradually, seepingly, as if time itself were a character in the narrative. "There is time enough for everything." As in his previous novel, *Waiting for the Barbarians*, Coetzee's landscapes of suffering are defined by the little-by-little art of moral disclosure—his stories might be about anyone and anyplace. At the same time they defy the vice of abstraction; they are engrossed in the minute and the concrete. It would be possible, following Coetzee's dazzlingly precise illuminations, to learn how to sow, or use a pump, or make a house of earth. The grain of his sentences is flat and austere, and so purifying to the senses that one comes away feeling that one's eye has been sharpened, one's hearing vivified, not only for the bright proliferations of nature, but for human unexpectedness.

If *Life & Times of Michael K* has a flaw, it is in the density of its own interior interpretations. In the final quarter we are removed, temporarily, from the plain seeing of Michael K to the self-indulgent diary of the prison doctor who struggles with the entanglements of an increasingly abusive regime. But the doctor's commentary is superfluous; he thickens the clear tongue of the novel by naming its "message" and thumping out ironies. For one thing, he spells out what we have long ago taken in with the immediacy of intuition and possession. He construes, he translates:

Michael K is "an original soul . . . untouched by doctrine, untouched by history . . . evading the peace and the war . . . drifting
through time, observing the seasons, no more trying to change the
course of history than a grain of sand does." All this is redundant.
The sister-melons and the brother-pumpkins have already had
their eloquent say. And the lip of the child kept from its mother's
milk has had its say. And the man who grows strong and intelligent
when he is at peace in his motherland has had his say.

Coetzee's subdued yet urgent lament is for the sadness of a South
Africa that has made dependents and parasites and prisoners of its
own children, black and white. (Not to mention more ambiguously
imprisoned groups: Indians, "coloreds," the troubled and precar-
ious Jewish community.) Moreover, Coetzee makes plain that the
noble endurances and passionate revelations of Michael K do not
mask a covert defense of terror; although he evades no horrors,
existing or to come, Coetzee has not written a symbolic novel about
the inevitability of guerrilla war and revolution in a country where
oppression and dependency are breathed with the air. Instead, he
discloses, in the language of imagination, the lumbering hoaxes
and self-deceptions of stupidity. His theme is the wild and merciless power of inanity. Michael K suffers from the obdurate cal-
lowness of both sides, rulers and rebels—one tramples the vines,
the other blows up the pump. At the end of the story, he dreams
of drinking the living water drawn out of his mother's earth, if
only drop by drop, if only from a teaspoon.

For the sake of the innocent, time is Coetzee's hope.

Primo Levi's Suicide Note

Primo Levi, an Italian Jewish chemist from Turin, was liberated from Auschwitz by a Soviet military unit in January of 1945, when he was twenty-five, and from that moment of reprieve (*Moments of Reprieve* was one of his titles) until shortly before his death in April of 1987, he went on recalling, examining, reasoning, recording—telling the ghastly tale—in book after book. That he saw himself as a possessed scribe of the German hell, we know from the epigraph to his final volume, *The Drowned and the Saved* —familiar lines taken from "The Rime of the Ancient Mariner" and newly startling to a merely literary reader, for whom the words of Coleridge's poem have never before rung out with such an anti-metaphorical contemporary demand, or seemed so cruel:

> Since then, at an uncertain hour,
> That agony returns,
> And till my ghastly tale is told
> This heart within me burns.

Seized by the survivor's heart, this stanza no longer answers to the status of Lyrical Ballad, and still less to the English Depart-

Published as "The Suicide Note," *The New Republic*, March 21, 1988

ment's quintessential Romantic text redolent of the supernatural; it is all deadly self-portrait. In the haven of an Italian spring— forty years after setting down the somber narrative called in Italian "If This Be a Man" and published in English as *Survival in Auschwitz*—Primo Levi hurled himself into the well of a spiral staircase four stories deep, just outside the door of the flat he was born in, where he had been living with his wife and aged ailing mother. Suicide. The composition of the last Lager manuscript was complete, the heart burned out; there was no more to tell.

There was no more to tell. That, of course, is an assumption nobody can justify, and nobody perhaps ought to dare to make. Suicide is one of the mysteries of the human will, with or without a farewell note to explain it. And it remains to be seen whether *The Drowned and the Saved* is, after all, a sort of suicide note.

Levi, to be sure, is not the first writer of high distinction to survive hell and to suggest, by a self-willed death, that hell in fact did not end when the chimneys closed down, but was simply freshening for a second run—Auschwitz being the first hell, and post-Auschwitz the second; and if "survival" is the thing in question, then it isn't the "survivor" whose powers of continuation are worth marveling at, but hell itself. The victim who has escaped being murdered will sometimes contrive to finish the job, not because he is attached to death—never this—but because death is under the governance of hell, and it is in the nature of hell to go on and on: inescapability is its rule, No Exit its sign. "The injury cannot be healed," Primo Levi writes in *The Drowned and the Saved*; "it extends through time, and the Furies, in whose existence we are forced to believe . . . perpetuate the tormentor's work by denying peace to the tormented."

Tadeusz Borowski, for instance, author of *This Way for the Gas, Ladies and Gentlemen*, eluded the gas at both Auschwitz and Dachau from 1943 to 1945; in Warsaw, in 1951, not yet thirty, three days before the birth of his daughter, he turned on the household gas. Suicide. The poet Paul Celan: a suicide. The Austrian-born philosopher Hans Mayer—another suicide—who later became Jean Améry by scrambling his name into a French anagram, was in Auschwitz together with Primo Levi, though the two never chanced on one another. Before his capture and deportation, Améry had been in the Belgian resistance and was subjected to Gestapo torture. After the war, Améry and Levi corresponded about their experiences. Levi esteemed Améry, appeared to understand him, but evidently could not like him—because, he says, Améry was a man who "traded blows." "A gigantic Polish criminal," Levi recounts, "punches [Améry] in the face over some trifle; he, not because of an animallike reaction but because of a reasoned revolt against the perverted world of the Lager, returns the blow as best he can." " 'Hurting all over from the blows, I was satisfied with myself,' " Levi quotes Améry; but for himself, Levi asserts,

"trading punches" is an experience I do not have, as far back as I can go in memory; nor can I say I regret not having it . . . go[ing] down onto the battlefield . . . was and is beyond my reach. I admire it, but I must point out that this choice, protracted throughout his post-Auschwitz existence, led [Améry] to such severity and intransigence as to make him incapable of finding joy in life, indeed of living. Those who "trade blows" with the entire world achieve dignity but pay a very high price for it because they are sure to be defeated.

Remarkably, Levi concludes: "Améry's suicide, which took place in Salzburg in 1978 [i.e., nine years before Levi's leap into the stairwell], like other suicides allows for a nebula of explanations, but, in hindsight, that episode of defying the Pole offers one interpretation of it."

This observation—that the rage of resentment is somehow linked to self-destruction—is, in the perplexing shadow of Levi's own suicide, enigmatic enough, and bears returning to. For the moment it may be useful to consider that Primo Levi's reputation—rather, the grave and noble voice that sounds and summons through his pages—has been consummately free of rage, resentment, violent feeling, or any overt drive to "trade blows." The voice has been one of pristine sanity and discernment. Levi has been unwilling to serve either as preacher or as elegist. He has avoided polemics; he has shrunk from being counted as one of those message-bearers "whom I view with distrust: the prophet, the bard, the soothsayer. That I am not." Instead, he has offered himself as a singular witness—singular because he was "privileged" to survive as a laboratory slave, meaning that German convenience, at least temporarily, was met more through the exploitation of his training as a chemist than it would have been through his immediate annihilation as a Jew; and, from our own point of view, because of his clarity and selflessness as a writer. It is selfless to eschew freely running emotion, sermonizing, the catharsis of anger, when these so plainly plead their case before an unprecedentedly loathsome record of criminals and their crimes. Levi has kept his distance from blaming, scolding, insisting, vilifying, lamenting, crying out. His method has been to describe—meticulously, analytically, clarifyingly. He has been a Darwin of the death camps: not the Virgil of the German hell but its scientific investigator.

Levi himself recognizes that he has been particularly attended to for this quality of detachment. "From my trade," he affirms in *The Drowned and the Saved*,

> I contracted a habit that can be variously judged and defined at will as human or inhuman—the habit of never remaining indifferent to the individuals that chance brings before me. They are human beings but also "samples," specimens in a sealed envelope to be identified, analyzed, and weighed. Now, the sample book that Auschwitz had placed before me was rich, varied, and strange, made up of friends, neutrals, and enemies, yet in any case food for my curiosity, which some people, then and later, have judged to be detached. . . . I know that this "naturalistic" attitude does not derive only or necessarily from chemistry, but in my case it did come from chemistry.

Whatever its source—chemistry, or, as others have believed, a lucent and humane restraint—this "naturalistic" approach has astonished and inspired readers and critics. Irving Howe speaks of Levi's "unruffled dignity" and "purity of spirit," James Atlas of his "magisterial equanimity." Rita Levi-Montalcini, a recipient of the 1986 Nobel Prize in medicine and a fellow Turinese, devotes an epilogue in her memoir, *In Praise of Imperfection*, to Levi's "detachment and absence of hatred." You, she addresses Levi, have "come out of the most atrocious of all experiences with an upright forehead and a spirit pure."

A temperament so transparent, so untainted, so unpolemical (indeed, so anti-polemical)—so like clear water—has, however, also provided a kind of relief, or respite, for those who hope finally to evade the gravamen of Levi's chronicle. The novelist Johanna Kaplan sets it out for us: "*Oh, that? Oh, that again?* . . . Because by now, after all the powerful, anguished novels . . . , after all the simple, heartrending documentary accounts, the stringent, haunting historians' texts, the pained and arduous movies—that shocking newsreel footage . . . after all the necessary, nightmare lists of involuntary martyrology, by now our response to the singular horrific barbarity of our time is—just the tiniest bit dutiful." This desire to recoil may describe all of us; and yet we—some of us—drag through these foul swamps, the documents, the films, the photos, the talks, the tales, the conferences, year after year, taking it in and taking it in: perhaps because we are dutiful, perhaps because the fury of outrage owns us, more likely because we are the children of mercy and will not allow the suffering to recede into mere past-ness, a time not ours, for which we are not responsible. We press on with the heartsick job of assimilating the imagination of savagery because in some seizure of helplessly belated justice we want to become responsible for the murdered. In short, guilt: in one form or another we are wounded by conscience. Either, as Jews, we were not there with the others who stood in for us as victims, or, as Christians, we were too much there, represented by the familiar upbringing of the criminals, with whose religious inheritance we have so much in common. Guilt in our absence, guilt in our presence. Jewish guilt; Christian guilt; English, French, Italian, Croatian, Ukrainian, American guilt. Guilt of the Germans whose patriotism gave birth to the criminals. Guilt of the Irish and the Swedes who hid behind neutrality. Guilt over zeal, guilt over apathy.

All of this Levi as naturalist skirts. He appears to have nothing to do with any of it. He is not in favor of a generalized anguish. His aim has been to erect a principled barrier against any show of self-appointed fanaticism, from any direction. Book after book has shied away from the emotive accusatory issues. Above all, Levi is careful not to blur victim and victimizer. He is wary of the sentimentalizers, preeners, hypothesizers: "I do not know," he writes, "and it does not much interest me to know, whether in my depths there lurks a murderer, but I do know that I was a guiltless victim and not a murderer. . . . to confuse [the murderers] with their victims is a moral disease or an aesthetic affectation or a sinister sign of complicity." He is a stringent taxonomist, on the side of precision: the crimes and the criminals have an identifiable habitation and name. This may be one reason—it is not the only one—it has been possible to read Levi with soul's pain (how could this be otherwise?), but without guilt. It is not that Levi absolves; rather, he mutes the question of absolution—a question always in the forefront for messengers as radically different from each other as, say, Elie Wiesel and Raul Hilberg. Hilberg's investigations in particular, coolly data-obsessed as they are, have erased the notion of "bystander" status in Nazi Germany. Levi has devoted himself less to social history and psychological motivation than to the microscope, with its exactingly circumscribed field of vision. Society-as-organism is not the area under his scrutiny, as it is for Hilberg; neither is suffering as metaphor, as with Wiesel's emblematic mourning madmen.

The advantage, for many of Levi's readers, has been—dare one say this?—a curious peacefulness: the consequence of the famous "detachment." Levi is far from being a peaceful witness, but because he has not harassed or harangued or dramatized or poetized or shaken a fist or shrieked or politicized (a little of the last, but only a little), because he has restricted himself to observation, notation, and restraint, it becomes alarmingly easy to force him into a false position. If it was futile for him to plead, as he once did, "I beg the reader not to go looking for messages," it is nevertheless disconcerting that of all the various "lessons" that might have been drawn from Levi's penetrations, the one most prevalent is also the coarsest and the most misleading: uplift. Rarely will you come on a publisher's jacket blare as shallow as the one accompanying *The Drowned and the Saved*: "a wondrous celebration of life . . . a testament to the indomitability of the human spirit and humanity's capacity to defeat death through meaningful work, morality and art." Contemptible puffery, undermining every paragraph of the text it ostensibly promotes; and if it is designed to counter *"Oh, that? Oh, that again?"* then it is even more contemptible. Celebration of life? Defeat of death? *Meaningful* work? Morality? Art? What callousness, what cravenness, before the subject at hand! In the Lager world, Levi tells us again and again, "work" was pointless, and deliberately so, in order to intensify torment; morality was reduced to staying alive as long as possible, and by any means; and art was non-existent. Applied to a place where murder claimed daily dominion, "celebration of life" can only be a mockery, or—if that phrase is meant to describe Levi's intent as witness—a double mockery: his intent is to let us see for ourselves the nature, extent, and depth of the German crime.

Yet "celebration of life," that falsifying balm, is hardly untypical of the illusory—or self-deluding—glow of good feeling (or, at worst, absence of bad feeling) that generally attaches to Levi's name. Of the scribes of the Holocaust, Levi appears to be the one who least troubles, least wounds, least implicates, the reader. A scientific or objective attitude will inform, certainly, but declines any show of agitation. What we have had from Levi, accordingly, is the portrait of a psychological oxymoron: the well-mannered cicerone of hell, mortal horror in a decorous voice. "Améry called me 'the forgiver,'" Levi notes. "I consider this neither insult nor praise but imprecision. I am not inclined to forgive, I never forgave our enemies of that time . . . because I know no human act that can erase a crime; I demand justice, but I am not able, personally"—here again is this insistent declaration of refusal— "to trade punches or return blows." All the same (untenable as he might consider it), Levi is widely regarded, if not quite as "the forgiver," then as the survivor whose books are, given their subject matter, easiest to take; one gets the impression (and from Levi's own pages) that he has been read in Germany far more willingly than have some others. He writes, as his countrywoman remarked, in the "absence of hatred."

And so it has seemed until this moment. *The Drowned and the Saved* reveals something else. It is a detonation, all the more volcanic because so unexpected. Yet "detonation" is surely, at least from Levi's point of view, the wrong word: concussion is an all-of-a-sudden thing. In *The Drowned and the Saved*, the change of tone is at first muted, faint. Gradually, cumulatively, rumble by rumble, it leads to disclosure, exposure—one can follow the sizzle flying along the fuse; by the last chapter the pressure is so powerful, the rage so immense, that "detachment" has long given way to convulsion. What was withheld before is now imploded in these pages. *The Drowned and the Saved* is the record of a man returning blows with all the might of human fury, in full knowledge that the pen is mightier than the fist. The convulsions of rage have altered the nature of the prose, and—if we can judge by Levi's suicide—the man as well. Almost no one, interestingly, has been disposed to say of Levi's final testimony that it is saturated in deadly anger—as if it would be too cruel to tear from him the veil of the spirit pure. It may be cruel; but it is Levi's own hand that tears away the veil and sets the fuse.

The fuse is ignited almost instantly, in the Preface. "No one will ever be able to establish with precision how many, in the Nazi apparatus, could *not not know* about the frightful atrocities being committed, how many knew something but were in a position to pretend they did not know, and, further, how many had the possibility of knowing everything but chose the more prudent path of keeping their eyes and ears (and above all their mouths) well shut." Here is the heralding of the indictment that will emerge: it is the German people whom Levi subjects to judgment, which may account for his rarely shrinking from the use of "German," where, nowadays, "Nazi" is usually the polite, because narrower, term. In the Preface also may be found the single most terrible sentence ever offered on the issue of what is variously called "res-

titution," "changed attitudes," "the new generation," and all the
rest: "The crematoria ovens themselves were designed, built, assembled, and tested by a German company, Topf of Wiesbaden
(it was still in operation in 1975, building crematoria for civilian
use, and had not considered the advisability of changing its name)."
Had not considered the advisability of changing its name: this applies
equally to Krupp, notorious for slave labor, and, in its most celebrated incarnation, to Hitler's "people's car," the ubiquitous
Volkswagen, driven unselfconsciously by half the world. (An un-
selfconscious irony, by the way, that Levi, or his admirable translator, should fall into the phrase "civilian use," meaning, one
supposes, the opposite of official governmental policy—i.e., ordinary funerals employing cremation. But who else other than
"civilians" were annihilated in the Lager?)

When Levi comes to speak of shame, it is nevertheless not the
absence of shame among Germans he invokes, though he condemns
the "complicity and connivance" of the "majority of Germans" just
before and during the Hitler years; rather, it is the loss of shame
in the victims of the Lager, dispossessed of any civilizing vestige,
reduced to the animal. The Lager "*anus mundi*," dominated "from
dawn to dusk by hunger, fatigue, cold, and fear," "ultimate drain-
age site of the German universe," was a condition without reciprocity, where you sought to succor and relieve only yourself, to
take care of yourself alone. Shame returned with the return of
freedom, retrospectively. In the "gray zone" of Lager oppression,
contaminated victims collaborated with contaminating persecutors. Arrival at Auschwitz meant "kicks and punches right away,
often in the face; an orgy of orders screamed with true or simulated
rage; complete nakedness after being stripped; the shaving off of
all one's hair; the outfitting in rags," and some of these depredations
were conducted by fellow victims appointed as functionaries.
Again and again Levi emphasizes the diminishment of every human
trait, the violated modesty, the public evacuation, the satanically
inventive brutality, the disorientation and desperation. He describes the absolute rule of "small satraps"—the common criminals
who became Kapos; the wretched *Bettnachzieher*, whose sole job

was to measure the orderliness of straw pillows with a maniacal
string and who had the power to punish "publicly and savagely";
the overseers of the "work that was purely persecutory"; the "Special Squads" that operated the crematoria for the sake of a few
weeks more of life, only to be replaced and thrown into the fire
in turn. These squads, Levi explains, "were made up largely of
Jews. In a certain sense this is not surprising, since the Lager's
main purpose was to destroy Jews, and, beginning in 1943, the
Auschwitz population was 90–95 percent Jews." (Here I interrupt
to remind the reader of William Styron's choice in *Sophie's Choice*,
wherein we are given, as the central genocidal emblem of Lager
policy in those years, a victim who is not a Jew.*) "From another
point of view," Levi continues, "one is stunned by this paroxysm
of perfidy and hatred: it must be the Jews who put the Jews into
the ovens; it must be shown that the Jews, the subrace, the submen,
bow to any and all humiliation, even to destroying themselves."
Levi admits that merely by virtue of his having stayed alive, he
never "fathomed [the Lager] to the bottom." The others, the
"drowned," he maintains, those who went down to the lees of
suffering and annihilation, were the only true fathomers of that
perfidy and hatred.

Levi's reflections appear to be fathomings enough. *The Drowned
and the Saved* is much less a book of narrative and incident than it
is of siftings of the most sordid deposits of the criminal
imagination—the inescapable struggle of a civilized mind to bore
through to the essence and consequence of degradation and atrocity. Levi is not the first to observe that "where violence is inflicted

---

*Let no one misconstrue this remark. The point is not that Jews suffered more
than anyone else in the camps, or even that they suffered in greater numbers;
concerning suffering there can be no competition or hierarchy. To suggest otherwise would be monstrous. Those who suffered at Auschwitz suffered with an
absolute equality, and the suffering of no one victimized group or individual weighs
more in human anguish than that of any other victimized group or individual.
But note: Catholic Poland, for instance (language, culture, land), continues, while
European Jewish civilization (language, culture, institutions) was wiped out
utterly—and that, for Jewish history, is the different and still more terrible central
meaning of Auschwitz. It is, in fact, what defines the Holocaust, and distinguishes
it from the multiple other large-scale victimizations of the Nazi period.

on man it is also inflicted on language," though he may be among the first to inform us of the life-or-death role of language in the Lager. Simply, not to understand German was to go under at once: "the rubber truncheon was called *der Dolmetscher*, the interpreter: the one who made himself understood to everybody." Levi had studied some German at the university to prepare himself as a chemist. He learned more in Auschwitz—grotesquely distorted barbarisms which he deliberately held on to years later, "for the same reason I have never had the tattoo removed from my left arm." As for the tattoo itself—"an autochthonous Auschwitzian invention," "gratuitous, an end in itself, pure offense," "a return to barbarism"—Levi, a secular Jew, is careful to note that Leviticus 19:28 forbids tattooing "precisely in order to distinguish Jews from the barbarians." Even newborn babies, he reports, were tattooed on arrival in Auschwitz.

All this, and considerably more, Levi gathers up under the chilling heading of "Useless Violence," which he defines as "a deliberate creation of pain that was an end in itself." What else was the purpose of the vindictive halt of a boxcar of Jews at an Austrian railroad station, where, while the guards laughed, "the German passengers openly expressed their disgust" at "men and women squatting wherever they could, on the platforms and in the middle of the tracks"? What else was the purpose of emptying out nursing homes filled with elderly sick people already near death and hauling them off to Auschwitz to be gassed? Or forcing grown men to lap up soup like dogs by depriving them of spoons (of which there were tens of thousands at Auschwitz)? Or using human ash from the crematoria to make "gravel" paths for the SS village that ruled the camp? Or selling human hair to the German textile industry for mattress ticking? Or locking human beings into decompression chambers "to establish at what altitude human blood begins to boil: a datum that can be obtained in any laboratory at minimum expense and without victims, or even can be deduced from common tables"?

A sparse sampling from Levi's meditation on the German abominations, some familiar, some not. Cardinal John O'Connor's the-

ologizing not long ago—which led him to identify the torments
of Auschwitz as a Jewish gift to the world—is no doubt indisputably valid Roman Catholic doctrine concerning the redemptive
nature of suffering; but, much as the observation was intended to
confer grace on the victims, it strikes me as impossible, even for
a committed Christian, even for an angel of God, to speak of
redemption and Auschwitz in the same breath. What we learn
overwhelmingly from Levi is this: if there is redemption in it, it
cannot be Auschwitz; and if it is Auschwitz, it is nothing if not
unholy. Let no one mistake Primo Levi. If an upright forehead
and a spirit pure mean forgoing outrage for the sake of one lofty
idea or another—including the renunciation of hatred for the de-
signers of the crematoria—then Primo Levi is as sullied as anybody
else who declines to be morally neutered in the name of superior
views.

He is in fact not morally neutered, and never was. He is not a
"forgiver" (only someone with a clouded conscience would presume to claim that right on behalf of the murdered), and he is not
dedicated, as so many believe, to an absence of rancor toward the
strategists of atrocity and their followers. He is, as he asserts, a
scientist and a logician: nowhere in Levi's pages will you find
anything even remotely akin to the notion of "hate the sin, not the
sinner." He is not an absurdist or a surrealist; nowhere does he
engage in such a severance. On the contrary, his preëminent theme
is responsibility: "The true crime, the collective, general crime of
almost all Germans of that time, was that of lacking the courage
to speak." One thinks, accordingly, of those unmoved German
citizens waiting for a train on a station platform, compelled to hold
their noses in revulsion as the freight cars, after passing through
miles of unpeopled countryside, disgorge their dehumanized
prey—a "relief stop" conceived in malice and derision. In his final
chapter, "Letters from Germans," Levi quotes a correspondent
who pleads with him "to remember the innumerable Germans who
suffered and died in their struggle against iniquity." This letter
and others like it bring Levi to the boiling point. He scorns the
apologists, the liars, the "falsely penitent." He recalls his feelings

when he learned that *Survival in Auschwitz* would be published in Germany:

> yes, I had written the book in Italian for Italians, for my children, for those who did not know, those who did not want to know, those who were not yet born, those who, willing or not, had assented to the offense; but its true recipients, those against whom the book was aimed like a gun, were they, the Germans. Now the gun was loaded. . . . I would corner them, tie them before a mirror. . . . Not that handful of high-ranking culprits, but them, the people, those I had seen from close up, those from among whom the SS militia were recruited, and also those others, those who had believed, who not believing had kept silent, who did not have the frail courage to look into our eyes, throw us a piece of bread, whisper a human word.

He quotes from *Mein Kampf*; he reminds his "polite and civil interlocutors, members of a people who exterminated mine," of the free elections that put Hitler into office, and of *Kristallnacht*; he points out that "enrollment in the SS was voluntary," and that heads of German families were entitled, upon application, to receive clothing and shoes for both children and adults from the warehouses at Auschwitz. "Did no one ask himself where so many children's shoes were coming from?" And he concludes with a *j'accuse* directed toward "that great majority of Germans who accepted in the beginning, out of mental laziness, myopic calculation, stupidity, and national pride, the 'beautiful words' of Corporal Hitler."

The Drowned and the Saved is a book of catching-up after decades of abstaining. It is a book of blows returned by a pen on fire. The surrender to fury in these burning chapters does not swallow up their exactness—the scientist's truthful lens is not dissolved—but Levi in the violated voice of this last completed work lets fly a biblical ululation that its predecessors withheld: *thy brother's blood cries up from the ground*. I do not mean that Levi has literally set down those words; but he has, at long last, unleashed their clamor.

And what of the predecessor-volumes? What of their lucid calm, absence of hatred, magisterial equanimity, unaroused detachment?

Readers have not misconstrued Levi's tone, at least not until now. *The Drowned and the Saved* makes it seem likely that the restraint of forty years was undertaken out of a consistent adherence to an elevated *idée fixe*, possibly to a self-deception: a picture of how a civilized man ought to conduct himself when he is documenting savagery. The result was the world's consensus: a man somehow set apart from retaliatory passion. A man who would not trade punches. A transparency; a pure spirit. A vessel of clear water.

I spoke earlier of creeping fuses, mutedness, the slow accretion of an insurmountable pressure. "The Furies . . . perpetuate the tormentor's work by denying peace to the tormented." But all that was subterranean. Then came the suicide. Consider now an image drawn from Primo Levi's calling. Into a vessel of clear water— tranquil, innocuous—drop an unaccustomed ingredient: a lump of potassium, say, an alkali metal that reacts with water so violently that the hydrogen gas given off by the process will erupt into instant combustion. One moment, a beaker of unperturbed transparency. The next moment, a convulsion: self-destruction.

The unaccustomed ingredient, for Levi, was rage. "Suicide," he reflects in *The Drowned and the Saved*—which may be seen, perhaps and after all, as the bitterest of suicide notes—"is an act of man and not of the animal. It is a meditated act, a noninstinctive, unnatural choice." In the Lager, where human beings were driven to become animals, there were almost no suicides at all. Améry, Borowski, Celan, and ultimately Levi did not destroy themselves until some time after they were released. Levi waited more than forty years; and he did not become a suicide until he let passion in, and returned the blows. If he is right about Améry—that Améry's willingness to trade punches is the key to his suicide— then he has deciphered for us his own suicide as well.

What we know now—we did not know it before *The Drowned and the Saved*—is that at bottom Levi could not believe in himself as a vessel of clear water standing serenely apart. It was not detachment. It was dormancy, it was latency, it was potentiality; it was inoperativeness. He was always conscious of how near to hand the potassium was. I grieve that he equated rage—the rage that speaks for mercifulness—with self-destruction. A flawed formula. It seems to me it would not have been a mistake—and could not have been misinterpreted—if all of Primo Levi's books touching on the German hell had been as vehement, and as pointed, as the last, the most remarkable.

What Drives Saul Bellow

A concordance, a reprise, a summary, all the old themes and obsessions hauled up by a single tough rope—does there come a time when, out of the blue, a writer offers to decode himself? Not simply to divert, or paraphrase, or lead around a corner, or leave clues, or set out decoys (familiar apparatus, art-as-usual), but to kick aside the maze, spill wine all over the figure in the carpet, bury the grand metaphor, and disclose the thing itself? To let loose, in fact, the secret? And at an hour no one could have predicted? And in a modestly unlikely form? The cumulative art concentrated, so to speak, in a vial?

For Saul Bellow, at age sixty-eight, and with his Nobel speech some years behind him, the moment for decoding is now, and the decoding itself turns up unexpectedly in the shape of *Him with His Foot in His Mouth*, a volume of five stories, awesome yet imperfect, at least one of them overtly a fragment, and none malleable enough to achieve a real "ending." Not that these high-pressure stories are inconclusive. With all their brilliant wiliness of predicament and

Published as "Farcical Combat in a Busy World," *The New York Times Book Review*, May 20, 1984

brainy language shocked into originality, they are magisterially the opposite. They tell us, in the clarified tight compass he has not been so at home in since *Seize the Day*, what drives Bellow.

What drives Bellow. The inquiry is seductive, because Bellow is Bellow, one of three living American Nobel laureates (the only one, curiously, whose natural language is English), a writer for whom great fame has become a sort of obscuring nimbus, intruding on the cleanly literary. When *The Dean's December* was published in 1982, it was not so much reviewed as scrutinized like sacred entrails: had this idiosyncratically independent writer turned "conservative"? Had he soured on Augiesque America? Was his hero, Albert Corde, a lightly masked Saul Bellow? Can a writer born into the Jewish condition successfully imagine and inhabit a WASP protagonist? In short, it seemed impossible to rid Bellow's novel of Bellow's presence, to free it as fiction.

In consequence of which, one is obliged to put a riddle: if you found this book of stories at the foot of your bed one morning, with the title page torn away and the author's name concealed, would you know it, after all, to be Bellow? Set aside, for the interim, the ruckus of advertised "models": that Victor Wulpy of "What Kind of Day Did You Have?" has already been identified as the art critic Harold Rosenberg, Bellow's late colleague at the University of Chicago's Committee on Social Thought; that the prodigy-hero of "Zetland: By a Character Witness" is fingered as the double of Isaac Rosenfeld, Bellow's boyhood friend, a writer and Reichian who died at thirty-eight. There are always anti-readers, resenters or recanters of the poetry side of life, mean distrusters of the force and turbulence of the free imagination, who are ready to demote fiction to the one-on-one flatness of photo-journalism. Omitting, then, extraterritorial interests not subject to the tractable laws of fiction—omitting *gossip*—would you recognize Bellow's muscle, his swift and glorious eye?

Yes, absolutely; a thousand times yes. It is Bellow's Chicago, Bellow's portraiture—these faces, these heads!—above all, Bellow's motor. That Bellow himself may acknowledge a handful of biographical sources—"germs," textured shells—does not excite.

The life on the page resists the dust of flesh, and is indifferent to external origins. Victor Wulpy is who he is as Bellow's invention; and certainly Zetland. These inventions take us not to Bellow as man, eminence, and friend of eminences (why should I care whom Bellow knows?), but to the private clamor in the writing. And it is this clamor, this sound of a thrashing soul—comic because metaphysical, metaphysical because aware of itself as a farcical combatant on a busy planet—that is unequivocally distinguishable as the pure Bellovian note. "The clever, lucky old Berlin Jew, whose head was like a round sourdough loaf, all uneven and dusted with flour, had asked the right questions"—if this canny sentence came floating to us over the waves, all alone on a dry scrap inside a bottle, who would not instantly identify it as Bellow's voice?

It is a voice demonized by the right (or possibly the right) questions. The characters it engenders are dazed by what may be called the principle of plenitude. Often they appear to take startled credit for the wild ingenuity of the world's abundance, as if they had themselves brought it into being. It isn't that they fiddle with the old freshman philosophy-course conundrum, Why is there everything instead of nothing? They ask rather: What is this everything composed of? What is it preoccupied with? They are knocked out by the volcanic multiplicity of human thought, they want to count up all the ideas that have ever accumulated in at least our part of the universe, they roil, burn, quake with cosmic hunger. This makes them, sometimes, jesters, and sometimes only sublime fools.

"What Kind of Day Did You Have?," the novella that is the centerpiece of this volume, also its masterpiece, gives us a day in the life of "one of the intellectual captains of the modern world" —Victor Wulpy, who, if love is sublime and lovers foolish, qualifies as a reacher both high and absurd. Reaching for the telephone in a Buffalo hotel, Victor calls his lover, Katrina Goliger, in suburban Chicago, and invites—commands—her to fly in zero weather from Chicago to Buffalo solely in order to keep him company on his flight from Buffalo to Chicago. "With Victor refusal was not one of her options," so Trina, sourly divorced, the mother of two unresponsive young daughters, acquiesces. Victor's egotism and self-indulgence, the by-blows of a nearly fatal recent illness and of a powerfully centered arrogance, are as alluring as his fame, his dependency, his brilliance, his stiff game leg "extended like one of Admiral Nelson's cannon under wraps," his size-sixteen shoes that waft out "a human warmth" when Trina tenderly pulls them off. Victor is a cultural lion who exacts, Trina surmises, ten thousand dollars per lecture. In Buffalo his exasperating daughter, a rabbinical school dropout who once advised her decorous mother to read a manual on homosexual foreplay as a means of recapturing Victor's sexual interest, hands him her violin to lug to Chicago for repairs; it is Trina who does the lugging. Victor is headed for Chicago to address the Executives Association, "National Security Council types," but really to be with Trina. Trina suffers from a carping angry sister, a doting hanger-on named Krieggstein, who carries guns and may or may not be a real cop, and the aftermath of a divorce complicated by psychiatric appointments, custody wrangling, greed. She is also wrestling with the perplexities of a children's story she hopes to write, if only she can figure out how to extricate her elephant from his crisis on the top floor of a department store, with no way down or out. At the same time Victor is being pursued, in two cities, by Wrangel, a white-furred Hollywood plot-concocter, celebrated maker of *Star Wars*–style films, a man hot with ideas who is impelled to tell Victor that "ideas are trivial" and Trina that Victor is a "promoter."

Meanwhile, planes rise and land, or don't take off at all; there is a bad-weather detour to Detroit and a chance for serendipitous sex in an airport hotel, and finally a perilous flight in a Cessna, where, seemingly facing death in a storm, Trina asks Victor to say he loves her. He refuses, they touch down safely at O'Hare, the story stops but doesn't exactly end. Wrangel has helped Trina dope out what to do about the trapped elephant, but Trina herself is left tangled in her troubles, submissively energetic and calculating, and with no way up or out.

What emerges from these fluid events, with all their cacophonous espousal of passion, is a mind at the pitch of majesty. The agitated, untamable, yet flagging figure of the dying Victor Wulpy, a giant in the last days of his greatness, seizes us not so much for the skein of shrewd sympathy and small pathos in which he is bound and exposed, as for the claims of these furious moments of insatiable connection: "Katrina had tried to keep track of the subjects covered between Seventy-sixth Street and Washington Square: the politics of modern Germany from the Holy Roman Empire through the Molotov-Ribbentrop Pact; what surrealist communism had *really* been about; Kiesler's architecture; Hans Hofmann's influence; what limits were set by liberal democracy for the development of the arts. . . . Various views on the crises in economics, cold war, metaphysics, sexaphysics."

Not that particular "subjects" appear fundamentally to matter to Bellow, though they thrillingly engage him. The young Zetland, discovering *Moby-Dick*, cries out to his wife: "There really is no human life without this poetry. Ah, Lottie, I've been starving on symbolic logic." In fact he has been thriving on it, and on every other kind of knowledge. "What were we here for, of all strange beings and creatures the strangest? Clear colloid eyes to see with, for a while, and see so finely, and a palpitating universe to see, and so many human messages to give and receive. And the bony box for thinking and for the storage of thought, and a cloudy heart for feelings."

It is the hound of heaven living in the bony box of intelligence that dogs Bellow, and has always dogged him. If the soul is the mind at its purest, best, clearest, busiest, profoundest, then Bellow's charge has been to restore the soul to American literature. The five stories in *Him with His Foot in His Mouth* are the distillation of that charge. Bellow's method is to leave nothing unobserved and unremarked, to give way to the unprogrammed pressure of language and intellect, never to retreat while imagination goes off like kites. These innovative sentences, famous for pumping street-smarts into literary blood vessels, are alive and snaky, though hot. And Bellow's quick-witted lives of near-poets, as recklessly confident in the play and intricacy of ideas as those of the grand Russians, are Russian also in the gusts of natural force that sweep through them: unpredictable cadences, instances where the senses fuse ("A hoarse sun rolled up"), single adjectives that stamp whole portraits, portraits that stamp whole lives (hair from which "the kink of high vigor had gone out"), the knowing hand on the ropes of how-things-work, the stunning catalogues of worldliness ("commodity brokers, politicians, personal-injury lawyers, bagmen and fixers, salesmen and promoters"), the boiling presence of Chicago, with its "private recesses for seduction and skulduggery." A light flavoring of Jewish social history dusts through it all: e.g., Victor Wulpy reading the Pentateuch in Hebrew in a cheder on the Lower East Side in 1912; or Zetland's immigrant father, who, in a Chicago neighborhood "largely Polish and Ukrainian, Swedish, Catholic, Orthodox, and Evangelical Lutheran . . . preferred the company of musical people and artists, bohemian garment workers, Tolstoyans, followers of Emma Goldman and of Isadora Duncan, revolutionaries who wore pince-nez, Russian blouses, Lenin or Trotsky beards."

What this profane and holy comedy of dazzling, beating, multiform profusion hints at, paradoxically, is that Bellow is as notable for what isn't in his pages as for what is. No preciousness, of the ventriloquist kind or any other; no carelessness either (formidably the opposite); no romantic aping of archaisms or nostalgias; no restraints born out of theories of form, or faddish tenets of experimentalism or ideological crypticness; no neanderthal flatness in the name of cleanliness of prose; no gods of nihilism; no gods of subjectivity; no philosophy of parody. As a consequence of these and other salubrious omissions and insouciant dismissals, Bellow's detractors have accused him of being "old-fashioned," "conventional," of continuing to write a last-gasp American version of the nineteenth-century European novel; his omnivorous "Russianness" is held against him, and at the same time he is suspected of expressing the deadly middle class.

The grain of truth in these disparagements takes note, I think, not of regression or lagging behind, but of the condition of local fiction, which has more and more closeted itself monkishly away in worship of its own liturgies—i.e., of its own literariness. Whereas Bellow, seeing American writing in isolation from America itself, remembered Whitman and Whitman's cornucopia: in homage to which he fabricated a new American sentence. All this, of course, has been copiously remarked of Bellow ever since Augie March; but these five stories say something else. What Bellow is up to here is nothing short of a reprise of Western intellectual civilization. His immigrants and children of immigrants, blinking their fetal eyes in the New World, seem to be cracking open the head of Athena to get themselves born, in eager thirst for the milk of Enlightenment. To put it fortissimo: Bellow has brain on the brain, which may cast him as *the* dissident among American writers.

But even this is not the decoding or revelation I spoke of earlier. It has not been enough for Bellow simply to have restored attention to society—the density and entanglements of its urban textures, viz.: "He [Woody Selbst in "A Silver Dish"] maintained the bungalow—this took in roofing, pointing, wiring, insulation, air-conditioning—and he paid for heat and light and food, and dressed them all out of Sears, Roebuck and Wieboldt's, and bought them a TV, which they watched as devoutly as they prayed." Nor has it been enough for Bellow to have restored attention to the over-riding bliss of learning: "Scholem and I [of "Cousins"], growing up on neighboring streets, attending the same schools, had traded books, and since Scholem had no trivial interests, it was Kant and Schelling all the way, it was Darwin and Nietzsche, Dostoyevsky and Tolstoy, and in our senior year it was Oswald Spengler. A whole year was invested in *The Decline of the West*."

To this thickness of community and these passions of mind Bellow has added a distinctive ingredient, not new on any landscape, but shamelessly daring just now in American imaginative prose. Let the narrator of "Cousins" reveal it: "We enter the world without prior notice, we are manifested before we can be aware of manifestation. An original self exists, or, if you prefer, an original soul. . . . I was invoking my own fundamental perspective, that of a person who takes for granted distortion in the ordinary way of seeing but has never given up the habit of referring all truly important observations to that original self or soul." Bellow, it seems, has risked mentioning—who can admit to this without literary embarrassment?—the Eye of God.

And that is perhaps what his intellectual fevers have always pointed to. "Cousins" speaks of it explicitly: "As a man is, so he sees. As the Eye is formed, such are its powers." Yet "Cousins" is overtly about "the observation of cousins," and moves from cousin Tanky of the rackets to cousin Seckel whose "talent was for picking up strange languages" to cousin Motty, who, "approaching ninety, still latched on to people to tell them funny things." All this reflects a powerfully recognizable Jewish family feeling—call it, in fact, family love, though it is love typically mixed with amazement and disorder. The professor-narrator of "Him with His Foot in His Mouth"—the title story—like cousin Motty is also a funny fellow, the author of a long letter conscientiously recording his compulsion to make jokes that humiliate and destroy: putdowns recollected in tranquillity. But the inescapable drive to insult through wit is equated with "seizure, rapture, demonic possession, frenzy, *Fatum*, divine madness, or even solar storm," so this lambent set of comic needlings is somehow more than a joke, and may touch on the Eye of Dionysus. "A Silver Dish," with its upside-down echo of the biblical tale of Joseph's silver cup, concerns the companionable trials of Woody Selbst and his rogue father, the two of them inextricably entwined, though the father has abandoned his family; all the rest, mother, sisters, aunt, and ludicrous immigrant reverend uncle, are Jewish converts to evangelicalism. Woody, like Joseph in Egypt, supports them all. The Eye of God gazes through this story too, not in the bathetic converts but in the scampish father, "always, always something up his sleeve." "Pop had made Woody promise to bury him among Jews"—neglected old connections being what's up that raffish sleeve. It is Woody's "clumsy intuition" that "the goal set for this earth was that it should be filled with good, saturated with it." All the same, the commanding image in this narrative is that of a buffalo calf snatched and devoured by a crocodile in the waters of the Nile, in that alien country where Joseph footed the family bills and his father Jacob kept his wish to be buried among Jews up his sleeve almost to the end.

The commanding image of this volume—the concordance, so to speak, to all of Bellow's work—turns up in the reflections of one of the cousins, Ijah Brodsky: " 'To long for the best that ever was': this was not an abstract project. I did not learn it over a seminar table. It was a constitutional necessity, physiological, temperamental, based on sympathies which could not be acquired. Human absorption in faces, deeds, bodies, drew me toward metaphysical grounds. I had these peculiar metaphysics as flying creatures have their radar."

This metaphysical radar (suspiciously akin to the Eye of God) "decodes" Saul Bellow; and these five ravishing stories honor and augment his genius.

Henry James's Unborn Child

Henry James is the only American writer whom our well-ingrained democratic literary conventions have been willing to call Master. Not even Emerson, who as philosopher of individualism stands as a kind of Muse to all subsequent American culture and society, has been granted that title. It fell to James—this acknowledgment of magisterial illuminations—not simply because of his Balzacian amplitude, although that would have been reason enough. From the oceanic plenitude of James's imagination and genius there rode out, with the aristocratic majesty of great seagoing ships, a succession of novels (20 of these), short stories (112; some, by contemporary standards, the size of novels), biographies and auto-biographies, critical and social essays (ranging from a book-length vision of Hawthorne to the 1905 Bryn Mawr College commencement speech), travel and museum impressions, a dozen plays, innumerable literary notebooks, dazzling letters bearing both difficult truths and what James himself termed "the mere twaddle of graciousness."

Published as "A Master's Mind," *The New York Times Magazine*, October 26, 1986

Like the Cunarders of his day, James's ambition was inter-continental. An expatriate who came of age in Cambridge, Mas-sachusetts, during the Civil War, he lived and wrote in hotels and lodgings in Rome, Venice, Florence, Paris. Eventually he took up residence in London, and finally he bought a house in the little English sea town of Rye. His themes too were international—Americans in Europe, Europeans in America. "Very special and very interesting," he once noted, "the state of being of the American who has bitten deep into the apple of 'Europe' and then been obliged to take his lips from the fruit." As it turned out, James never did take his lips from the fruit; he died an American bachelor who was also a patriotic British subject. Numbers of his short stories—like "Hugh Merrow"—are about English people in England.

Yet what marks James as Master is not his Europeanized cosmopolitan eye, or even the cornucopia of his cascading novels and tales—masterpiece after masterpiece. Well before the advent of what we now call Modernism, James's prose began to exhale the most refined and secret psychological processes and nuances; and it is these exquisite techniques of insight that distinguish him from other late-nineteenth-century writers. Mysteriously, with the passing of each new decade, James becomes more and more our contemporary—it is as if our own sensibilities are only just catching up with his. We can recognize him now as a powerful symbolist, one of the supreme literary innovators of consciousness.

"Hugh Merrow," an unfinished short story written in the densely reverberating style of James's "late manner," was dis-covered in 1937 by Leon Edel, James's unsurpassed interpreter and biographer, in an old sea chest at the bottom of Harvard's Widener Library. It lay there "neatly tied with red and blue cotton strips" among the last of the Notebooks and in the company of several commercial pocket diaries (in one of which James could view the Jewish liturgical calendar for the year 5671 amid the eclipses and tides of 1911). A fragment had, of course, no place in Edel's twelve-volume definitive edition of James's

Tales. For fifty years—though "Hugh Merrow" was there for the asking, catalogued, readily accessible—no one came forward to publish it, comment on it, or even marvel at its uniquely truncated condition. An unaccountable absence of scholarly curiosity, given the always bustling university industry represented by Jamesian studies. (A Jamesian wonderment: is it only artists who are lured by the inchoate, and never scholars?) In bringing out *The Complete Notebooks of Henry James*—the sea-chest residue of James's pen—Leon Edel and his collaborator, Lyall H. Powers, have put into our hands the text of an acute psychological riddle: why did James, whose brilliant consummations did not fail him in 112 completed stories, break off in the middle of this one?

That he could have been discouraged by any falling off in tone or brio is unlikely. The style of "Hugh Merrow" is James at his steadiest and most assured. The comedy is burnished and fully self-aware. The progression of the plot is as finely calculated as anything James ever wrote. And it was not his habit, as the output of half a century testifies, to leave work unfinished. Nor was there anything casual about the design of "Hugh Merrow"—the Notebooks reveal at least six separate foreshadowings of this eccentric tale.

The first appears in the fall of 1895, in the form of a subject James calls "The Child," a story about a painter told to him thirdhand by friends of the Italian novelist Luigi Gualdo. In May of 1898, James begins to imagine a "woman who wants to have *been* married—to *have become* a widow," who approaches a painter for a portrait of the husband she has never had. A tendril of this motif turned into "The Tone of Time," chiefly about rival lovers—but what seems to have been brewing here, and to have kept on brewing, is the idea of the life never lived, the missed experience. (This was to become the reigning theme of *The Ambassadors*, a novel at the summit of James's art, also written during this period.) Two years later, in 1900, "the little 'Gualdo' notion" is still haunting James, and now he jots down the version he will finally pursue: "a young childless couple comes to a painter and asks him to *paint* them a little girl (or a child *quelconque*) whom they can have as their own—since they so want one and can't come by it otherwise. My subject is what I get out of *that*."

That same day, setting down a long row of names (over a hundred of them) for possible future use in stories, James lists "Archdean," which will emerge as Captain Archdean, the young would-be father in "Hugh Merrow." Two other names on that list—"Marcher" and "Bartram"—will empower one of James's most shocking psychological horror tales, "The Beast in the Jungle," published the following year: about a man whose life, tragically hollow, passes him by solely because he has wilfully missed the chance to live it. John Marcher does not marry May Bartram, and ends in devastating loneliness.

James was at this time preoccupied with his own loneliness. Not long after the names Archdean, Marcher, and Bartram were entered into his Notebook, he confessed, in a letter, to *"the essential loneliness of my life"*—the emphasis is his. "This loneliness," he inquired, "what is it still but the deepest thing about one? Deeper about *me*, at any rate, than anything else; deeper than my 'genius,' deeper than my 'discipline,' deeper than my pride, deeper, above all, than the deep counterminings of art." Loneliness, he said, was to be his final port. He was fifty-seven.

The bachelor painter Hugh Merrow is presented cheerfully as "our young man," and yet he too is described as ultimately solitary. "He was single, he was, behind everything, lonely, and it had been given him so little to taste of any joy of perfect union, that he was, as to many matters, not even at one with himself. The joy of perfect union, nevertheless, had hovered before him like a dream. . . ." Again the theme of the missed experience. In the story's original scheme it was not to have been in the artist, this sense of the lost life, but rather in the childless couple. It is as if James had inadvertently sketched himself in: a fleeting self-portrait in a corner of the canvas.

On the other hand, James's self-scrutiny is everywhere on the canvas. Captain and Mrs. Archdean are hoping to commission a portrait of a child that doesn't exist, the child they cannot have. Adoption won't do; a real son or daughter will fall short of the ideal. "Hugh Merrow," from its confident start to its abrupt stop, is a meditation on the nature of imagination. How close to reality is the artist's invention? Can there be invention without at least partial grounding in actuality—some hint or model? Is there an ideal beauty that solid flesh can never duplicate? Can one live on fantasy just as well as on reality? Is there "such a drawback as [the artist's] having *too* free a hand?" Is imagination only a tricky disguise for the actual and the known? Is art the same as forgery?

But these questions point to only half the riddle of "Hugh Merrow." The other half may come nearer to the marrow of the self. (Is it unimportant, by the way, that "Hugh" can be heard as "you," and "Merrow" as "marrow"?) The other half is psychosexual. It is Mrs. Archdean's intelligence that Hugh Merrow draws close to; she asks him to combine with her in the making of her child. Looking around his studio at "things on easels, started, unfinished, but taking more or less the form of life," she vividly implores him to give birth to an imagined child on her account, in her place. And what is the sex of the child to be? Captain Archdean wants a boy who will look like his wife; Mrs. Archdean wants a girl in the image of her husband. Since they can't agree on which it is to be—*they* aren't a perfect union—they leave it up to Hugh Merrow: the sexual choice is his. Girl or boy? The painter must decide.

Here the fragment ends. There is no climax. "It was wonderful how he pleased them. . . . If only he could keep it up!"

Yet James had often before made such choices. His novels and stories are full of little girls understood—and inhabited—from within. Sensitive little boys are somewhat fewer, but they are dramatically there. He continually chose one or the other—in effect he chose both. But in "Hugh Merrow" he was pressing the artist—himself—to give birth to pure imagining, roused from the artist's inmost being and equivalent to it. If the painting is the painter, then James was pressing the artist—he was pressing himself—to decide his own sex, a charge impossible to satisfy. James had never married; he had never achieved perfect union with anyone. He counted his solitude the deepest thing about him. As for sexual union, he was apparently wholly inexperienced, a true celibate. He was at various times attracted to artistic young men, and there has always been speculation about suppressed homoerotic inclinations. Some have even gone so far as to hint at a castrating accident, the notorious "obscure hurt" of James's youth.

James, for his part, burned all the papers and letters he wished to keep from us. He intended to close the door on his privacy. It is a door that we, out of respect for the Master, ought not to force. But "Hugh Merrow" may, after all, be a crack of light from under the door. If James did not go on with "Hugh Merrow," it may be that it required him to resolve, once and for all, the unspoken enigma of his sexual identity. And this, as protean artist, as imaginative tenant of the souls of both women and men, he could not do.

There is more. In the figurations of "Hugh Merrow," James put to himself in its most radical form the question of his own missed experience. In life he had chosen not to be husband or father. But "Hugh Merrow" demanded more than symbolic fatherhood. It demanded that the artist become, through the visionary organization of his art, a mother. It equated the artist with the embryo-bearing woman—while at the same time urging the substitution of art for life. The aesthetic birth was to be an explicit stand-in for an impossible biological fruition. And here the intrinsic contradictions may have grown too stressful for James; the metaphor burst and could not be sustained. He could not keep it up, he could not deliver. In "Hugh Merrow" —a tale seemingly easy and comic, and surely rich with the recognitions of its own bizarreness—James was flinging himself past the threshold of the erotic into the very birth canal itself. In the face of psychological pressure so plainly insupportable, he withdrew.

The question for us is whether *we* will withdraw. Given the enchantment of an unfinished story by Henry James brought to light almost a century after the Master first conceived "the little 'Gualdo' notion," how many writers and readers will be tempted to complete the artist's birth rites? Who now will dare to paint the unimaginable unborn Child?

Emerging Dreiser

Theodore Dreiser: At the Gates of the City, 1871–1907, the first volume of Richard Lingeman's two-part biography, reaches only seven years beyond the initial publication of *Sister Carrie*, when, in the wake of early neglect, the book was successfully reissued. Its 1907 revival—and victorious arrival—is an appropriate biographical climax. A first novel by the son of a German Catholic immigrant, *Sister Carrie* is also the first recognizably "American" novel—urban American in the way we feel it now. Springing up in a period when the novel's tone was governed chiefly by aristocrats of English-speaking stock—William Dean Howells, Edith Wharton, Henry James—Dreiser's driven prose uncovers the unmistakable idiom of a raw Chicago and the New York of dumbwaiters and flophouses. To find one's way into the streets and flats of Dreiser's two cities is to experience the unfolding of literary history—to see how the English novel, itself an immigrant, finally pocketed its "papers" and became naturalized.

But to enter these cramped flats and teeming streets is to re-

Published as "Miracle on Grub Street," *The New York Times Book Review*, November 9, 1986

experience personal history as well. Dreiser's salesmen and managers, his factory girls and two-dollar-a-week boarders, his images of shirtwaists, sweatshops, horsecars, are the fabric of our grandparents' world; we know it with the kind of intimacy we cannot bring to Hawthorne's Puritans or James's high-caste international visitors. *Sister Carrie* is a turn-of-the-century vat boiling with the hot matter—and cold materialism—of old Broadway, West Side apartment houses newly built, glimmers of restaurants, hotels, and theaters that once were remote names out of newspapers in our own households. Unless you are descended from John Quincy Adams—unless no one in your family ever passed through Castle Garden—*Sister Carrie*, read now and for the first time, is an oddly private voyage home: a time machine into the harrowings of an era not yet dimmed, when jobs meant unbroken drudgery, and when the eight-hour working day, Social Security, and publicly funded relief were futuristic socialist visions. Into just such confusions and predicaments our immigrant relations tumbled.

Richard Lingeman's impressive marshalings build toward the consummation of this landmark work, and if a new life of Dreiser needs any justification at all, then the unremitting veracity and inclusiveness of *Sister Carrie* are reason enough. It is strengthening to Mr. Lingeman's undertaking that he is preceded by an already admirable procession of biographers and critics—among the latter the late Ellen Moers, unsurpassed in robust Dreiserian advocacy. Still, a fresh biography becomes a necessity only if more life is imagined for it, more than there was before. Biography remains, after all, the one form where the chronological empowerment of character, in the way of the nineteenth-century novel, continues to dominate—with the difference, of course, that the life in it is "real." Some biographies require no successors—Leon Edel's *Henry James* springs to mind—because their subjects are permeated with the conviction of sufficiency. It is not that they have been recorded merely; they have "come to life," and break through the page once and for all. In this sense there is still plenty of room, and opportunity, for the psychological illumination of Theodore Dreiser—for a biography with the blood-force of a novel.

Lingeman's representation of Dreiser is scrupulously, mas-sively—devotedly—constructed; everything is in it, including a clear passion for the social issues of the period. And it is immac-ulately rendered, free of tendentiousness of any kind. But it is an expository library construction, not an elastically breathing imag-inative reanimation. The great Dreiserian riddle is not even so much as approached, still less appraised: how is it that a workhorse daily journalist—a needy and febrile Grub Street factotum grind-ing out newspaper copy at fire-truck speed—could transform him-self into a novelist of such encompassing gritty recalcitrant power? Lingeman asserts this miracle without examining it. "Dreiser's greatest strength," he tells us at the halfway mark, "is his empathy with his characters, which reaches its peak [in *Sister Carrie*] in the final scenes about Hurstwood. In the supreme effort to make be-lievable the climactic downfall of this, the most strongly imagined figure in the book, Dreiser *became* Hurstwood, producing his every thought, his every emotion, from inside himself." (That Dreiser would "become Hurstwood" again later on, and far less meta-phorically, is a vivid connection with the future Lingeman crucially lets slip.)

Yet Lingeman, from inside *him*self, offers no comparable be-coming. His Dreiser is for the most part a product of strong in-formation, not strong imagining. Hence "Theodore," as Lingeman calls his subject—with undelivered intimations of insight—remains just that: a subject, a datum on the surface of the text. Theodore—the living Dreiser—is not exactly *there*. But his evi-dences are everywhere, and they are rich and dense. A biography of information is not overwhelmingly inferior to a biography of psychological re-creation; and flashy re-creation (such a thing is possible) without the dedicated accumulation of a store of diligent accuracies is a cheat. Lingeman's biography of information is never a cheat. On the contrary. Such patient assimilation of old and new particularity not only earns our homage, but, on its own terms, exhilarates. Once warned that Theodore—i.e., Dreiser as *mind*—is not exactly there, we can marvel at what is.

And what is there, punctiliously there, is a chronicle of

emergence—of an especially American kind. Dreiser was an obsessive reader of Balzac, but his own story is tonally different from that of Balzac's young man from the provinces who sets out to seize literary fame in the glorious city. In much of Dreiser's America, city and boondocks were alike in newness and rootlessness; both were more provisional than traditional, more contingent than composed. The Midwest was only just fashioning itself; a family line was often no longer than a single generation. Dreiser's father was himself, to use that striking old immigrant's tag, right off the boat; his English was never unblemished. All ten of his children (Theodore was the ninth) were given combinations of names that would have been more at home in his native Mayen in Alsace-Lorraine than in Terre Haute, Indiana. All the children eventually anglicized their Christian names—Alphons Joachim, for instance, became Al—and the oldest, Johann Paul, Jr., changed Dreiser to Dresser and ended as Paul Dresser, the celebrated songwriter. The mother of this first-generation family came of an earlier German-American migration. A Mennonite, she abandoned the "plain people" strictures of her sect and converted to Catholicism to please her rigidly devout husband.

These shifts of vowels and allegiances, these fresh and strange alliances, would have been unthinkable in any society less bent on mutation. Emerging from the American backwater was not so much a matter of making one's way as it was of finding a way to make oneself up. Dreiser was determined to emerge—he allowed himself no other course—because he was born, so to speak, sunk. His father, a wool worker, rose briefly to mill manager and then, after a head injury, descended into unbalanced religious fanaticism and irreversible joblessness and poverty. The mother moved the children from Hoosier town to Hoosier town, taking in washing and boarders. Dreiser's brother Paul sang in blackface and for a time lived with the madam of a prosperous bordello. Dreiser's sisters went off to be "kept." One gave birth to an out-of-wedlock child. Another, Emma, fled first to Canada and then to New York with a Chicago thief and absconder named Hopkins: the flagrant domestic seed of *Sister Carrie*. In New York, Hopkins, like the fictional Hurstwood, collapsed into indigent apathy. So finally did Dreiser's father. Respectability was no part of Dreiser's family inheritance; he grew up on the underside, among the spurned. At twenty he stole money to buy himself an overcoat. If, in later years, he wrote with a journalist's detachment of the "curious shifts of the poor," it was nevertheless out of bitter familiarity. For Dreiser, being poor was life, not hypothesis.

The instruments of his emergence were two. The first was social gentility: Sara White, nicknamed Jug, the woman he romantically fixed on to marry (he went on dreaming and letter-writing through a drawn-out courtship), belonged to a prominent small-town Missouri family of transplanted Virginia aristocrats. The second instrument was journalism. Dreiser's climb from legman to free lance to full-time reporter to "magazinist" to editor, with pratfalls and loss of footing along the way, is the sovereign thread of Lingeman's narrative. It includes Dreiser's peculiarly dependent friendship—an entrance into psychological twinship—with his fellow journalist Arthur Henry: "If he had been a girl, I would have married him," Dreiser once remarked. Instead, Henry moved in with the newly-weds, Dreiser and Jug, on West 102nd Street, and the pair—Dreiser and Henry—formed a writing partnership, sharing assignments and fees. The summer before, they had shared Henry's house on the idyllic Maumee, in Ohio. Urged on by Henry—with whom he eventually broke—Dreiser began writing his first fiction.

Lingeman's meticulous account of Dreiser's work history—covering Pittsburgh, St. Louis, Chicago, New York, a progression of cities in growth—yields also a masterly impressionist history of American journalism in the preëminent age of newspapers, and in the heyday of a variety of popular periodicals now obsolete: song sheets, song magazines, and even dress-pattern magazines. The sale of song sheets made Paul Dresser rich; his hit, "On the Banks of the Wabash," partly written by Dreiser, quickly acquired the credentials of a folk melody. *Ev'ry Month*, a song magazine for the parlor piano that had been launched by the success of "The Sidewalks of New York," took Dreiser on as editor; he soon transformed it, and even found room for an essay by Arthur Henry entitled "The Philosophy of Hope." This was in 1897; that same year Dreiser was fired. A decade beyond saw him editor of the Butterick pattern periodical, *The Delineator*, which he authoritatively refashioned into a more comprehensive women's magazine. He had risen to become a major editor in New York, quartered in genteelly plush offices. In between, he was successively at the helm of *Smith's* and *Broadway*—"a prototype of *Vanity Fair* and the *New Yorker*"—where his assistant, a young intellectual fresh out of Bryn Mawr, "thought her boss a commercial hack—until she read *Sister Carrie* and became a worshiper."

Sister Carrie had been grudgingly brought out in 1900 against the wishes of its own publisher, Frank Doubleday, who had accepted the novel on the basis of Frank Norris's enthusiasm, and then precipitately changed his mind midway. A libertine according to conventional judgment, Dreiser's heroine not only goes unpunished, but ascends to become a brilliant figure in the world. To Doubleday this was "indecent," and though both Jug and Arthur Henry worked at softening—bowdlerizing—certain problematical passages, the publisher, fearing scandal, barely fulfilled his contract; the novel was stillborn. Dreiser, however, was counting on William Dean Howells, who had the power of making reputations. No review by Howells appeared. When Dreiser ran into him by chance, Howells told him brusquely: "I didn't like *Sister Carrie*."

With the failure of his novel, Dreiser's morale gradually foundered, and from this moment—a hundred pages or so before the close of this first volume, and the harbinger perhaps of larger resonances in the second—Lingeman increases in psychological force and imaginative presence. His record of Dreiser's extraordinary decline, after a period of pointless wandering—"an aching desire to be forever on the move," Dreiser called it—into the lost life of lodging-house hall bedrooms is a cutting portrait of mental depression and the disintegrations of "neurasthenia." But it is also something more. Dreiser as railway crew member, Dreiser spending the night in a Bowery flophouse—here is the mystery of a vigorous and self-disciplined writer melting into the character and fate of his creation: Dreiser astoundingly turning himself into his own Hurstwood. Lingeman is able to penetrate this eerie and prodigious darkness, I think, because he lets it unfold almost novelistically on its own: he surrenders to its unaccountability.

Earlier, Lingeman had plausibly reminded us of "Dreiser's sense of the economic tragedy at the heart of American life." In a Prologue, he sketches the stringent atmosphere of Dreiser's ripening years—"the mass migration to the cities, the widening fissure between rich and poor, the rise of industry, the centralization of economic (and political) power in the corporations and trusts," and more. It is true that much of this entered Dreiser's fictional domestic scenery. An anonymous reviewer of *Sister Carrie* observed how the downward course of Hurstwood illustrated a rule: that "civilization is at bottom an economic fact," that "if the economic pilings on which . . . lives are built are swept away, they will sink into destitution, loss of self-respect, moral squalor." Lingeman appears to attribute this altogether programmatic position to Dreiser himself. Possibly. (Toward the end of his life Dreiser did become markedly programmatic, to the extent of endorsing Communism and supporting Earl Browder's opposition to the war against Hitler.)

And yet something there is in the enigma of literary dreaming that eludes even the most searching social thesis. Those economic pilings cannot be made to sustain or explain the whole range of the human predicament, and it is hard to believe that Dreiser— as novelist—ever took such a view. Dreiser sinking into the very vision his art foretold—Dreiser becoming Hurstwood—is in a place where socioeconomic theory cannot reach. His recovery and return to achievement, followed by the gratifying reissue of *Sister Carrie*, stand poignantly apart from any determinist social analysis. *Sister Carrie*—the story of a woman dreaming her way out of poverty—may powerfully exemplify the migration to the cities and the fissure between rich and poor, and indeed the entire American "economic tragedy" of a century ago; but what Carrie exemplifies hardly accounts for her. And Hurstwood too is governed as much by his own threadbare imagination as by any external collapse of "economic pilings." Carrie is Dreiser's dream of the

spirit incandescent, Hurstwood of the snuffed. It is not a contradiction that Dreiser is signally recorded among the realists.

I spoke at the start of the rare chance of encountering *Sister
Carrie* now and for the first time. Who, after so many school
assignments, will have such good luck? But to come to *Sister Carrie*
minus the baggage of unripe exposure and stale critical disparagements—to cut loose from Dreiser's reputation for ponderous
eyesore sentences—is to fall into a living heat, the truth of things.
The well-accepted abuse of Dreiser's style—how relieving it is
that Lingeman steers clear of any of this—seems a calumny. Taken
by itself and for itself, Dreiser's novel is life-hard: stubborn, nervy,
gaudy and bawdy, full of weather, sex, hope, inertness, toil, sadness, dirt, dream. A work with no lying—toward which Mr.
Lingeman's lucid sympathies and resourceful labor form a strong
and granite corridor.

George Steiner's Either / Or

In an essay pointedly called "The Archives of Eden," George
Steiner makes a case for America (a case against, actually) as the
great museum hall of Europe. Almost no element of American
cultural expression, he argues, is indigenously American. Even
American literature is compelled to come under the heading of
fundamental parasitism: "Strictly regarded," Steiner avers, "American English and the literature it produces is one of the branches,
if statistically the most forceful, of the prodigal ramifications of
the mother-tongue." Among the latter he lists "the language and
literature of Canada, Australia, New Zealand, of the Anglo-Indian
community of the West Indies [and] of the English-speaking nations of Africa." These, along with American English, continue
to depend on "the eroded but still canonic primacy of the motherland." American letters are, in fact—and in spite of "claims
to classic occasion"—a manifestation of a "continentally regional
literature."

Originally a talk at a conference, "Art and Intellect in America," at Skidmore
College, April 1980. Published (in somewhat different form) in *Salmagundi*, Fall
1980–Winter 1981

"The [literary] summits," Steiner finds, "are *not* American: they are Thomas Mann, Kafka, Joyce and Proust."

As for painting and music, "American museums and art collections are brimful of classical and European art. . . . American orchestras, chamber groups, opera companies, perform European music." In philosophy and social thought, "American philosophers edit, translate, comment upon and teach Heidegger, Wittgenstein or Sartre but do not put forth a major metaphysics. . . . the pressure of presence throughout the world of the mind and moral feeling exercised on civilization by a Marx, a Freud, even a Lévi-Strauss, is of a caliber which American culture does not produce."

The reason, in a word, is democracy; or, rather, democracy's indifference to high culture. Genius of this kind, Steiner believes, cannot be nurtured in a society lacking an "elite model": "It does look, and this is a somewhat perplexing phenomenon, as if the number of human beings capable of responding intelligently, with any genuine commitment of sensibility, to, say, a Mozart sonata, a Gauss theorem, a sonnet by Dante, a drawing by Ingres or a Kantian proposition and deductive chain is, in any given time and community, very restricted." And he concludes: "The first thing a coherent culture will do, therefore, is to maximalize the chances for the quantum leap, for the positive mutation which is genius."

But American culture has chosen to concentrate on something else: democratic meliorism, the broad hope of social progress. Steiner hardly denies the value of such a choice: "The flowering of the humanities is not worth the circumstance of the inhuman. No play by Racine is worth a Bastille, no Mandelstam poem an hour of Stalinism." Nor does he deny the harsh cost of a Periclean age; for the sake of honesty, the cost is what he insists on. Willingly, Steiner summons up the dark landscape that is likely, he assures us, to surround the gold:

> . . . the fabric of high literacy in the Periclean and European vein offers little protection against political oppression and folly. Civilization, in the elevated and formal sense, does not guarantee civility,

does not inhibit social violence and waste. No mob, no storm-troop has ever hesitated to come down the Rue Descartes.

And yet for a moment he opens a chink into a possibly different notion of what high literacy might command: "An authentic culture," he tells us, focuses

> on the understanding, the enjoyment, the transmission forward, of the best that reason and imagination have brought forth in the past and are producing now. An authentic culture is one which makes of this order of response a primary moral and political function. It makes "response" "responsibility," it makes echo "answerable to" the high occasions of the mind.

This second glimpse, which for an instant demotes despair, offers a view of authentic high culture commensurate with, and even giving rise to, ideas of "moral function," of "responsibility," of "answerability"—in short, all those signposts of the kind of liberal society we usually call "democratic humanism."

It is the second glimpse that makes me wonder about Steiner's conclusion—his Kierkegaardian Either/Or. The choice of democratic humanism, he grants, is "thoroughly justifiable." But it is "puerile hypocrisy" to want it both ways. Either the democratic society or the Periclean: one or the other. Still, Steiner's second glimpse suggests that at least for the space of that glimpse, he too sees a hope for having it both ways: visualizes it as possible, in fact, to have an "authentic culture" with a "fabric of high literacy" not only flourishing in a context of morality, responsibility, and answerability, but actually determining and stimulating these. When Steiner ascends, however fleetingly, to this vision (or maybe, in his view, is distracted by it), the meliorist American in me wants to cheer.

He does not allow a meliorist American (which anyhow is not what I usually think I am) to cheer for long. It would indeed be puerile to imagine that Steiner supposes the interest of the KGB to be a validation of the worth of culture. He leads us into the profoundest thickets of irony when he writes: "They order these matters better in the world of the gulag. . . . The KGB and the serious writer are in total accord when both know, when both *act on the knowledge* that a sonnet . . . , a novel, a scene from a play can be the power-house of human affairs." And earlier, Steiner aptly quotes Borges: "Censorship is the mother of metaphor." That is a maxim to gasp at; but Aesopian responses to oppression, however brilliant, can have only a limited life. Finally oppression destroys literature because it eats away at words, so that eventually an abused language will be of no use to an artist, no matter how metaphorical and Aesopian his devices. These are lessons that, following Orwell, Steiner was among the first to teach us. In "The Hollow Miracle," an essay on post-Holocaust Germany, he warned: "Something will happen to the words."* Namely: when the public language is hanged in the public square, it will ultimately put the noose around the interior language. The sublime Mandelstam, to take one of Steiner's own examples, was martyred and perished because of a poem in which he compared Stalin's mustache to an insect. Of course Steiner doesn't mean us to think that tyranny, in its acknowledgment of the power in the poem—in its ceding importance to the poem—is "good for" culture. All the same, he reminds us that even when the barbarians were upon him, Archimedes did not flee; he stuck to his meditations and kept working on his theorem. Here is Plutarch's account:

> Archimedes was then, as fate would have it, intent upon working out some problem by a diagram, and having fixed his mind alike and his eyes upon the subject of speculation, he never noticed the incursion of the Romans, nor that the city was taken. In this transport of study and contemplation, a soldier unexpectedly coming up to him, commanded him to follow; which he declined to do before he had worked out his problem to a demonstration; the soldier, enraged, drew his sword and ran him through.

*In response to this allusion, Steiner comments: "I was entirely mistaken, more than twenty years ago, when I conjectured that the German language and its literatures (there are, of course, several) would not recover from Nazi evisceration. Poetry, fiction, drama and philosophic argument are intensely alive in both Germanies." Among "writers of the first rank" he cites "Thomas Bernhard, Ingeborg Bachmann, Christa Wolf, Günter Grass." But if German culture has indeed wholly recovered, and is now to be judged by the usual standards of civilization, and if Steiner requires American writing to be measured against "Thomas Mann, Kafka,

Yet elsewhere in his own demonstration Steiner counts up all those mathematical thinkers of foreign birth who flourished in America precisely because they *did* flee the barbarians.

But leaving all that aside, doesn't history grant us at least one miraculous age when the munificence of "high literacy" came to pass in a vigorously open society, sans barbarians or storm troopers? Steiner himself urges us to remember that "the passionate outpouring of popular interest in the often competitive, agonistic achievements of Renaissance artists and men of learning, of the complex manifold of adherence which made possible the Elizabethan theater audience, is not nostalgic fiction." Would it then be futuristic fiction—and not an instance of "puerile hypocrisy"—to imagine that absolute thought and absolute art might one day happen in America, despite the absence of popular interest and adherence? Despite all the horrendously recognizable descriptions Steiner has given us of America as a busy, vulgarized, well-stocked, but sterile warehouse for the fossils of European civilization?

I want to make a small quick—perhaps comical—case for such a futuristic fiction, based not on any idea of my own, but on Steiner's own portrait of the "matrix of creation"—of the genius. Here, culled at random, are some phrases and fragments that represent Steiner's depiction of genius:

"Privacy *in extremis*"
"A leprosy which seeks apartness"
"The inebriate of thought"
"The *cordon sanitaire* which a Wittgenstein could draw around himself in order to secure minimal physical survival and autonomy of spirit"
"Obsession"

Joyce and Proust" (two of whom emerge from two of the German "literatures"), then why will he not demand the same measure of grandeur for a recovered Germany? And if the vitality of the new German democracy contributes to this lack—just as American democracy is seen to be responsible for American high-cultural barrenness—why should Steiner find himself so easily satisfied by a Bernhard, a Bachmann, a Wolf, a Grass, when he is not at all satisfied by their American equivalents?

"Contagion"
"Craziness"
"Ecstatic lives"
"Calling"
"Talisman of true clerisy"
"Transcendence"
"Ontological astonishment"
"Artistic absolutes of possession and self-possession"
  The pursuit of art characterized as "pathological"
  The use of the word "espouse" with its accompanying gloss:
    "a justly sacramental verb"
  Obsession "that overrides the claims of social justice"
"A cultivation of solitude verging on the pathological"
"Absolute thought" as "antisocial, resistant to gregariousness,
    perhaps autistic"
"Personal apartness, self-exile"

It would be diminishing, and not to Steiner, to characterize these particles of portraiture as "romantic." He may seem momentarily romantic in that special sense when he speaks of "Montaigne's tower, Kierkegaard's room, Nietzsche's clandestine peregrinations." But Steiner himself warns us not to mistake his meaning for mere romanticism: "one need not mouth romantic platitudes on art and infirmity, on genius and madness, on creativity and suffering, in order to suppose that absolute thought, the commitment of one's life to a gamble on transcendence, the destruction of domestic and social relations in the name of art and 'useless' speculation, *are* part of the phenomenology which is, in respect of the utilitarian, social norm, pathological."

It would also be diminishing to make a joke about the extremely American tone of Steiner's ultimately anti-American, if I may use that term, essay. How would one buttress such a joke? As follows, with still more fragments on the necessary isolation and antisocial pathology of genius:

   . . . truly it demands something godlike in him who has cast off the
  common motives of humanity and has ventured to trust himself for

a taskmaster. High be his heart, faithful his will, clear his sight, that he may in good earnest be doctrine, society, law, to himself, that a simple purpose may be to him as strong as iron necessity is to others! . . . Your isolation must not be mechanical, but spiritual, that is, must be elevation. . . . Be it known unto you that henceforward I will obey no law less than the eternal law. . . . I will so trust that what is deep is holy, that I will do strongly before the sun and moon whatever inly rejoices me and the heart appoints.

Here again is Archimedes in concentration the moment before the barbarian sword runs him through. But you have already recognized the joke. These words are almost paraphrases of Steiner's "cultivation of solitude verging on the pathological," his "absolute thought" as "antisocial, resistant to gregariousness, perhaps autistic." You know that they are from Emerson's "Self-Reliance." The joke, if one were looking for a joke, would be to point out that Steiner's chord, with all its antipathy for the American culture-warehouse, carries nearly breath-for-breath the heartbeat of the quintessentially American essay.

But the reason I cannot accept Steiner's delineation of the absolute thinker and artist has nothing to do with any specious accusation of romanticism, and still less to do with Emersonian ironies and echoes. I cannot accept his portrait of the artist because I am willing to take his portrait as seriously as he himself takes it: the artist as a kind of shaman or holy figure, set apart from the tribe by special powers and magickings. Steiner alludes, at one point, to the sacramental valuation set on epileptics, who in some societies are automatically regarded as shamans. "There *is* a strategy of chosen illness in Archimedes' decision to die rather than relinquish a geometric deduction (this gesture being the talisman of a true clerisy)." These last three words—"talisman," "true," "clerisy"—are a trinity testifying to the priestly position Steiner accords the absolute artist, the absolute thinker. He endows his genius with godlike concentration; he agrees that "common sense, civics, and political humanity" can make no such espousal.

But consider another path. Believing as thoroughly and as passionately as he does in the artist as thaumaturge, in the nearly

autistic, obsessive, privacy-seeking autonomy of the creative genius, perhaps Steiner may be genuinely led not to decry American
philistinism, but to see it as a wry opportunity. Unlike the KGB,
Steiner notes, American culture is totally indifferent to the claims
of high art. "What text," Steiner asks, "what painting, what sym-
phony, could shake the edifice of American politics? What act of
abstract thought really matters at all? Who *cares*?"

If it is true that the answer is *nobody cares*—and *nobody cares* is
the answer Steiner certainly gives us—then American society
ought to be the ideal seedbed, the perfect fertilization dish, for the
genius for whom isolation is the *sine qua non*. What is more isolating
than our philistinism? What offers a deeper privacy? I am afraid
that what I am saying now will come to you with a touch of the
sardonic: a joke, you may think, like Emerson. But it is not a joke
and I am not aiming for the merely sardonic. If high culture is
really a matter, as Steiner has it, of *nascitur non fit*, born-not-made
(the philosopher, say, in whom complex and arduous thought is
latent, and who cannot be trained into his idiosyncratic calling);
if high culture is really a matter of obsessive privacy, originality,
autonomy, then the surrounding indifference makes everything
possible. What is missing, of course, is that "competitive, agonistic" Elizabethan responsiveness; but does a shaman need that?
Isn't a shaman complete in himself, a circle of fire, torch and
conflagration both, the dancer and the dance? Isn't the theorem
its own reward, the living note of music its own delight, the line
of a poem its own rapture? Everything Steiner reports to us about
his conception of the requirements of absolute (and absolutely
elitist) art would have us believe this. Why then should he deplore
the absence of an animate and responsive culture as a context for
his godlike creator?* Isn't it more than enough for the thinker to
say, Let there be light, and to see for himself that the light is good?

---

*To this Steiner has replied: "There is a great difference between an isolation
which remains so because the surrounding community could not care less and
one which is instrumental toward work which the community waits for and regards
as central (the isolation of a Webern, of a Heidegger, of a Wittgenstein, of a
Borges)." But if this is so, then Steiner must surrender his admiration for the

But if Steiner asserts—and he has magnificently asserted it—that a society must be more than a storehouse for the culture of another continent, that a society must answer back the claims of art and science with appropriate understanding and joy, gratitude and gratification—then should he not require for this responsiveness, this seizing and answering, a different definition of the artist, the thinker, the "matrix of creation," the genius? A definition less dependent on holy pathology?

---

death of Archimedes; or at least surrender it as an emblem of the original thinker's isolated obsessiveness. Archimedes keeps up his concentration, sticks to his work, even when the "surrounding community" is no more welcoming than a single murderous barbarian soldier. The point of the story for Steiner, if I properly understand his use of it, is precisely the absolute thinker's consummate indifference to the idea of a community that waits for his work and regards it as central. Who will care less for Archimedes' demonstration than that barbarian?

O Spilling Rapture!
O Happy Stoup!

Jonathan Cott's subject in *Pipers at the Gates of Dawn: The Wisdom of Children's Literature* is early reading and lore—the mind poised at the source of all discovery. In a way this is the only subject there is. It seizes the transcendent secret that lies within the innermost folds of science, philosophy, religion, poetry, art, and laughter. Its themes are not only magic, myth, tale, origins and causes, fates and subversions, psychological and animal nature (i.e., what is the world like, and how, and why, and why not), but the beating urgency that wells and spurts below even these: imagination itself. Or, more exactly, the shudder of bliss-tinged awe we feel when we come close enough to imagination to smell its absolute strangeness.

This strangeness, endlessly inquired after, is so endlessly protean that it is not at all surprising to find it take even the humdrum form Cott assigns it: a series of interviews with six makers of contemporary children's literature and two collectors of children's oral transmittance, accompanied by what amounts to a scattered

Published as "Talks with the Gods Who Lure Children," *The New York Times Book Review*, May 1, 1983

anthology of pertinent quotations. Cott, quoting one Gaston Ba-
chelard, defines the strangeness: "There are moments in childhood
when every child is the astonishing being, the being who realizes
the *astonishment of being.* . . . In every dreamer there lives a child,
a child whom reverie magnifies and stabilizes. Reverie tears it away
from history, sets it outside time, makes it foreign to time. One
more reverie and this permanent, magnified child is a god."

It is the gods, after all, who lure children, as they lure us: the
sensible god-out-of-the-machine that is science and diurnal miracle,
and is also Mary Poppins descending by umbrella; the whimsical
god (an insouciant Cat wearing a Hat) who first brings mess and
destruction and then proffers the dazzling olive branch of magical
cleanup. But also, according to Cott, it is gods—permanent, magnified children—who invent these reveries, who turn mundane
families and figures into receptacles for the astonishment of being.
And it appears to be the point of Jonathan Cott's interviews to
learn from these god-making dreamers—fashioners of celebrated
adventures everyone recognizes and children claim and reclaim—
whether they know themselves to be a species of god.

The disconcerting answer is: mainly yes. Sometimes the answer
is the storyteller's; more often it is Cott's own assertion imposed
on the storyteller. The answer becomes even more disconcerting
when the range of writers Cott has questioned is spread before
us—Dr. Seuss (who is really Theodor Geisel), Maurice Sendak,
William Steig, Astrid Lindgren, Chinua Achebe, P. L. Travers;
and, finally, a pair of bracingly sane scholars who, nevertheless,
hang around playgrounds to eavesdrop on rope-skippers and stuff
their house with staggering quantities of old toys. The two last
are the redoubtable Opies, Iona and the late Peter. Of the half-
dozen storytellers, Dr. Seuss begins and ends, entirely properly,
as a clown, sans any divine or vatic voice; from him Cott can draw
nothing more cosmically seductive than "When I was young . . .
I used to go to the zoo a lot, and when I returned home I would
try to draw animals. . . . You see, my father, among other things,
ran a zoo in Springfield, Massachusetts."

These words, one would think, resist conversion to lambent

mythmaking; yet Cott persists in giving us Seuss as seer. His intoxicated assessment of "The Glunk That Got Thunk," from Dr. Seuss's *I Can Lick 30 Tigers! and Other Stories*, derives, with a straight face, from Wordsworth's description of imagination as "but another name for absolute power / And clearest insight, amplitude of mind, / And Reason in her most exalted mood . . . [an] awful Power [that] rose from the mind's abyss." This flight is quickly followed, in the same paragraph, by a lofty sentence from Italo Calvino: "Our true element extends without shores, without boundaries," applied by Cott to Dr. Seuss's *On Beyond Zero* and, more darkly, to the tragic gunk that rains down in *Bartholomew and the Oobleck*. But if Wordsworth and Calvino are not enough to suggest Dr. Seuss's mind's abyss's awful Power, Cott, still in the same breath, tops them both with: "As Brian Sutton-Smith remarked in a conversation with me: 'I think that Dr. Seuss is packaging flexibility and possibility.' "

Though these dizzying juxtapositions seem to have the flat-footed out-of-the-blue energy of the Cat in the Hat himself, they are tempered by the term-paper sobriety and abundance of Cott's thousand-and-one apt quotations, which pepper the text everywhere. To wit: "It is incorrect to think fantasy is useful only to the poet. This is an insipid prejudice! It is useful even in mathematics—even differential and integral calculus could not have been discovered without it. Fantasy is a quality of the highest importance." Thus Nikolai Lenin, founder of the Soviet state, who also turns up in the chapter on Dr. Seuss.

I admit that Lenin as an authority on the mind's free play made me laugh out loud: the consequence, no doubt, of an insipid prejudice. Yet these quotations, inspirational and explicative, are both the pestilence and the unresolved purpose of this earnest volume, inserted at the most awkward moments conceivable, with the most embarrassingly omniscient lead-ins—"As Yeats said," "The fourteenth-century Japanese writer Kenko comments," "The folklorist Richard M. Dorson states," "In the New Testament we read," "In a famous letter that Mozart wrote," "Selma G. Lanes tells," "It reminds me of an extraordinary statement by Meister Eckhart,"

"As a Gnostic text says," "There's a story about a Taoist saint who," etc., etc. It is all serious and clumsy, and pancultural and pantheist, but—after a while—not an occasion for raillery. Behind the unflinching waterfall of Cott's citations there can be descried the bright phantom of a passionate aspiration. It is to write a book (this is not yet the one) about imagination expressed as universal myth; about storytellers as Primal Explainers, as priests of the Old, the First, Religion; about fairies as fallen gods and goddesses; and, more than anything, about fallen belief, diminished now to the shiver of enchantment. Just such a book has already been written, though by somebody else, and a generation ago; it is C. S. Lewis's *Surprised by Joy*, a remarkable meditation on childhood longing for magic potencies and sensations.

Pipers at the Gates of Dawn (the title is from Kenneth Grahame's *The Wind in the Willows*: "Such music I never dreamed of, and the call in it is stronger than the music is sweet!") is saturated with that longing—or, rather, with a longing for such a longing. Meanwhile, and instead, there are the interviews. But these are too maneuvered, too anticipatory, too adulatory, in fact too "informative," to catch the elusive heel of imagination on the fly. Only the wonderfully thumping Opies manage to take hold of the interview format as a declarative artifact of their own making. The result is a cascade of family background, personal history, rich accounts of their astonishing compilations of nursery rhymes and street chants, and so on: they are anthropologists in the continually replenishing country of children. And because they are scholars of lore rather than shamans or inventors, with the kind of capacious authority that objectivity confers, the long chapter on the Opies is the most gratifying and the most successful.

The interview with P. L. Travers, progenitrix (she refuses the word "creator") of Mary Poppins, on the other hand, is dumbfounding—designed, it would seem, by Dr. Seuss in an atypically mean, but representatively coarse, mood. (There *is* a coarseness to Seuss deeper than the jollifications of the intended coarseness: a touch of self-institutionalized hard sell—or hard soul.) "I recall your saying," Cott tells Travers, " 'I'm a mere kitchenmaid in the

house of myth and poetry.' " And Travers replies, "Yes, indeed
. . . or rather that is what I would like to be: to take a stoup of
wine to Homer or polish Pallas Athene's sandals!" And adds soon
after: "I'm happy to be poured. Happy to be a flagon that is poured
out." Cott, citing an ancient Christian Gnostic text, eggs her on:
"It's a very deep passage, and I don't think I understand it fully."
Travers: "Nor do I. I wait to be told. . . . Having written certain
things, I sometimes think to myself, 'How did *she* learn that? It's
so *true*.' " Cott: "You mean Mary Poppins?" Travers: "No, P. L.
Travers. And I long to meet her. And then I wonder: Am I she?"
By the next page Cott is exclaiming, "You yourself have such
intense blue eyes!" A stoup, so to speak, of oil. Earlier, Cott points
out to Travers that M.P., the initials of Mary Poppins, can be
found in Wordsworth's Immortality Ode: "Mighty Prophet! Seer
blest!"

Whereupon Travers, enraptured, cries out, "Oh, I never
thought of that! How very perceptive of you! I'm reminded of a
letter I received from a young woman threatened by a fatal disease
who apparently had been deeply affected by Mary Poppins. . . .
'Dear Mother Nature, thank you for altering my life. Dear Snow-
storm, thank you for beautifying the world.' "

Ah, Holden Caulfield, you hardly knew your peril when you
told us how badly you wanted to call up the author of any book
that really knocked you out.

If it is unsettling to learn that Mary Poppins was born of a coy
mind made coyer by exposure to Gurdjieff and "a Zen roshi," as
well as by a proclivity for the portentous paradox, then it is time
to consider the engaging visions of William Steig—e.g., *Sylvester
and the Magic Pebble*, a loving fable of eerie loneliness, with a happy
ending that teaches the meaning of salvational blessing (I begin to
sound like one of Cott's citations); its "energy," we are told, comes
from Wilhelm Reich's orgone theories. Steig has *sat* in that box—
the magically scientific Reichian "accumulator." After which, it is
a relief to find that Astrid Lindgren's powers (*Pippi Longstocking*)
reverberate out of a spunky childhood recaptured, and Maurice
Sendak's (*Outside Over There*) out of a ruminating childhood regen-

erated, with an admixture of Mozart. (Cott to Sendak: " 'D. H. Lawrence,' I interject, 'used to describe the pregnant mother as feeling at one with the world.' " Sendak, unindulgent: "The *maven* on how women felt!") The Nigerian novelist Chinua Achebe, more nuanced than the Opies, is able to represent an unfamiliar culture with robust penetration; his command of Igbo belief, and his percipient exposition of its moral and metaphorical values, have a firm essaylike influence over the softness of the loquacious interview form. Like the Opies, he does not wholly fall prey to it.

It isn't that Cott's interviews are not, by and large, worthy journalism. It doesn't matter that an interview, framed not by the dream of the artist but by an exterior summarizer and instigator, will inexorably reduce the most impressive gift to a kind of potboilerdom. The chaotic though interesting difficulty with *Pipers at the Gates of Dawn* is that it is so clearly short-circuited by being what it is, instead of what it longed to be—an instance of its own sublime themes, a book about enchantment and awe. Cott's Niagara-floods of quotations are so many prooftexts of the reach of his desire.

Cott, citing Picasso: "Any man can make the sun into a yellow ball. Ah, but to make a yellow ball into the sun!" Any reporter can make literature into subject matter. Ah, but to make subject matter into literature!

A Short Note on
"Chekhovian"

"Chekhovian." An adjective that had to be invented for the new voice Chekhov's genius breathed into the world—elusive, inconclusive, flickering; nuanced through an underlying disquiet, though never morbid or disgruntled; unerringly intuitive, catching out of the air mute inferences, glittering motes, faint turnings of the heart, tendrils thinner than hairs, drift. But Chekhov's art is more than merely Chekhovian. It is dedicated to explicit and definitive portraiture and the muscular trajectory of whole lives. Each story, however allusive or broken off, is nevertheless exhaustive —like the curve of a shard that implies not simply the form of the pitcher entire, but also the thirsts of its shattered civilization.

And yet it is an odd misdirection that we have come to think of Chekhov mainly as a writer of hints and significant fragments, when so much of his expression is highly colored and abundant, declaratively open, even noisy. He is not reticent, and his people are often charged with conviction, sometimes ludicrously, sometimes with the serious nobility of Chekhov himself. But even when

Published by the Ecco Press, in Volume 5 of its Chekhov short stories series, *The Tales of Chekhov*, 1985

his characters strike us as unwholesome, or exasperating, or enervated, or only perverse (especially then), we feel Chekhov's patience, his clarity—his meticulous humanity, lacking so much as a grain of malevolence or spite. At bottom Chekhov is a writer who has flung his soul to the side of pity, and sees into the holiness and immaculate fragility of the hidden striver below. Perhaps this is why we know that when we are with Chekhov, we are with a poet of latency. He is an interpreter of the underneath life, even when his characters appear to be cut off from inwardness.

He is also an artist of solidity and precision. Here is Aksinya (from "In the Ravine"): "a handsome woman with a good figure, who wore a hat and carried a parasol on holidays, got up early and went to bed late, and ran about all day long, picking up her skirts and jingling her keys, going from the granary to the cellar and from there to the shop." That is the vigor of outerness; Chekhov is as much a master of the observed as he is of the unobserved. And he is, besides, the source of unusual states of wisdom, astonishing psychological principles. He can transfigure latency into drama, as in "Ward No. Six," which belongs with Conrad's "The Secret Sharer" among the great expositions of self-disclosure. And this too is Chekhov: he teaches us us.

Crocodiled Moats
in the Kingdom of Letters

> For constantly I felt I was moving among two
> groups—comparable in intelligence, identical
> in race, not grossly different in social origin,
> earning about the same incomes, who had al-
> most ceased to communicate at all, who in in-
> tellectual, moral and psychological climate had
> so little in common that . . . one might have
> crossed an ocean.
>
> C. P. SNOW, *The Two Cultures*
> *and the Scientific Revolution*

Disraeli in his novel *Sybil* spoke of "two nations," the rich and the
poor. After the progress of more than a century, the phrase (and
the reality) remains regrettably apt. But in the less than three decades since C. P. Snow proposed his "two cultures" thesis—the gap
of incomprehension between the scientific and literary elites—the
conditions of what we still like to call culture have altered so drasti-
cally that Snow's arguments are mostly dissolved into pointless-
ness. His compatriot and foremost needler, the Cambridge critic
F. R. Leavis, had in any case set out to flog Snow's hypothesis from
the start. Snow, he said, "rides on an advancing swell of cliché,"
"doesn't know what literature is," and hasn't "had the advantage of

Published as "Science and Letters—God's Work and Ours," *The New York Times
Book Review*, September 27, 1987

an intellectual discipline of any kind." And besides—here Leavis
emitted his final boom—"there is only one culture."

In the long run both were destined to be mistaken—Leavis
perhaps more than Snow. In 1959, when Snow published *The Two
Cultures*, we had already had well over a hundred years to get used
to the idea of science as a multi-divergent venture—dozens and
dozens of disciplines, each one nearly a separate nation with its
own governance, psychology, entelechy. It might have been possible to posit, say, a unitary medical culture in the days when
barbers were surgeons; but in recent generations we don't expect
our dentist to repair a broken kneecap, or our orthopedist to practice cardiology. And nowadays we are learning that an ophthal-
mologist with an understanding of the cornea is likely to be a bit
shaky on the subject of the retina. Engineers are light-years from
astrophysicists. Topology is distinct from topography, paleo-
botany from paleogeology. In reiterating that scientific culture is
specialist culture—who doesn't know this?—one risks riding an
advancing swell of cliché. Yet science, multiplying, fragmented,
in hot pursuit of split ends, is in a way a species of polytheism,
or, rather, animism: every grain of matter, every path of concep-
tualization, has its own ruling spirit, its differentiated lawgiver and
traffic director. Investigative diversity and particularizing empiricism have been characteristic of science since—well, since
alchemy turned into physical chemistry (and lately into super-
conductivity); since the teakettle inspired the locomotive; since
Icarus took off his wax wings to become Pan Am; since Archimedes
stepped out of his tub into Einstein's sea.

Snow was in command of all this, of course—he was pleased
to identify himself as an exceptional scientist who wrote novels—
and still he chose to make a monolith out of splinters. Why did
he do it? In order to have one unanimity confront another. While
it may have been a polemical contrivance to present a diversiform
scientific culture as unitary, it was patently not wrong, thirty years
ago, to speak of literary culture as a single force or presence. That
was what was meant by the peaceable word "humanities." And it
was what Leavis meant, too, when he growled back at Snow that

one culture was all there was worth having. "Don't mistake me," Leavis pressed, "I am not preaching that we should defy, or try to reverse, the accelerating movement of external civilization (the phrase sufficiently explains itself, I hope) that is determined by advancing technology. . . . What I *am* saying is that such a concern is not enough—disastrously not enough." Not enough, he argued, for "a human future . . . in full intelligent possession of its full humanity." For Leavis, technology was the mere outer rind of culture, and the job of literature (the hot core at the heart of culture) was not to oppose science but to humanize it. Only in Snow's wretchedly deprived mind did literature stand apart from science; Snow hardly understood what literature was *for*. And no wonder: Snow's ideas about literary intellectuals came, Leavis sneered, from "the reviewing in the Sunday papers."

It has never been easy to fashion a uniform image of science— which is why we tend to say "the sciences." But until not very long ago one could take it for granted (despite the headlong decline of serious high art) that there was, on the humanities side, a concordant language of sensibility, an embracing impulse toward integration, above all the conviction of human connectedness— even if that conviction occasionally partook of a certain crepuscular nostalgia we might better have done without. Snow pictured literature and science as two angry armies. Leavis announced that there was only one army, with literature as its commander in chief. Yet it was plain that both Leavis and Snow, for all their antagonisms, saw the kingdom of letters as an intact and enduring power.

This feeling for literary culture as a glowing wholeness—it *was* a feeling, a stirring, a flush of idealism—is now altogether dissipated. The fragrant term that encapsuled it—belles-lettres—is nearly archaic and surely effete: it smacks of leather tooling for the moneyed, of posturing. But it was once useful enough. "Belles-lettres" stood for a binding thread of observation and civilizing emotion. It signified not so much that letters are beautiful as that the house of letters is encompassingly humane and undivisive, no matter how severally its windows are shaped, or who looks out or in. Poets, scholars, journalists, librarians, novelists, playwrights, art critics, philosophers, writers for children, historians, political theorists, and all the rest, may have inhabited different rooms, differently furnished, but it was indisputably one house with a single roof and plenty of connecting doors and passageways. And sometimes—so elastic and compressive was the humanist principle—poet, scholar, essayist, philosopher, etc., all lived side by side in the same head. Seamlessness (even if only an illusion) never implied locked and separate cells.

And now? Look around. Now "letters" suggests a thousand enemy camps, "genres" like fortresses, professions isolated by croc-odiled moats. The living tissue of intuition and inference that nurtured the commonalty of the humanities is ruptured by an abrupt invasion of specialists. In emulation of the sciences? But we don't often hear of astronomers despising molecular biologists; in science, it may be natural for knowledge to run, like quicksilver, into crannies.

In the ex-community of letters, factions are in fashion, and the business of factions is to despise. Matthew Arnold's mild and venerable dictum, an open-ended, open-armed definition of liter-ature that clearly intends a nobility of inclusiveness—"the best that is known and thought in the world"—earns latter-day assaults and jeers. What can all that mean now but "canon," and what can a received canon mean but reactionary, racist, sexist, elitist closure? Politics presses against disinterestedness; what claims to be intrinsic is counted as no more than foregone conclusion. All categories are suspect, no category is allowed to display its wares without the charge of vested interest or ideological immanence. What Arnold called the play of mind is asked to show its credentials and prove its legitimacy. "Our organs of criticism," Arnold com-plained in 1864 (a period as uninnocent as our own), "are organs of men and parties having practical ends to serve, and with them those practical ends are the first thing and the play of mind the second."

And so it is with us. The culture of the humanities has split and split and split again, always for reasons of partisan ascendancy and scorn. Once it was not unusual for writers—Dreiser, Stephen Crane, Cather, Hemingway!—to turn to journalism for a taste of the workings of the world. Today novelists and journalists are alien breeds reared apart, as if imagination properly belonged only to the one and never to the other; as if society and instinct were designed for estrangement. The two crafts are contradictory even in method: journalists are urged to tell secrets in the top line; novelists insinuate suspensefully, and wait for the last line to spill the real beans. Dickens, saturated in journalism, excelled at shorthand; was a court reporter; edited topical magazines.

In the literary academy, Jacques Derrida has the authority that Duns Scotus had for medieval scholastics—and it is authority, not literature, that mainly engages faculties. In the guise of maverick or rebel, professors kowtow to dogma. English departments have set off after theory, and use culture as an instrument to illustrate doctrinal principles, whether Marxist or "French Freud." The play of mind gives way to signing up and lining up. College teachers were never so cut off from the heat of poets dead or alive as they are now; only think of the icy distances separating syllables by, say, Marianne Moore, A. R. Ammons, May Swenson, or Amy Clampitt from the papers read at last winter's Modern Language Association meeting—viz., "Written Discourse as Dialogic Interaction," "Abduction, Transference, and the Reading Stage," "The Politics of Feminism and the Discourse of Feminist Literary Criticism."

And more: poets trivialize novelists, novelists trivialize poets. Both trivialize critics. Critics trivialize reviewers. Reviewers retort that they *are* critics. Short-story writers assert transfigurations unavailable to novelists. Novelists declare the incomparable glories of the long pull. Novelizing aestheticians, admitting to literature no claims of moral intent, ban novelizing moralists. The moralists condemn the aestheticians as precious, barren, solipsist. Few essayists essay fiction. Few novelists hazard essays. Dense-language writers vilify minimalists. Writers of plain prose ridicule complex sentences. Professors look down on commercial publishers. Fiction writers dread university presses. The so-called provinces envy and despise the provinciality of New York. New York sees sour grapes in California and everywhere else. The so-called mainstream judges which writers are acceptably universal and which are to be exiled as "parochial." The so-called parochial, stung or cowardly or both, fear all particularity and attempt impersonation of the acceptable. "Star" writers—recall the 1986 International PEN Congress in New York—treat lesser-knowns as invisible, negligible. The lesser-knowns, crushed, disparage the stars.

And even the public library, once the unchallenged repository of the best that is known and thought, begins to split itself off, abandons its mandate, and rents out Polaroid cameras and videotapes, like some semi-philanthropic Crazy Eddie. My own local library, appearing to jettison the basic arguments of the age, flaunts shelf after shelf prominently marked Decorating, Consumer Power, How To, Cookery, Hooray for Hollywood, Accent on You, What Makes Us Laugh, and many more such chitchat categories. But there are no placards for Literature, History, Biography; and Snow and Leavis, whom I needed to moon over in order to get started on this essay, were neither one to be had. (I found them finally in the next town, in a much smaller if more traditionally bookish library.)

Though it goes against the grain of respected current belief to say so, literature is really *about* something. It is about us. That may be why we are drawn to think of the kingdom of letters as a unity, at least in potential. Science, teeming and multiform, is about how the earth and the heavens and the microbes and the insects and our mammalian bodies are constructed, but literature is about the meaning of the finished construction. Or, to set afloat a more transcendent vocabulary: science is about God's work; literature is about our work. If our work lies untended (and what is our work but aspiration?), if literary culture falls into a heap of adversarial splinters—into competing contemptuous clamorers for turf and mental dominance—then what will be left to tell us that we are one human presence?

To forward that strenuous telling, Matthew Arnold (himself now among the jettisoned) advised every reader and critic to "try and possess one great literature, at least, besides his own; and the more unlike his own, the better." Not to split off from but to add on to the kingdom of letters: so as to uncover its human face.

An idea that—in a time of ten thousand self-segregating literary technologies—may be unwanted, if not obsolete.

Portrait of the Artist as a Bad Character

Finally there is something new to say about Mona Lisa's smile. A current theory holds that La Gioconda is a self-portrait—Leonardo without his beard—and that the smile is, in fact, a trickster's derisive glimmer, a transvestite joke: five centuries of pulling the wool over everyone's eyes.

Well, all right, suppose it's really so: a da Vinci witticism unmasked at last. What would that mean for all those duped dead generations who marveled at Mona Lisa for her harmonious specificity as a woman, or, more romantically, as Woman? If they believed in the innocence they saw, was it a lie they were seeing? Or, because he fooled the ages, ought we to send the hangman after Leonardo's ghost? And what of us—we who are advantaged, or, conceivably, deprived—in the wake of this putative discovery? In recognizing the artist's ruse, are we seeing Mona Lisa plain for the first time in the history of her unflagging secret laughter? Or do we tamper with intention when we superimpose what we may now know on that unaccoutered loveliness? Mona Lisa mustached! The graffiti vandal's dream.

Published as "Good Novelists, Bad Citizens," *The New York Times Book Review*, February 15, 1987

Moonings like these may be of little use to da Vinci scholars, but they are charged with a certain literary irritation. They prod us to recall that the work of art is in its nature figment and fraud—but figment and fraud we have pointedly agreed to surrender to. If the fraud ends up a screw-twist more fraudulent than bargained for, that is what happens when you strike a bargain with someone dressed up in cap and bells. The Mona Lisa is made out of five-hundred-year-old paint, no matter who the model was, and it's the viewer who assents to the game of her being there at all. A portrait, like a novel, is a fiction, and what we call fiction is rightly named. In the compact between novelist and reader, the novelist promises to lie, and the reader promises to allow it.

These are notations so conspicuous and so stale that they are inscribed, no doubt, among the sacred antlers on neolithic cave walls; but they raise somewhat less obvious questions about the writer's potential for decent citizenship—the writer, that is, of fiction. Literary essayists, critical and social thinkers, historians, journalists, and so forth, don't in general, or at least not ideally, set out to defraud. The essayist's contract is exactly contrary to the novelist's—a promise to deliver ideas and "issues," implicit in which is a promise to show character. Fiction writers may easily begin as persons of character—more easily, say, than political columnists who are tempted to put a finger lightly on the scale—but the likelihood is that in the long run fiction bruises character. Novelists invent, deceive, exaggerate, and impersonate for several hours every day, and frequently on the weekend. Through the creation of bad souls they enter the demonic as a matter of course. They usurp emotions and appropriate lives.

As to the latter: "We all like to pretend we don't use real people," E. M. Forster once confessed, "but one does actually. I used some of my family. Miss Bartlett was my Aunt Emily—they all read the book but none of them saw it. . . . Mrs. Honeychurch was my grandmother. The three Miss Dickinsons condensed into two Miss Schlegels. Philip Herriton I modeled on Professor Dent. He knew this, and took an interest in his own progress." That may sound benign, but more often Professor Dent turns out to be sour and litigious, eager to muzzle, maim, or brain the writer into whose inspirations he has been unfortunate enough to fall. Saul Bellow's ingenious Shawmut, the put-down expert of "Him with His Foot in His Mouth," a self-described vatic type who stands for the artist, deduces that "I don't have to say a word for people to be insulted by me . . . my existence itself insults them. I come to this conclusion unwillingly, for God knows that I consider myself a man of normal social instincts and am not conscious of any will to offend." Yet Shawmut acknowledges he is in the grip of a manic force—a frenzy—signifying "something that is inaccessible to revision."

Good citizens are good—the consequence of normal social instincts—because they are usually accessible to revision; they are interested in self-improvement. Fiction writers have a different program for ego: not to polish it up for public relations, but to make it serve rapture—the rapture of language and drama, and also the rapture of deceit. The drive to rapture is resistant to revision in a big way, and will nail grandmothers and condense ladies no matter what. Professor Dent is right to look sweetly to his progress; he never had a chance to escape it. A well-worked fable is nothing but outright manipulation of this sort, not simply because it is all theater—what seems to be happening never actually happened—but because readers of fiction are forcibly dispossessed of a will of their own, and are made to think and feel whatever the writer commands. The characters in a novel are ten thousand times freer than their readers. Characters are often known to mutiny against the writer by taking charge of their books; readers, never. Readers are docile in succumbing to the responses prescribed for them; or else the book uncompromisingly closes its gates and shuts them out. In either case the writer is master.

Letters and diaries are not necessarily less fraudulent than works of fiction. It might be worthwhile for a scholar of deception— some ambitious graduate student in American literature, say—to compare a writer's journal entry on a particular day with a letter sent that same day. "Dear W: Your new poems have just come. Supernal stuff! You surpass yourself," the letter will start off. And the journal entry: "This A.M. received bilgewater from W; wrote him some twaddle." But even journals may not be trustworthy; a journal is a self-portrait, after all, and can white out the wens. I once met a young novelist who admitted that he was ashamed to tell his private diary his real secrets. On the other hand, the absence of abashment in a writer's diary is not the same as truth: who will measure Thomas Mann by the record of his flatulence, or the bite of Edmund Wilson by his compulsive nature pastels ("Mountains stained by blue shade—and, later, the pale brown rungs of the eucalyptus screens all pink in the setting sun")?

Storytellers and novelists, when on the job, rely on a treacherous braid of observation and invention; or call it memory and insinuation. Invention despoils observation, insinuation invalidates memory. A stewpot of bad habits, all of it—so that imaginative writers wind up, by and large, a shifty crew, sunk in distortion, misrepresentation, illusion, imposture, fakery. Those who— temporarily—elude getting caught out as bad characters are the handful of mainly guileless writers who eat themselves alive, like Kafka or Bruno Schulz. Such creatures neither observe nor invent. They never impersonate. Instead, they use themselves up in their fables, sinew by sinew. They are not in the world at all, or, if for a time they seem to be, it is only a simulacrum of a social being, and another lie.

Who will blame Leonardo for fooling us? The work was a sham to begin with. Those granules of chemicals on canvas were never Mona Lisa. She comes to life only with our connivance. And if the artist shows no character at all, and piles a second trick on the first, isn't he exactly the rascal we know him for?

On Permission to Write

> I hate everything that does not relate to liter-
> ature, conversations bore me (even when they
> relate to literature), to visit people bores me,
> the joys and sorrows of my relatives bore me
> to my soul. Conversation takes the importance,
> the seriousness, the truth, out of everything I
> think.
>
> FRANZ KAFKA, from his diary, 1918

In a small and depressing city in a nearby state there lives a young
man (I will call him David) whom I have never met and with whom
I sometimes correspond. David's letters are voluminous, vehe-
mently bookish, and—in obedience to literary modernism—without capitals. When David says "I," he writes "i." This does not
mean that he is insecure in his identity or that he suffers from a
weakness of confidence—David cannot be characterized by
thumbnail psychologizing. He is like no one else (except maybe
Jane Austen). He describes himself mostly as poor and provincial,
as in Balzac, and occasionally as poor and black. He lives alone
with his forbearing and bewildered mother in a flat "with imaginary
paintings on the walls in barren rooms," writes stories and novels,
has not yet published, and appears to spend his days hauling heaps
of books back and forth from the public library.

He has read, it seems, everything. His pages are masses of flashy
literary allusions—nevertheless entirely lucid, witty, learned, and

Published as "Writers Domestic and Demonic," *The New York Times Book Review*,
March 25, 1984

sane. David is not *exactly* a crank who writes to writers, although he is probably a bit of that too. I don't know how he gets his living, or whether his letters romanticize either his poverty (he reports only a hunger for books) or his passion (ditto); still, David is a free intellect, a free imagination. It is possible that he hides his manuscripts under a blotter, Jane-Austenly, when his mother creeps mutely in to collect his discarded socks. (A week's worth, perhaps, curled on the floor next to Faulkner and Updike and Cummings and *Tristram Shandy*. Of the latter he remarks: "a worthy book. dare any man get offspring on less?")

On the other hand, David wants to be noticed. He wants to be paid attention to. Otherwise, why would he address charming letters to writers (I am not the only one) he has never met? Like Joyce in "dirty provincial Dublin," he says, he means to announce his "inevitable arrival on the mainland." A stranger's eye, even for a letter, is a kind of publication. David, far from insisting on privacy, is a would-be public man. It may be that he pants after fame. And yet in his immediate position—his secret literary life, whether or not he intends it to remain secret—there is something delectable. He thirsts to read, so he reads; he thirsts to write, so he writes. He is in the private cave of his freedom, an eremite, a solitary; he orders his mind as he pleases. In this condition he is prolific. He writes and writes. Ah, he is poor and provincial, in a dim lost corner of the world. But his lonely place (a bare cubicle joyfully tumbling with library books) and his lonely situation (the liberty to be zealous) have given him the permission to write. To be, in fact, prolific.

I am not like David. I am not poor, or provincial (except in the New York way), or unpublished, or black. (David, the sovereign of his life, invents an aloofness from social disabilities, at least in his letters, and I have not heard him mythologize "negritude"; he admires poets for their words and cadences.) But all this is not the essential reason I am not like David. I am not like him because I do not own his permission to write freely, and zealously, and at will, and however I damn please; and abundantly; and always.

There is this difference between the prolific and the non-prolific: the prolific have arrogated to themselves the permission to write.

By permission I suppose I ought to mean *inner* permission. Now "inner permission" is a phrase requiring high caution: it was handed to me by a Freudian dogmatist, a writer whose energy and confidence depend on regular visits to his psychoanalyst. In a useful essay called "Art and Neurosis," Lionel Trilling warns against the misapplication of Freud's dictum that "we are all ill, i.e., neurotic," and insists that a writer's productivity derives from "the one part of him that is healthy, by any conceivable definition of health . . . that which gives him the power to conceive, to plan, to work, and to bring his work to a conclusion." The capacity to write, in short, comes from an uncharted space over which even all-prevailing neurosis can have no jurisdiction or dominion. "The use to which [the artist] puts his power . . . may be discussed with reference to his particular neurosis," Trilling concedes; yet Trilling's verdict is finally steel: "But its essence is irreducible. It is, as we say, a gift."

If permission to write (and for a writer this is exactly equal to the power to write) is a gift, then what of the lack of permission? Does the missing "Go ahead" mean neurosis? I am at heart one of those hapless pre-moderns who believe that the light bulb is the head of a demon called forth by the light switch, and that Freud is a German word for pleasure; so I am not equipped to speak about principles of electricity or psychoanalysis. All the same, it seems to me that the electrifying idea of inward obstacle— neurosis—is not nearly so often responsible for low productivity as we are told. Writer's permission is not something that is switched off by helpless forces inside the writer, but by social currents— human beings and their ordinary predilections and prejudices— outside. If David writes freely and others don't, the reason might be that, at least for a while, David has kidnapped himself beyond the pinch of society. He is Jane Austen with her hidden manuscript momentarily slipped out from under the blotter; he is Thoreau in his cabin. He is a free man alone in a room with imaginary pictures on the walls, reading and writing in a private rapture.

There are some writers who think of themselves as shamans, dervishes of inspiration, divinely possessed ecstatics—writers who believe with Emerson that the artist "has cast off the common motives of humanity and has ventured to trust himself for a task-master": himself above everyone. Emerson it is who advises writers to aspire, through isolation, to "a simple purpose . . . as strong as iron necessity is to others," and who—in reply to every contingency—exhorts, "O father, O mother, O wife, O brother, O friend, I have lived with you after appearances hitherto. Hence-forward I am the truth's." These shaman-writers, with their cult of individual genius and romantic egoism, may be self-glamorizing holy madmen, but they are not maniacs; they know what is good for them, and what is good for them is fences. You cannot get near them, whatever your need or demand. O father, O mother, O wife, O brother, O friend, they will tell you—*beat it*. They call themselves caviar, and for the general their caviar is a caveat.

Most writers are more modest than this, and more reasonable, and don't style themselves as unbridled creatures celestially priv-ileged and driven. They know that they are citizens like other citizens, and have simply chosen a profession, as others have. These are the writers who go docilely to gatherings where they are required to marvel at every baby; who yield slavishly to the ukase that sends them out for days at a time to scout a samovar for the birthday of an elderly great-uncle; who pretend to overnight guests that they are capable of sitting at the breakfast table without being consumed by print; who craftily let on to in-laws that they are diligent cooks and sheltering wives, though they would sacrifice a husband to a hurricane to fetch them a typewriter ribbon; and so on. In short, they work at appearances, trust others for task-masters, and do not insist too rigorously on whose truth they will live after. And they are honorable enough. In company, they do their best to dress like everyone else: if they are women they will tolerate panty hose and high-heeled shoes, if they are men they will show up in a three-piece suit; but in either case they will be concealing the fact that during any ordinary row of days they sleep in their clothes. In the same company they lend themselves, decade after decade, to the expectation that they will not lay claim to unusual passions, that they will believe the average belief, that they will take pleasure in the average pleasure. Dickens, foreseeing the pain of relinquishing his pen at a time not of his choosing, reportedly would not accept an invitation. "Thank God for books," Auden said, "as an alternative to conversation." Good-citizen writers, by contrast, year after year decline no summons, refuse no banquet, turn away from no tedium, willingly enter into every anecdote and brook the assault of any amplified band. They will put down their pens for a noodle pudding.

And with all this sterling obedience, this strenuous courtliness and congeniality, this anxious flattery of unspoken coercion down to the third generation, something goes wrong. One dinner in twenty years is missed. Or no dinner at all is missed, but an "attitude" is somehow detected. No one is fooled; the cordiality is pronounced insincere, the smile a fake, the goodwill a dud, the talk a fib, the cosseting a cozening. These sweating citizen-writers are in the end always found out and accused. They are accused of elitism. They are accused of snobbery. They are accused of loving books and bookishness more feelingly than flesh and blood.

Edith Wharton, in her cool and bitter way, remarked of the literary life that "in my own family it created a kind of restraint that grew with the years. None of my relations ever spoke to me of my books, either to praise or to blame—they simply ignored them; . . . the subject was avoided as if it were a kind of family disgrace, which might be condoned but could not be forgotten."

Good-citizen writers are not read by their accusers; perhaps they cannot be. "If I succeed," said Conrad, "you shall find there according to your deserts: encouragement, consolation, fear, charm—all you demand—and, perhaps, also that glimpse of truth for which you have forgotten to ask." But some never demand, or demand less. "If you simplified your style," a strict but kindly aunt will advise, "you might come up to par," and her standard does not exempt Conrad.

The muse-inspired shaman-writers are never called snobs, for the plain reason that no strict but kindly aunt will ever get within a foot of any of them. But the good-citizen writers—by virtue of their very try at citizenship—are suspect and resented. Their work will not be taken for work. They will always be condemned for

not being interchangeable with nurses or salesmen or schoolteach-
ers or accountants or brokers. They will always be found out.
They will always be seen to turn longingly after a torn peacock's
tail left over from a fugitive sighting of paradise. They will always
have hanging from a back pocket a telltale shred of idealism, or a
cache of a few grains of noble importuning, or, if nothing so
grandly quizzical, then a single beautiful word, in Latin or Hebrew; or else they will tip their hand at the wedding feast by
complaining meekly of the raging horn that obliterates the human
voice; or else they will forget not to fall into Montaigne over the
morning toast; or else they will embarrass everyone by oafishly
banging on the kettle of history; or else, while the room fills up
with small talk, they will glaze over and inwardly chant "This
Lime-Tree Bower My Prison"; or else—but never mind. What is
not understood is not allowed. These citizen-pretenders will never
be respectable. They will never come up to par. They will always
be blamed for their airs. They will always be charged with superiority, disloyalty, coldness, want of family feeling. They will
always be charged with estranging their wives, husbands, children.
They will always be called snob.

   They will never be granted the permission to write as serious
writers are obliged to write: fanatically, obsessively, consumingly,
torrentially, above all comically—and for life.

   And therefore: enviable blissful provincial prolific lonesome
David!

The Seam of the Snail

In my Depression childhood, whenever I had a new dress, my cousin Sarah would get suspicious. The nicer the dress was, and especially the more expensive it looked, the more suspicious she would get. Finally she would lift the hem and check the seams. This was to see if the dress had been bought or if my mother had sewed it. Sarah could always tell. My mother's sewing had elegant outsides, but there was something catch-as-catch-can about the insides. Sarah's sewing, by contrast, was as impeccably finished inside as out; not one stray thread dangled.

My uncle Jake built meticulous grandfather clocks out of rosewood; he was a perfectionist, and sent to England for the clockworks. My mother built serviceable radiator covers and a serviceable cabinet, with hinged doors, for the pantry. She built a pair of bookcases for the living room. Once, after I was grown and in a house of my own, she fixed the sewer pipe. She painted ceilings, and also landscapes; she reupholstered chairs. One summer she planted a whole yard of tall corn. She thought herself

Published as "Excellence," *Ms.*, January 1985

capable of doing anything, and did everything she imagined. But nothing was perfect. There was always some clear flaw, never visible head-on. You had to look underneath, where the seams were. The corn thrived, though not in rows. The stalks elbowed one another like gossips in a dense little village.

"Miss Brrrroooobaker," my mother used to mock, rolling her Russian *r*'s, whenever I crossed a *t* she had left uncrossed, or corrected a word she had misspelled, or became impatient with a *v* that had tangled itself up with a *w* in her speech. ("*Vv*ventriloquist," I would say. "*Vvv*entriloquist," she would obediently repeat. And the next time it would come out "wiolinist.") Miss Brubaker was my high school English teacher, and my mother invoked her name as an emblem of raging finical obsession. "Miss Brrrroooobaker," my mother's voice hoots at me down the years, as I go on casting and recasting sentences in a tiny handwriting on monomaniacally uniform paper. The loops of my mother's handwriting—it was the Palmer Method—were as big as soup bowls, spilling generous splashy ebullience. She could pull off, at five minutes' notice, a satisfying dinner for ten concocted out of nothing more than originality and panache. But the napkin would be folded a little off center, and the spoon might be on the wrong side of the knife. She was an optimist who ignored trifles; for her, God was not in the details but in the intent. And all these culinary and agricultural efflorescences were extracurricular, accomplished in the crevices and niches of a fourteen-hour business day. When she scribbled out her family memoirs, in heaps of dog-eared notebooks, or on the backs of old bills, or on the margins of last year's calendar, I would resist typing them; in the speed of the chase she often omitted words like "the," "and," "will." The same flashing and bountiful hand fashioned and fired ceramic pots, and painted brilliant autumn views and vases of imaginary flowers and ferns, and decorated ordinary Woolworth platters with lavish enameled gardens. But bits of the painted petals would chip away.

Lavish: my mother was as lavish as nature. She woke early and saturated the hours with work and inventiveness, and read late into the night. She was all profusion, abundance, fabrication. Angry at her children, she would run after us whirling the cord of the electric iron, like a lasso or a whip; but she never caught us. When, in seventh grade, I was afraid of failing the Music Appreciation final exam because I could not tell the difference between "To a Wild Rose" and "Barcarole," she got the idea of sending me to school with a gauze sling rigged up on my writing arm, and an explanatory note that was purest fiction. But the sling kept slipping off. My mother gave advice like mad—she boiled over with so much passion for the predicaments of strangers that they turned into permanent cronies. She told intimate stories about people I had never heard of.

Despite the gargantuan Palmer loops (or possibly because of them), I have always known that my mother's was a life of—intricately abashing word!—excellence: insofar as excellence means ripe generosity. She burgeoned, she proliferated; she was endlessly leafy and flowering. She wore red hats, and called herself a gypsy. In her girlhood she marched with the suffragettes and for Margaret Sanger and called herself a Red. She made me laugh, she was so varied: like a tree on which lemons, pomegranates, and prickly pears absurdly all hang together. She had the comedy of prodigality.

My own way is a thousand times more confined. I am a pinched perfectionist, the ultimate fruition of Miss Brubaker; I attend to crabbed minutiae and am self-trammeled through taking pains. I am a kind of human snail, locked in and condemned by my own nature. The ancients believed that the moist track left by the snail as it crept was the snail's own essence, depleting its body little by little; the farther the snail toiled, the smaller it became, until it finally rubbed itself out. That is how perfectionists are. Say to us Excellence, and we will show you how we use up our substance and wear ourselves away, while making scarcely any progress at all. The fact that I am an exacting perfectionist in a narrow strait only, and nowhere else, is hardly to the point, since nothing matters to me so much as a comely and muscular sentence. It is my narrow strait, this snail's road; the track of the sentence I am writing now; and when I have eked out the wet substance, ink or blood, that is its mark, I will begin the next sentence. Only in treading out sentences am I perfectionist; but then there is nothing else I know how to do, or take much interest in. I miter every pair of abutting sentences as scrupulously as Uncle Jake fitted one strip of rosewood against another. My mother's worldly and bountiful hand has escaped me. The sentence I am writing is my cabin and my shell, compact, self-sufficient. It is the burnished horizon—a merciless planet where flawlessness is the single standard, where even the inmost seams, however hidden from a laxer eye, must meet perfection. Here "excellence" is not strewn casually from a tipped cornucopia, here disorder does not account for charm, here trifles rule like tyrants.

I measure my life in sentences pressed out, line by line, like the lustrous ooze on the underside of the snail, the snail's secret open seam, its wound, leaking attar. My mother was too mettlesome to feel the force of a comma. She scorned minutiae. She measured her life according to what poured from the horn of plenty, which was her own seamless, ample, cascading, elastic, susceptible, inexact heart. My narrower heart rides between the tiny twin horns of the snail, dwindling as it goes.

And out of this thinnest thread, this ink-wet line of words, must rise a visionary fog, a mist, a smoke, forging cities, histories, sorrows, quagmires, entanglements, lives of sinners, even the life of my furnace-hearted mother: so much wilderness, waywardness, plenitude on the head of the precise and impeccable snail, between the horns. (Ah, if this could be!)

Pear Tree and Polar Bear:
A Word on Life and Art

Inventing a secret, then revealing it in the drama of entanglement—this is what ignites the will to write stories. The creation of forms has no part in this; I have no interest in "the new." Rupture doesn't attract me: I would rather inherit coherence than smash and start over again with enigma. The secrets that engage me— that sweep me away—are generally secrets of inheritance: how the pear seed becomes a pear tree, for instance, rather than a polar bear. Ideas are emotions that penetrate the future of coherence— in particular the idea of genesis. You cannot have Philip Roth without Franz Kafka; you cannot have Kafka without Joseph the dreamer. You cannot have William Gass without Walter Pater; you cannot have Pater without Pindar.

As for life, I don't like it. I notice no "interplay of life and art." Life is that which—pressingly, persistently, unfailingly, imperially—interrupts.

Published as "How Writers Live Today," *Esquire*, August 1985

Washington Square, 1946

> . . . this portion of New York appears to many
> persons the most delectable. It has a kind of
> established repose which is not of frequent oc-
> currence in other quarters of the long, shrill
> city; it has a riper, richer, more honorable look
> than any of the upper ramifications of the great
> longitudinal thoroughfare—the look of having
> had something of a social history.
>
> HENRY JAMES, *Washington Square*

I first came down to Washington Square on a colorless February
morning in 1946. I was seventeen and a half years old and was
carrying my lunch in a brown paper bag, just as I had carried it
to high school only a month before. It was—I thought it was—
the opening day of spring term at Washington Square College,
my initiation into my freshman year at New York University. All
I knew of N.Y.U. then was that my science-minded brother had
gone there; he had written from the Army that I ought to go there
too. With master-of-ceremonies zest he described the Browsing
Room on the second floor of the Main Building as a paradisal
chamber whose bookish loungers leafed languidly through magazines and exchanged high-principled witticisms between classes.
It had the sound of a carpeted Olympian club in Oliver Wendell
Holmes's Boston, Hub of the Universe, strewn with leather chairs
and delectable old copies of *The Yellow Book*.

Published as "The First Day of School: Washington Square 1946," *Harper's*,
September 1985

On that day I had never heard of Oliver Wendell Holmes or *The Yellow Book*, and Washington Square was a faraway bower where wounded birds fell out of trees. My brother had once brought home from Washington Square Park a baby sparrow with a broken leg, to be nurtured back to flight. It died instead, emitting in its last hours melancholy faint cheeps, and leaving behind a dense recognition of the minute explicitness of mortality. All the same, in the February grayness Washington Square had the allure of the celestial unknown. A sparrow might die, but my own life was luminously new: I felt my youth like a nimbus.

Which dissolves into the dun gauze of a low and sullen city sky. And here I am flying out of the Lexington Avenue subway at Astor Place, just a few yards from Wanamaker's, here I am turning the corner past a secondhand bookstore and a union hall; already late, I begin walking very fast toward the park. The air is smoky with New York winter grit, and on clogged Broadway a mob of trucks shifts squawking gears. But there, just ahead, crisscrossed by paths under high branches, is Washington Square; and on a single sidewalk, three clear omens; or call them riddles, intricate and redolent. These I will disclose in a moment, but before that you must push open the heavy brass-and-glass doors of the Main Building, and come with me, at a hard and panting pace, into the lobby of Washington Square College on the earliest morning of the freshman year.

On the left, a bank of elevators. Straight ahead, a long burnished corridor, spooky as a lit tunnel. And empty, all empty. I can hear my solitary footsteps reverberate, as in a radio mystery drama: they lead me up a short staircase into a big dark ghost-town cafeteria. My brother's letter, along with an account of the physics and chemistry laboratories (I will never see them), has already explained that this place is called Commons—and here my heart will learn to shake with the merciless newness of life. But not today; today there is nothing. Tables and chairs squat in dead silhouette. I race back through a silent maze of halls and stairways to the brass-and-glass doors—there stands a lonely guard. From the pocket of my coat I retrieve a scrap with a classroom number on it and ask the way. The guard announces in a sly croak that the first day of school is not yet; come back tomorrow, he says.

A dumb bad joke: I'm humiliated. I've journeyed the whole way down from the end of the line—Pelham Bay, in the northeast Bronx—to find myself in desolation, all because of a muddle: Tuesday isn't Wednesday. The nimbus of expectation fades off. The lunch bag in my fist takes on a greasy sadness. I'm not ready to dive back into the subway—I'll have a look around.

Across the street from the Main Building, the three omens. First, a pretzel man with a cart. He's wearing a sweater, a cap that keeps him faceless—he's nothing but the shadows of his creases—and wool gloves with the fingertips cut off. He never moves; he might as well be made of papier-mâché, set up and left out in the open since spring. There are now almost no pretzels for sale, and this gives me a chance to inspect the construction of his bare pretzel poles. The pretzels are hooked over a column of gray cardboard cylinders, themselves looped around a stick, the way horseshoes drop around a post. The cardboard cylinders are the insides of toilet paper rolls.

The pretzel man is rooted between a Chock Full o' Nuts (that's the second omen) and a newsstand (that's the third).

The Chock Full: the doors are like fans, whirling remnants of conversation. *She will marry him. She will not marry him.* Fragrance of coffee and hot chocolate. *We can prove that the senses are partial and unreliable vehicles of information, but who is to say that reason is not equally the product of human limitation?* Powdered doughnut sugar on their lips.

Attached to a candy store, the newsstand. Copies of *Partisan Review*: the table of the gods. Jean Stafford, Mary McCarthy, Elizabeth Hardwick, Irving Howe, Delmore Schwartz, Alfred Kazin, Clement Greenberg, Stephen Spender, William Phillips, John Berryman, Saul Bellow, Philip Rahv, Richard Chase, Randall Jarrell, Simone de Beauvoir, Karl Shapiro, George Orwell! I don't know a single one of these names, but I feel their small conflagration flaming in the gray street: the succulent hotness of their promise. I mean to penetrate every one of them. Since all the money I have is my subway fare—two nickels—I don't buy a copy (the price of *Partisan* in 1946 is fifty cents); I pass on.

I pass on to the row of houses on the north side of the Square. Henry James was born in one of these, but I don't know that either. Still, they are plainly old, though no longer aristocratic: haughty last-century shabbies with shut eyelids, built of rosy-ripe respectable brick, down on their luck. Across the park bulks Judson Church, with its squat squarish bell tower; by the end of the week I will be languishing at the margins of a basketball game in its basement, forlorn in my blue left-over-from-high-school gym suit and mooning over Emily Dickinson:

> There's a certain Slant of light,
> Winter Afternoons—
> That oppresses, like the Heft
> Of Cathedral Tunes—

There is more I don't know. I don't know that W. H. Auden lives just down *there*, and might at any moment be seen striding toward home under his tall rumpled hunch; I don't know that Marianne Moore is only up the block, her doffed tricorn resting on her bedroom dresser. It's Greenwich Village—I know *that*— no more than twenty years after Edna St. Vincent Millay has sent the music of her name (her best, perhaps her only, poem) into these bohemian streets: bohemia, the honey pot of poets.

On that first day in the tea-leafed cup of the town I am ignorant, ignorant! But the three riddle-omens are soon to erupt, and all of them together will illumine Washington Square.

Begin with the benches in the Park. Here, side by side with students and their loose-leafs, lean or lie the shadows of the pretzel man, his creased ghosts or doubles: all those pitiables, half-women and half-men, neither awake nor asleep, the discountable, the re-pudiated, the unseen. No more notice is taken of any of them than of a scudding fragment of newspaper in the path. Even then, even so long ago, the benches of Washington Square are pimpled with this hell-tossed crew, these Mad Margarets and Cokey Joes, these volcanic coughers, shakers, groaners, tremblers, droolers, blas-

phemers, these public urinators with vomitous breath and rusted
teeth-stumps, dead-eyed and self-abandoned, dragging their makeshift junkyard shoes, their buttonless layers of raggedy ratfur. The
pretzel man with his toilet paper rolls conjures and spews them
all—he is a loftier brother to these citizens of the lower pox, he
is guardian of the garden of the jettisoned. They rattle along all
the seams of Washington Square. They are the pickled City, the
true and universal City-below-Cities, the wolfish vinegar-Babylon
that dogs the spittled skirts of bohemia. The toilet paper rolls are
the temple-columns of this sacred grove.

Next, the whirling doors of Chock Full o' Nuts. Here is the
marketplace of Washington Square, its bazaar, its roiling gossip
parlor, its matchmaker's office and arena—the outermost wing, so
to speak, evolved from the Commons. On a day like today, when
the Commons is closed, the Chock Full is thronged with extra
power, a cello making up for a missing viola. Until now, the fire
of my vitals has been for the imperious tragedians of the *Aeneid*;
I have lived in the narrow throat of poetry. Another year or so of
this oblivion, until at last I am hammer-struck with the shock of
Europe's skull, the bled planet of death camp and war. Eleanor
Roosevelt has not yet written her famous column announcing the
discovery of Anne Frank's diary. The term "cold war" is new.
The Commons, like the college itself, is overcrowded, veterans in
their pragmatic thirties mingling with the reluctant dreamy young.
And the Commons is convulsed with politics: a march to the docks
is organized, no one knows by whom, to protest the arrival of
Walter Gieseking, the German musician who flourished among
Nazis. The Communists—two or three readily recognizable can-
tankerous zealots—stomp through with their daily leaflets and
sneers. There is even a Monarchist, a small poker-faced rectangle
of a man with secretive tireless eyes who, when approached for
his views, always demands, in perfect Bronx tones, the restoration
of his king. The engaged girls—how many of them there seem to
be!—flash their rings and tangle their ankles in their long New
Look skirts. There is no feminism and no feminists; I am, I think,
the only one. The Commons is a tide: it washes up the cold war,

it washes up the engaged girls' rings, it washes up the several
philosophers and the numerous poets. The philosophers are all
Existentialists; the poets are all influenced by "The Waste Land."
When the Commons overflows, the engaged girls cross the street
to show their rings at the Chock Full.

Call it density, call it intensity, call it continuity: call it, finally,
society. The Commons belongs to the satirists. Here, one afternoon, is Alfred Chester, holding up a hair, a single strand, before
a crowd. (He will one day write stories and novels. He will die
young.) "What is that hair?" I innocently ask, having come late
on the scene. "A pubic hair," he replies, and I feel as Virginia
Woolf did when she declared human nature to have "changed in
or about December 1910"—soon after her sister Vanessa explained
away a spot on her dress as "semen."

In or about February 1946 human nature does not change;
it keeps on. On my bedroom wall I tack—cut out from *Life*
magazine—the wildest Picasso I can find: a face that is also a belly.
Mr. George E. Mutch, a lyrical young English teacher twenty-
seven years old, writes on the blackboard: "When lilacs last in the
dooryard bloom'd," and "Bare, ruined choirs, where late the sweet
birds sang," and "A green thought in a green shade"; he tells us
to burn, like Pater, with a hard, gemlike flame. Another English
teacher—his name is Emerson—compares Walt Whitman to a
plumber; next year he will shoot himself in a wood. The initial
letters of Washington Square College are a device to recall three
of the Seven Deadly Sins: Wantonness, Sloth, Covetousness. In
Commons they argue the efficacy of the orgone box. Eda Lou
Walton, sprightly as a bird, knows all the Village bards, and is a
Village bard herself. Sidney Hook is an intellectual rumble in the
logical middle distance. Homer Watt, chairman of the English
Department, is the very soul who, in a far-off time of bewitchment,
hired Thomas Wolfe.

And so, in February 1946, I make my first purchase of a "real"
book—which is to say, not for the classroom. It is displayed in
the window of the secondhand bookstore between the Astor Place
subway station and the union hall, and for weeks I have been

coveting it: *Of Time and the River.* I am transfigured; I am pierced through with rapture; skipping gym, I sit among morning mists on a windy bench a foot from the stench of Mad Margaret, sinking into that cascading syrup: "Man's youth is a wonderful thing: It is so full of anguish and of magic and he never comes to know it as it is, until it is gone from him forever. . . . And what is the essence of that strange and bitter miracle of life which we feel so poignantly, so unutterably, with such a bitter pain and joy, when we are young?" Thomas Wolfe, lost, and by the wind grieved, ghost, come back again! In Washington Square I am appareled in the "numb exultant secrecies of fog, fog-numb air filled with solemn joy of nameless and impending prophecy, an ancient yellow light, the old smoke-ochre of the morning. . . ."

The smoke-ochre of the morning. Ah, you who have flung Thomas Wolfe, along with your strange and magical youth, onto the ash heap of juvenilia and excess, myself among you, isn't this a lovely phrase still? It rises out of the old pavements of Washington Square as delicately colored as an eggshell.

The veterans in their pragmatic thirties are nailed to Need; they have families and futures to attend to. When Mr. George E. Mutch exhorts them to burn with a hard, gemlike flame, and writes across the blackboard the line that reveals his own name,

> The world is too much with us; late and soon,
> Getting and spending, we lay waste our powers,

one of the veterans heckles, "What about getting a Buick, what about spending a buck?" Chester, at sixteen, is a whole year younger than I; he has transparent eyes and a rosebud mouth, and is in love with a poet named Diana. He has already found his way to the Village bars, and keeps in his wallet Truman Capote's secret telephone number. We tie our scarves tight against the cold and walk up and down Fourth Avenue, winding in and out of the rows of secondhand bookshops crammed one against the other. The proprietors sit reading their wares and never look up. The books in all their thousands smell sleepily of cellar. Our envy of them is speckled with longing; our longing is sick with envy. We are the sorrowful literary young.

Every day, month after month, I hang around the newsstand near the candy store, drilling through the enigmatic pages of *Partisan Review*. I still haven't bought a copy; I still can't understand a word. I don't know what "cold war" means. Who is Trotsky? I haven't read *Ulysses*; my adolescent phantoms are rowing in the ablative absolute with *pius* Aeneas. I'm in my mind's cradle, veiled by the exultant secrecies of fog.

Washington Square will wake me. In a lecture room in the Main Building, Dylan Thomas will cry his webwork syllables. Afterward he'll warm himself at the White Horse Tavern. Across the corridor I will see Sidney Hook plain. I will read the Bhagavad Gita and Catullus and Lessing, and, in Hebrew, a novel eerily called *Whither?* It will be years and years before I am smart enough, worldly enough, to read Alfred Kazin and Mary McCarthy.

In the spring, all of worldly Washington Square will wake up to the luster of little green leaves.

The Function of the
Small Press

What, nowadays, is a small press? Partly it is really a *press*: one thinks of the burgeoning, all over America, of those artists who are active artisans, who care for beautiful paper (and sometimes fabricate their own) and beautiful type (and sometimes set it themselves, the old-fashioned way), and with their own hands turn out pleasing sewn folios that, while they are certainly books, are at the same time art objects of high dedication. In the crush of a lightning technology that slams out computerized volumes stuck together with a baleful glue, it is good now and then to be reminded of a book as something worthy of body-love. The nostrils also read.

A small press means something else as well: a publisher who is a woman or a man (or a living handful of men and women), not a "corporate entity." Big companies are compelled to attend to "markets"; the bigger the house, the deeper the compulsion. Small-press publishers, unless they operate out of the pocket of some maverick philanthropist indifferent to the pinch of economics, are

---

Published (in somewhat different form) as the Introduction to *The Pushcart Prize, XI: Best of the Small Presses*, ed. Bill Henderson (Pushcart Press, 1986–87)

not averse to a bit of profit either; but more than on making money, they concentrate on making *room*: for eccentricity, for risk, for the *idée fixe*, for poetry, for the odd essay and the odder fiction; for the future. They are on the watch for originality—even though originality, like any watched pot, often ends by blowing off steam identical to all other steam. It is a vigilance, a readiness, for which nothing can be predicted: one day (the saying goes) a tedium, the next a Te Deum. Still, when the big publishers are looking for a miracle, they are usually thinking of dollars. For the small presses a miracle is more often a literary dream: Willa Cather rising out of an unlikely Red Cloud; the obscure Bernard Malamud, teacher and father in Oregon, patiently constructing his magic barrel of stories—sprinkling out shavings of a kind never shaped in the world before; Donald Barthelme, editor of a forgotten organ called *locations*, closeted in a dusky cubicle at the top of a staircase in New York, imagining new locutions for a new art. Unexpectedness is what the small presses are open to. They are like the little shoemakers who come unseen at night to stitch the leather no one else can master. No wonder they have Rumpelstiltskin goldspinner names—*Unmuzzled Ox*, and *Mho and Mho Works*, and *Unspeakable Visions of the Individual*, and *Cosmic Information Agency*, and *Shankpainter*, and *Mr. Cogito Press*, and *Antaeus* and *Persea* and *Shantih* and *Orim* and *Pequod* and *Sun and Moon*—names that announce their intent to turn the invisible visible. (They can also be called by straightforward names like *The Quarterly*, *Southwest Review*, *Fiction*.) Some of these little-shoemaker presses are in fact conventionally ambitious publishing houses working on a shoestring. But many are little magazines.

Little magazines. These may not be the real right words any more; they have a faintly anachronistic resonance, and have been sensibly replaced by the more capacious term small press, which in its democratic egalitarianism omits nothing on the American scene, whatever its aim, mood, tone, "school," literary or political coloration. But with the words "little magazine" we are in another place; we are in the history of our literary culture. It is not simply that without *Poetry*, without the fabled *Dial*, those antique particularist precursors of our current abundance, we would not have had a vehicle for the first glimmers of modernism in American poetry and criticism. The little magazines began as an elitist movement favoring high art, in contradistinction to the big popular magazines; in this sense they were programmatic, didactic. They were intended as sanctuaries away from what was once thought of, dismissively and uncomplicatedly, as "midcult" (an out-of-date notion in a time when even kitsch is a resource, when graduate students in philosophy solemnly deconstruct the language of McDonald's hamburger advertisements and serious literary critics look to reruns of *The Honeymooners* for cultural signifiers). It was not so much what they were, or what they were meant to be—they were meant to be an aristocracy of letters, and sometimes they were. But their best case lay in what they weren't. They weren't *Life* or *Look* or the *Saturday Evening Post* or *Esquire*, or even *Harper's* or the *Atlantic*. They were, by and large (I am reflecting now on the little magazines of the forties and fifties), coterie journals: all, however, with the same ideal— the loftiest peaks of what was known and thought. In a 1946 essay, "The Function of the Little Magazine," Lionel Trilling undertook to defend the little magazines against "populist critics" who "denounce the coterie and the writer who does not write for 'the many' ":

> The matter is not so simple as these earnest minds would have it. From the democratic point of view, we must say that in a true democracy nothing should be done *for* the people. The writer who defines his audience by its limitations is indulging in the unforgivable arrogance. The writer must define his audience by its abilities, by its perfections. . . . He does well, if he cannot see his right audience within immediate reach of his voice, to direct his words to his spiritual ancestors, or to posterity, or even if need be, to a coterie. The writer serves his daemon and his subject. And the democracy that does not know that the daemon and the subject must be served is not, in any ideal sense of the word, a democracy at all.

"The word coterie should not frighten us too much," Trilling warned. "Neither should it charm us too much; writing for a small group does not insure integrity any more than writing for the many; the coterie can corrupt as surely, and sometimes as quickly, as the big advertising appropriation."

If anything has changed in the life of the little magazines in the last four decades, it is their proliferation; and also the meaning of their proliferation. The little magazine as a form no longer stands for a single idea: the retreat to art and high culture. If Trilling's justification for the coterie journal—that "the daemon and the subject must be served"—is still even minimally viable, if little magazines are still founded to promote and pursue an "agenda" (and surely they are), then what has happened is the multiplication of coteries, hence of purposes and agendas. Not every daemon will be congenial.

It may be that the little magazines no longer define themselves as uniformly as they once did because they cannot. Once they were the heralds and couriers of modernism—in advance of modernism's inclusion in the literary curricula of the universities. Their agenda, prevalent and single-minded, *was* modernism, and with it the now-archaic passions of the New Criticism, inspiring ranks and ranks of tertiary imitators—every poet a sub-Pound, every writer of fiction a neo-Kafka, every critic a pseudo-Eliot. Not that, forty or fifty years later, we have left the parrots behind, but the question is: parrot whom, parrot what? With the famous exhaustion of modernism, who knows where we are now? Aspiring to the cadences of James Joyce or Virginia Woolf or Gertrude Stein or Samuel Beckett is one thing; aspiring to the sound of Ann Beattie or Anne Tyler is another, and may represent us more honestly. We live on a nameless planet. To give it a name—postmodernism—is only to confirm these thickets in the wilderness of no-man's-land, which turns out to be everyone's turf.

And so the little magazines increase their numbers. Where there were twenty little magazines with a single modernist idea, there are now a hundred, with a hundred different daemons. If you

believe in the power of the Zeitgeist, then they may be more alike
than they realize, these different daemons; but they assume singularity. This puts me in mind of my five zealously individualistic
uncles. Each uncle demanded to be regarded as absolutely unlike
the others; yet they *all* demanded this, and in just the same style.
And so they march by, our Rumpelstiltskins, some devoted to
intellectual puzzlements of a recognizably professorial kind, others
to startling Pan into kicking up his goat feet: *Salmagundi, Raritan,
Grand Street, Granta, Parnassus; Holy Cow!, Home Planet News, Crawl
Out Your Window, Toothpaste Press.* The range in reviews is from
Anaesthesia to *Yale*, with *Lowlands, Mulch, Nada,* and *Ploughshares* in
between. And just here it may be salubrious to look at still another
passage in Trilling's small-press report:

> To the general lowering of the status of literature and of the interest
> in it [and Trilling is writing before television], the innumerable "little
> magazines" have been a natural and heroic response. Since the be-
> ginning of the century, meeting difficulties of which only their ed-
> itors can truly conceive, they have kept our culture from being
> cautious and settled, or merely sociological, or merely pious. They
> are snickered at and snubbed, sometimes deservedly, and no one
> would venture to say in a precise way just what effect they have—
> except that they keep the new talents warm until the commercial
> publisher with his customary air of noble resolution is ready to take
> his chance, except that they make the official representatives of
> literature a little uneasy, except that they keep a countercurrent
> moving which perhaps no one will be fully aware of until it ceases
> to move.

Some years later, Trilling, having invented the term "adversary
culture," would show how the established institutions of society
have digested their opposition. Bohemia and all its works are
vanished out of America; or, more exactly, bohemia has migrated
to the middle class, and is alive and well in condo and suburb.
The countercurrent has become the main current. So the little
magazines have not only lost their elitism—beginning, one supposes, with the turning from Eliot and the long-range impact
of Allen Ginsberg's *Howl.* They have also lost (though some of

them may resist admitting to it) their bohemianism, the glamour of outsiderness and marginality. Citizens of a free country with a free press, we are luckily without a *samizdat*; anybody can publish anything, including righteous rage of a political sort, which rather limits the spectrum of anti-establishment emotion. All this—the swallowing up of the counterculture—Trilling more or less predicted.

The loss of elitism, the loss of bohemianism—the loss, in short, of a universal or unifying agenda or ideology. What, then, remains of the function of the little magazine? Three annual literary anthologies attest to what used to be called "the cultural situation": *O. Henry Prize Stories*, edited by William Abrahams; *The Best American Short Stories*, edited by Shannon Ravanel; and *The Pushcart Prize*, subtitled *Best of the Small Presses* and edited, since he founded it a dozen years ago, by Bill Henderson, with the aid of nearly two hundred contributing editors. Of the three, only the last draws solely from the little magazines, collecting poets and essayists along with fiction writers—the whole American writing sound. Multiple chords, but not in open yawping Whitman fashion. The new writers in these volumes epitomize private lives: the secret, the idiosyncratic, nuanced and tendril-like, rife with hints and whispers. Flashes of *What Maisie Knew*, or the river scene in *The Ambassadors*. Aloneness. Contemplation and calculation, so many lonesome night-breathings. Every poem, story, essay charged with the solitary. The essay in particular cultivates the voice of the single mind, of an indivisible temperament.

The American essay has been dormant for a long time, though its history is brilliant enough: Emerson to Edmund Wilson. For a long time it hardly recognized itself for what it was, and was often confused with the magazine article—that shabby, team-driven, ugly, truncated, undeveloped, speedy, breezy, cheap thing. Through the vehicle of the small press, the essay is waking up and turning muscular. It knows that Hazlitt lived.

"They keep the new talents warm," Trilling rightly said of the little magazines. They still do. They may also keep talents warm that would be better off put on the shelf to cool. More to the point today is not who writes for the small presses, or what their prospects are, but in which genre they are writing. What the small presses keep warm, and alive, are those very forms "the cultural situation" tends to submerge: essay, story, poem.

Of Basilisks and Barometzes

Is reality necessary?

Light-hearted, light-footed reader, do not flee! Our subject is no tough ontological rind. (Philosophers, go home.) It is, rather, the mazy gossamer of make-believe; the desire to be invisible; the longing for strange histories that never were; the urge to slip loose from one's own life. In short, the overcrowded precincts of nonexistence.

To wit: A celebrated American novelist recently sought to vanish—or, if not precisely to vanish, then to be transformed, as in any tale of magic, from true and accessible being to the arcane grottoes of subterranean fancy. Joyce Carol Oates, casting a spell over her husband's name—Raymond Smith—became Rosamond Smith, who doesn't exist. ("I wanted to escape from my own identity," Rosamond Smith's inventor explained.) The imaginary Smith instantly signed a contract with a publisher for a first novel. Almost as instantly, the ruse was aborted—it may be that the literary famous are forbidden clandestine play, and too bad. It is

Published as "The Library of Nonexistent Classics," *The New York Times Book Review*, April 12, 1987

easy to find Joyce Carol Oates in any bookshop; but Rosamond Smith has yet to be read, and now never will be. To protest that it makes no difference, that the very same novel will be published anyhow, is not to the point. A book by Rosamond Smith is in no way a book by Joyce Carol Oates, even if the words are identical. We know, after all, what to expect of Joyce Carol Oates, however unexpected her devisings: the imprint of reputation inheres in every phrase. But what kind of writer might Rosamond Smith have turned out to be?

The brief materialization and speedy vaporization of the phantom Smith will leave a melancholy mark in literary history, yet hardly an anomalous one. There are whole phalanxes of nonexistent writers who have written real books—among them Lewis Carroll, Mark Twain, George Orwell; and some would even dare to charge Homer, Shakespeare, and David the Psalmist with the scam of attaching phony names to popular hits. Still, the assurance of corporeal authenticity—half a dozen writers more or less in the world—will scarcely shake society. Far more significant are the vast libraries, corridors stretching into infinity, of books that have never been written. We ought to declare our gratitude for these non-existent works on two counts: first, writing that is confined to mere potentiality is in almost all instances reliably superior to words actually on a page. What drudging novelist has not been alarmed by the corruption of a visionary text the moment it begins to creep from the satanically forked nib of a fountain pen, or to solidify on a gelid green screen? And second, if every volume dreamed of were committed to paper ("I could write a book!" cry landlady, doorman, and cabby), our crammed and diminutive planet would have to choose, ecologically speaking, between new publishing houses and new generations.

Non-existent books offer relief in other ways. For example, a disappointed writer whose own novels have sunk into nullity (without the advantage of prior non-existence) can saturate himself in the putative bliss of fame simply by tossing off a romance about an illustrious author of genius. All that is required in such a scheme is to *name* the glorious works in question; toiling at a facsimile of, say, *The Magic Mountain* will be superfluous, since the delectable emoluments of acclaim rush in to be relished as early as Chapter Two. Compensation for the ache of mediocrity, no doubt—a notion swiped, I admit, not from the immortal Emerson but from the indispensable Max Beerbohm. Beerbohm deserves to be kept on the kitchen counter along with other household helps; he is as valuable for appeasing the consciences of people who hate giving dinner parties (see his "Hosts and Guests") as for having produced an actual *list* of non-existent books. The handful of volumes that he regards as first-rate (there are many more judged inferior though seductive) seems to have sprung mainly from the heads of non-existent writers who have sprung from the head of Henry James; we are provocatively reminded that the ectoplasmic passions promised in "The Middle Years," "Shadowmere," and "The Major Key," not to mention the magisterial "Beltraffio," are all grievously beyond our reach.

But if it is a sad thing to know there are books we will never be allowed to read for no better reason than that they do not exist, this does not imply we are to learn nothing of the careers of their spectral authors. Jorge Luis Borges, the century's most flagrant, ingenious, and industrious compiler of manuscripts that fall short of reality (including their plots, footnotes, and commentaries), is even more intent on fathoming the curious minds of his imaginary scribes. One of these, Jaromir Hladík, author of an unfinished tragedy in verse, is about to be shot by a firing squad; in the final seconds of consciousness his electrified brain is able to revise and complete his play—a full year's labor—down to its last turn and syllable. Pierre Menard—whose definitive if counterfeit bibliography Borges meticulously catalogues—attempts, in 1934, to rewrite Cervantes's *Don Quixote*, though in language painstakingly unaltered from the sixteenth-century original. ("The archaic style of Menard," Borges pedantically notes, "suffers from a certain affectation. Not so that of his precursor, who handles easily the ordinary Spanish of his time.") Borges also introduces a novel by a non-existent Bombay lawyer named Mir Bahadur Ali, along with an analysis of its publishing history, theology, and mythological derivations. Similarly, he describes the astounding erudition of the non-existent author of "The God of the Labyrinth," Herbert Quain, who unfortunately died "totally used to failure" at the age of forty. All these writers have in common not only their commanding non-existence, but also their confidence in the power of the insubstantial. As the courageous Hladík puts it, "unreality . . . is the necessary condition of art."

It should not be assumed, however, that it is solely authors and books that are eligible for non-existence. Not at all; such a claim would be parochial. One has only to consult Borges's own *Book of Imaginary Beings* to encounter chimeras, phoenixes, basilisks, barometzes (the last a kind of vegetable lamb), and the like. As for the geography of non-being—here the terrain is very wide indeed—every sleepless tourist is familiar with the Land of Cockaigne; but for directions to such sites as Icaria, Limanora, Amneran Heath, the Waq Archipelago, or Wastepaperland, one must go to the exhaustive *Dictionary of Imaginary Places*, an encyclopedic work admirably edited by Alberto Manguel and Gianni Guadalupi. The objection may be raised that make-believe creatures and make-believe localities are themselves a branch of the library of non-existence, and will inevitably be classified as bookish—but that is a tedious and literal-minded quibble. Popefigs' Island is currently without a single bookshop, and hippogriffs are notorious for fearing librarians.

Of course, it must be conceded that the non-existent—while admittedly necessary—is not always more inviting, original, interesting, or praiseworthy than what is stocked in the more limited warehouse of reality. To be persuaded of this truth, merely recall, from *Middlemarch*, the desiccated Mr. Casaubon's huge manuscript volumes: those deadly notes for his appalling "Key to All Mythologies." Though we may regret that we will never get the chance to read the exquisite "Beltraffio," or Pierre Menard's punctilious "Don Quixote," there are some non-existent books we can well do without.

The Apprentice's Pillar

There was an ominously anxious watch of eyes visible and invisible over the infancy of W——, fifth in descent from Simon Patterne, of Patterne Hall, premier of this family, a lawyer, a man of solid acquirements and stout ambition. . . .[1]

On the walls of the large dining room of the T—— home at Y—— hung blackened ancestral portraits—seventeenth- and eighteenth-century men in wigs, uniforms, ribbons, and decorations, and women in their stiff gowns, laces, and powdered hair. At first the T—— children were rather alarmed by these painted specta-tors. . . .[2]

The family of D—— had been long settled in Sussex. Their estate was large, and their residence was at Norland Park, in the center of their property, where for many generations they had lived in so respectable a manner as to engage the general good opinion of their surrounding acquaintance.[3]

Published as "Where Orphans Can Still Become Heiresses," *The New York Times Book Review*, March 8, 1987

The B——s of Hampshire lived, at the turn of the eighteenth century, in a place called Gavelacre on the banks of the River Test, some eleven miles from Winchester along the old Roman road to the east of Salisbury plain.[4]

The four passages above—each preoccupied with ancestry, place, family—are all beginnings, the opening sentences of volumes pulled out here and there from the shelves nearest my writing table. Despite their randomness, they are craftily entangled in a didactic trick: two are "true" and two are "false." Or, to point the riddle more explicitly, a pair of nineteenth-century novels are mixed up with a pair of twentieth-century biographies. Which is transparently which?

Start with literary history. As between biography and the novel, which is the apprentice, which the master? If it is true that the novel in its infancy set out to imitate real life, then one might say that biography's narrative-of-fact is the first form, the Ur-Gestalt, the predecessor-pattern: Plutarch's *Lives*, for instance, engendering *Robinson Crusoe*. But if biography is the art of organizing a coherent tale out of the chancy scatterings and sunderings of any individual life, then surely biography would seem to be the imitator, and the novel its model.

For a very long time—until the novel took its idiosyncratic and apparently irreversible turn away from supposedly historical narration toward self-illumination (or call it anti-objectivity, jagged, fitful, willfully erratic)—biography and novel were kin, and sometimes more than that. The forms had the occasional habit of converging to near-fusion: certainly a little of one had got into the other. Novel and biography were genetically piebald, or else were designed for mistaken identity, on the style of the Chinese philosopher who awoke one morning in an unsettled condition: "Now I do not know," he complained, "whether I am a man dreaming I am a butterfly or a butterfly dreaming I am a man."

Recall that familiar narrative centered on the incandescent character of a single extraordinary young woman, yet labyrinthine enough to touch also on famine and emigration; the deaths of a father and two sons; three widows; remarriage and a triumphant birth. Is the biblical Book of Ruth novella or biography? Or jump ahead three millennia to Samuel Butler: "When I was a small boy at the beginning of the century I remember an old man who wore knee-breeches and worsted stockings, and who used to hobble about the street of our village with the help of a stick." Who is recording that vivid old man—an autobiographer or a novelist? Is it memory that governs here, or fabrication? If *The Way of All Flesh* is an autobiography, we are being asked to pretend it is a novel. If it is a novel, we are being asked to pretend it is an autobiography. The motivation is the same: to evoke believability in a story about the perilous span between birth and death.

And still the two forms—two ways of imagining True Being— seem always, in their mutual mirrorings, to have been jealous of each other. The apprentice jealous of the master? The master jealous of the apprentice? A brilliant medieval legend (reincarnated, perhaps, in the virtuoso coinages of Harold Bloom) begins in romantic ambition and ends in bloody envy: the prideful tale of the architect of the castle chapel at Rosslyn, who hopes to erect a pillar so beautiful that it will surpass every other on the face of the earth. In search of inspiration (his is an age of tradition and emulation), he travels through many lands, sketching pillar after comely pillar, but not yet satisfied. At last he arrives in Rome, and there he finds it: a noble pillar of exquisite grace, incontestably lovelier than any other. Ah, but during all the years of his absence, his boy apprentice, a mere sub-mason, has been similarly aspiring to the perfect pillar, and has, in fact, succeeded in constructing it—according to a vision vouchsafed him in a dream, of course. Then the architect, returning home, ready to execute what he beheld in the Holy See, comes upon the apprentice's pillar, recognizes that it is a supernal conception, grander than any column that ever rose up in all the world before, and instantly bashes in the apprentice's skull.

The legend, cropping up in various guises throughout Europe, is never in doubt about who killed off whom: it is always the expert who brains the disciple, and not (as in Freud and Bloom) the other way around. In the competitive relations between biography and novel, we are less certain about which did the other in. The novel—like the apprentice—sought at length to go off on its own hook, away from emulation and into the proto-visionary. Biography—like the master architect—stuck to received designs. The traditional novel, with its chronological representations and its claim to imitation-of-life, is as remote from contemporary serious writing as the likelihood of a fresh Edda. Should we conclude, then, that biography, which has lasted with its lineaments unchanged since Cain and Abel, and seems as nearly permanent as any form we can imagine, is the ultimate master and victor? On the other hand, metamorphosis is not the same as death (ask any Chinese butterfly), and a case can be made that it is precisely the novel that is the living master, while biography is moribund, or, worse, an exhausted rite doggedly repeating stale configurations, with the spirit dashed out of it. A zombie. Brained.

This may be something we need to sort out, because one of the literary secrets of our time is that we miss the nineteenth-century novel. We miss it intensely, urgently. Simply *reading* it doesn't bring it back—we are always aware that it is an excursion, however humanly universal, into lost conventions. No matter that we crave, now and for ourselves, those wholehearted gratifications, moral and technical; we can't have them. The Zeitgeist is against it. It allows us, to be sure, an inventive diadem or two—the unique prose-creases of Donald Barthelme, say—but it withholds a *Middlemarch* or a *Great Expectations* of our own.

Hence our unslakable infatuation with the rich-blooded old novel's royal cousin. Biography alone delivers the chance to read and write "linear" lives, and caters to our natural inquisitiveness about pedigree, locality, ancestral cause-and-effect, genetic and adoptive influences, orphans turning into heiresses, generational unfolding. With genius as its frequent subject, biography is the one remaining form that can—old-fashioned thought!—inspire. Biography contrives to let us see the world elapse, as in the three acts of a play: it draws us to the hurdles, hidings, underminings, regenerations and full clockwork of a life. If there is covert instruction in it, it is chiefly the precept of chronicle—the idea that every life is not only a trajectory but also a teleology, that every character, intuitively addressed, will press out the passionate ichor of "theme." What we continue to prize in biography is the honest constancy of its narrative ripeness: the trustworthy satisfactions of a still-coherent form, the ancient name of which is Story.

As for determining finally whether biography vis-à-vis the novel is vitally intact or fractured—is, in short, master or apprentice— observe that the architect of Rosslyn destroyed his uppity sub-mason, but never the work of art itself. The apprentice's pillar stands, even now, sublime.

1. *The Egoist*, George Meredith, 1879.
2. *Leo Tolstoy*, Ernest J. Simmons, 1946.
3. *Sense and Sensibility*, Jane Austen, 1811.
4. *Ivy: The Life of Ivy Compton-Burnett*, Hilary Spurling, 1984.

The Muse,
Postmodern and Homeless

If you're a writer and if you're by nature Sublime and
    Magisterial,
but you need cash—lots and lots—
don't try to change your literary spots.
Spot-changing won't get you any dough or even any cereal.
You'll only end up feeling gypped, not to mention funereal.
So if you're a hifaluting ineffable Artist of noble intent,
    you might as well stick to your last,
since nobody who reads for fun will read *you* for fun
    because it's impossible to read you fast.

These are lines Ogden Nash did not write. Henry James did, sort
of, in the form of a melancholy comic tale called "The Next Time."
Its hero is a genius novelist who, in the hope of making his fortune,
attempts to become a popular hack. Again and again he feels sure
he has finally gotten the hang of it—grinding out a best-selling
quick read—but each time, to his disappointment, what emerges
is only another masterpiece.

Published in *The New York Times Book Review*, January 18, 1987

James himself once contrived to write a letter of Paris chat for the New York *Tribune*. He managed to keep it going for months, but the column was a failure. He could not "entertain." When the editor complained that James's themes were "too remote from popular interests," James snapped back: "If my letters have been 'too good' I am honestly afraid that they are the poorest I can do, especially for the money!" "I thought in all conscience," he said privately, "they had been flimsy enough."

"The Next Time" appeared in 1895; modernism was not yet born. But in his portrait (however teasing) of the artist as a sovereign and unbetrayable focus of authenticity, James had put his finger on what modernism was going to be mainly about.

"Things fall apart; the center cannot hold." That, we used to think, was the whole of modernism—Yeats mourning the irrecoverable old assurances while the surprising new shapes of things, symbols and fragments, flashed by in all their usurping alterations. Now we know better, and also, in a way, worse. Yeats hardly foresaw how our dissolutions would surpass his own—but where we are now is, after all, what he was describing.

And where we are now is the no-man's-land that more and more begins to inherit the name postmodern—atomized, leveled, thoroughly democratic turf where anything goes, everything counts, significance is what I say it is, literature is what's there for the exegetes: comic strips, 1950s sitcoms, fast-food hamburger ads. The elitism of High Art was vanquished long ago, and not only by the Marxists. The divide between Bob Dylan and Dylan Thomas is plugged by critical egalitarianism; so is the difference between poet and critic. *Allee samee*, as Allen Ginsberg once remarked of the great religions—as if wanting to repair the world and wanting to get out of it were indistinguishable. History is whatever selection most favors your cultural thesis. Movements move so rapidly that their direct ancestors are on to something else before they can be undermined and undone as rival precursors. Whether in painting or in literary theory, there is the glee of plenitude and proliferation along these postmodern boulevards, and a dogged pluralism, and individualism splintering off into idiosyncratic fits of unconventionality desperate to pass for original. With so much originality at hand (originality without an origin), and no center (or any number of centers, one to a customer), what's left to be called eccentric?

Modernism had its own widening gyres and ruptures—ruptures enough, hollow men and waste lands, the smashing of every rooted assumption and literary guaranty—but one center did hold, one pledge stuck. This was the artist's pledge to the self. Joyce, Mann, Eliot, Proust, Conrad (even with his furies): they *knew*. And what they knew was that—though things fall apart—the artist is whole, consummate. At bottom, in the deepest brain, rested the supreme serenity and masterly confidence of the sovereign maker.

Prior to modernism, genius scarcely needed to be centered—self-centered, "magisterial"—in this way. Jane Austen and Trollope had their village certainties to keep the balance, to pull toward the center: society, tradition, "realism," the solid verity of the vicar's wife. Even the Romantics, haunting the lonely periphery, deserting the matrix, still had a matrix to desert. The moderns looked all around, saw that nothing held, and began to make themselves up as law, and sometimes as religion. James, preparing in his Notebooks for a new piece of work, secretly crooned down at his pen: *mon bon, caro mio*. His dearest good angel, his faithful Muse, was housed in himself.

Almost no writer, not even the most accomplished, is like that now. Postmodernism, for writers, means fear and flux, unsureness, inward chaos, self-surprise. Virginia Woolf's *Common Reader* in full sail may suggest she is among the moderns, but her diaries show her trembling. Of contemporaries we read in English, only Nadine Gordimer, Joseph Brodsky, and V. S. Naipaul seem to own that central stillness, pride, and genuinely autocratic play of the humors that the moderns had; all three have been embattled by dislocations (Naipaul aggressively, by choice), and it is hard to tell whether it is the seizures of history we feel in these writers, or a true residue of modernist authority.

Those born into American indulgences are less flinty. John Updike in an interview last year spoke of the writer's work as "a little like handwriting. It comes out to be you no matter what you do. That is, it's recognizably Updike." A tendril of astonishment in that, as if there might reasonably have been an alternative. The moderns were unsurprised by their consistencies, and expected to come out what they were: inviolable. The characters in Philip Roth's *The Counterlife* are so wilily infiltrated by postmodernist inconstancy that they keep revising their speeches and their fates: you can't trust them even to stay dead. It goes without saying that we are forbidden to speculate whether the writer who imagined them is as anxiously protean, as cleft by doubt, as they.

Literary modernism, despite clangor and disjunction, was gilded by a certain voluptuousness: it came of the writer's self-knowledge—or call it self-anointment, a thing that properly embarrasses us today. But there was mettle in it; and also prowess, and defiance, and accountability. If the raggedy improvisations of postmodernism have killed off the idea of the Sublime and Magisterial Artist, it suits and gratifies our democratic temperament; the Sublime and the Magisterial were too long on their deathbeds anyhow.

Still, without modernism to give her shelter in the supernal confidence of genius, where can the Muse lodge now?

North

One dark wet November afternoon a few years ago, I flew in a small plane from Copenhagen to Aarhus, Jutland, and landed in a cold and pelting storm. The wind drove more powerfully than any wind I had ever known before; it struck with a mythic moan, like that of the wind in the nursery rhyme: *The North Wind will blooowww, and soon we'll have snooowww*. Afterward, shivering over tea in the refuge of a snug little hotel, I looked around the dining room, all shining mahogany, and felt myself a desolate stranger. I was traveling alone. The hotel had once been a way station for missionaries heading for foreign parts; no New Yorker, I thought, could be at ease in such a place. I was banished, lost. I ached with forlornness. The people in the dining room seemed enviably at home. They shuffled their newspapers and hardly spoke, and when they did, the alien syllables shut me decisively out.

And suddenly, just then, I found myself assaulted by a brilliant eeriness; enchantment swept me through and through. It was very

Published as "The Apparition of Northernness," *The New York Times Magazine*, Part II: *The Sophisticated Traveler*, October 4, 1987

nearly a kind of seizure: an electrifying pang that shook me to tears of recognition. It was, to choose the palest term for it, a moment of *déjà vu*, but also something vaster, more tumultuous, bottomless. Though I was incontrovertibly new to this wind-ghosted place, it came to me all at once that north was where I had once belonged, north was the uncanny germ of my being.

Northernness—the shrouded poetry of northernness—is why we crave the Scandinavian autumn and winter. It may be that July and August beam down on Copenhagen, Stockholm, Oslo, and Helsinki as attractively as they do elsewhere—who can doubt it? But say it outright: summer in Sweden is for the homebody Swedes. The imagination of a Stockholm-bound traveler is transfixed by a crystal dream of low, cold, tilted light.

We go north "enamored of a season . . . cold, spacious, severe, pale and remote," misted over by "trouble, ecstasy, astonishment"—C. S. Lewis's apparition of Northernness, drawn from childhood susceptibility, and from the icy glimmer of Norse fable. We go north to reclaim something buried, clouded, infiltrating, unsure, or else as sure as instantaneous sensation.

For me, it was, I think, a grain of historical memory in the gleam of that little hotel, a secret idiosyncratic autobiographical Jutland jot: a thousand ancestral years lived to the east, just across the Baltic, along the same latitude, in old Russia's Minsk province. But there are more universal reasons to seek out the north when it is most northern in aspect. The blinding late-October sun-slant on Copenhagen walks; the pewter pavements of Stockholm under a days-long autumn rain—in all of that there lurks a time-before, whirling up from storybooks and pictures and legends, and from some idea we have of our hot inward life set against a rind of frosted light.

Mystically, in sheets of clarified air, the north reminds.

The Shock of Teapots

One morning in Stockholm, after rain and just before November, a mysteriously translucent shadow began to paint itself across the top of the city. It skimmed high over people's heads, a gauzy brass net, keeping well above the streets, skirting everything fabricated by human arts—though one or two steeples were allowed to dip into it, like pens filling their nibs with palest ink. It made a sort of watermark over Stockholm, as if a faintly luminous river ran overhead, yet with no more weight or gravity than a vapor.

This glorious strangeness—a kind of crystalline wash—was the sunlight of a Swedish autumn. The sun looked *new*: it had a lucidity, a texture, a tincture, a position across the sky that my New York gape had never before taken in. The horizontal ladder of light hung high up, higher than any sunlight I had ever seen, and the quality of its glow seemed thinner, wanner, more tentatively morning-brushed; or else like gold leaf beaten gossamer as tissue —a lambent skin laid over the spired marrow of the town.

"Ah yes, the sun *does* look a bit different this time of year," say

Published as "Enchantments at First Encounter," *The New York Times Magazine*, Part II: *The Sophisticated Traveler*, March 17, 1985

the Stockholmers in their perfect English (English as a second first language), but with a touch of ennui. Whereas I, under the electrified rays of my whitening hair, stand drawn upward to the startling sky, restored to the clarity of childhood. The Swedes have known a Swedish autumn before; I have not.

Travel returns us in just this way to sharpness of notice; and to be saturated in the sight of what is entirely new—the sun at an unaccustomed slope, stretched across the northland, separate from the infiltrating dusk that always seems about to fall through clear gray Stockholm—is to revisit the enigmatically lit puppet-stage outlines of childhood: those mental photographs and dreaming woodcuts or engravings that we retain from our earliest years. What we remember from childhood we remember forever—permanent ghosts, stamped, imprinted, eternally seen. Travelers regain this ghost-seizing brightness, eeriness, firstness.

They regain it because they have cut themselves loose from their own society, from every society; they are, for a while, floating vagabonds, like astronauts out for a space walk on a long free line. They are subject to preternatural exhilarations, absurd horizons, unexpected forms and transmutations: the matter-of-fact (a battered old stoop, say, or the shape of a door) appears beautiful; or a stone that at home would not merit the blink of your eye here arrests you with its absolute particularity—just because it is what your hand already intimately knows. You think: a stone, a stone! They have stones here too! And you think: how uncannily the planet is girdled, as stone-speckled in Sweden as in New York. For the vagabond-voyeur (and for travelers voyeurism is irresistible), nothing is not for notice, nothing is banal, nothing is ordinary: not a rock, not the shoulder of a passerby, not a teapot.

Plenitude assaults; replication invades. Everything known has its spooky shadow and Doppelgänger. On my first trip anywhere—it was 1957 and I landed in Edinburgh with the roaring of the plane's four mammoth propellers for days afterward embedded in my ears—I rode in a red airport bus to the middle of the city, out of which ascended its great castle. It is a fairy-book castle, dreamlike, Arthurian, secured in the long-ago. But the shuddery

red bus—hadn't I been bounced along in an old bus before, perhaps
not so terrifically red as this one?—the red bus was not within
reach of plain sense. Every inch of its interior streamed with
unearthliness, with an undivulged and consummate witchery. It
put me in the grip of a wild Elsewhere. This unexceptional vehicle,
with its bright forward snout, was all at once eclipsed by a rush
of the abnormal, the unfathomably Martian. It was the bus, not
the phantasmagorical castle, that clouded over and bewildered our
reasoned humanity. The red bus was what I intimately knew:
only I had never seen it before. A reflected flicker of the actual.
A looking-glass bus. A Scottish ghost.

This is what travelers discover: that when you sever the links
of normality and its claims, when you break off from the quotidian,
it is the teapots that truly shock. Nothing is so awesomely unfamiliar as the familiar that discloses itself at the end of a journey.
Nothing shakes the heart so much as meeting—far, far away—
what you last met at home. Some say that travelers are informal
anthropologists. But it is ontology—the investigation of the nature
of being—that travelers do. Call it the flooding-in of the real.

There is, besides, the flooding-in of character. Here one enters
not landscapes or streetlit night scenes, but fragments of drama:
splinters of euphoria that catch you up when you are least de-
serving. Sometimes it is a jump into a pop-up book, as when a
cockney cabdriver, of whom you have asked directions while leaning out from the curb, gives his native wink of blithe goodwill.
Sometimes it is a mazy stroll into a toy theater, as when, in a
museum, you suddenly come on the intense little band following
the lecturer on Mesopotamia, or the lecturer on genre painting,
and the muse of civilization alights on these rapt few. What you
are struck with then—one of those mental photographs that go on
sticking to the retina—is not what lies somnolently in the glass
case or hangs romantically on the wall, but the enchantment of a
minutely idiosyncratic face shot into your vision with indelible
singularity, delivered over forever by your own fertile gaze. When
travelers stare at heads and ears and necks and beads and mus-
taches, they are—in the encapsuled force of the selection—making

art: portraits, voice sonatinas, the quick haiku of a strictly trian-
gular nostril.

Traveling is seeing; it is the implicit that we travel by. Travelers
are fantasists, conjurers, seers—and what they finally discover is
that every round object everywhere is a crystal ball: stone, teapot,
the marvelous globe of the human eye.

The Question of Our Speech: The Return to Aural Culture

When I was a thirteen-year-old New Yorker, a trio of women from the provinces took up, relentlessly and extravagantly, the question of my speech. Their names were Miss Evangeline Trolander, Mrs. Olive Birch Davis, and Mrs. Ruby S. Papp (pronounced *pop*). It was Mrs. Papp's specialty to explain how to "breathe from the diaphragm." She would place her fingers tip-to-tip on the unyielding hard shell of her midriff, hugely inhaling: how astonishing then to see how the mighty action of her lungs caused her fingertips to spring apart! This demonstration was for the repair of the New York voice. What the New York voice, situated notoriously "in the throat," required above everything was to descend, pumping air, to this nether site, so that "Young Lochinvar came out of the WEST" might come bellowing out of the pubescent breast.

The New York palate, meanwhile, was consonantally in neglect. *T*'s, *d*'s, and *l*'s were being beaten out against the teeth, European-fashion—this was called "dentalization"—while the homeless *r* and *n* went wandering in the perilous trough behind the front incisors.

Published in *Partisan Review*, Fiftieth Anniversary Issue, 1984–85

There were corrective exercises for these transgressions, the chief one being a liturgical recitation of "Tillie the Toiler took Tommy Tucker to tea," with the tongue anxiously flying up above the teeth to strike precisely on the lower ridge of the upper palate.

The diaphragm; the upper palate; and finally the arena in the cave of the mouth where the vowels were prepared. A New Yorker could not say a proper *a*, as in "paper"—this indispensable vibration was manufactured somewhere back near the nasal passage, whereas civility demanded the *a* to emerge frontally, directly from the lips' vestibule. The New York *i* was worst of all: how Mrs. Davis, Mrs. Papp, and Miss Trolander mimicked and ridiculed the New York *i*! "Oi loik oice cream," they mocked.

All these emendations, as it happened, were being applied to the entire population of a high school for girls in a modest Gothic pile on East Sixty-eighth Street in the 1940s, and no one who emerged from that pile after four years of daily speech training ever sounded the same again. On the eve of graduation, Mrs. Olive Birch Davis turned to Mrs. Ruby S. Papp and said: "Do you remember the *ugliness* of her *diction* when she came to us?" She meant me; I was about to deliver the Class Speech. I had not yet encountered Shaw's *Pygmalion*, and its popular recrudescence in the form of *My Fair Lady* was still to occur; all the same, that night, rehearsing for commencement, I caught in Mrs. Davis and Mrs. Papp something of Professor Higgins's victory, and in myself something of Eliza's humiliation.

Our teachers had, like young Lochinvar, come out of the West, but I had come out of the northeast Bronx. Called on to enunciate publicly for the first time, I responded with the diffidence of secret pleasure; I liked to read out loud, and thought myself not bad at it. Instead, I was marked down as a malfeasance in need of overhaul. The revisions and transformations that followed were not unlike an evangelical conversion. One had to be willing to be born again; one had to be willing to repudiate wholesale one's former defective self. It could not be accomplished without faith and shame: faith in what one might newly become, shame in the degrading process itself—the dedicated repetition of mantras. "Tillie the Toiler took Tommy Tucker to tea," "Oh! young LOCHinvar has come out of the WEST, Through all the wide BORDER HIS steed was the BEST." All the while pneumatically shooting out one's diaphragm, and keeping one's eye (never one's *oi*) peeled for the niggardly approval of Miss Evangeline Trolander.

In this way I was, at an early age, effectively made over. Like a multitude of other graduates of my high school, I now own a sort of robot's speech—it has no obvious native county. At least not to most ears, though a well-tutored listener will hear that the vowels hang on, and the cadence of every sentence has a certain laggardly northeast Bronx drag. Brooklyn, by contrast, is divided between very fast and very slow. Irish New York has its own sound, Italian New York another; and a refined ear can distinguish between Bronx and Brooklyn Irish and Bronx and Brooklyn Jewish: four separate accents, with the differences to be found not simply in vowels and consonants, but in speed and inflection. Nor is it so much a matter of ancestry as of neighborhood. If, instead of clinging to the green-fronded edge of Pelham Bay Park, my family had settled three miles west, in a denser "section" called Pelham Parkway, I would have spoken Bronx Jewish. Encountering City Island, Bronx Jewish said Ciddy Oilen. In Pelham Bay, where Bronx Irish was almost exclusively spoken in those days, it was Ciddy Allen. When Terence Cooke became cardinal of New York, my heart leaped up: Throggs Neck! I had assimilated those sounds long ago on a pebbly beach. No one had ever put the cardinal into the wringer of speech repair. I knew him through and through. He was my childhood's brother, and restored my orphaned ear.

Effectively made over: these noises that come out of me are not an overlay. They do not vanish during the free play of dreams or screams. I do not, cannot, "revert." This may be because Trolander, Davis, and Papp caught me early; or because I was so passionate a devotee of their dogma.

Years later I tried to figure it all out. What did these women have up their sleeves? An aesthetic ideal, perhaps: Standard American English. But behind the ideal—and Trolander, Davis, and

Papp were the strictest and most indefatigable idealists—there must have been an ideology; and behind the ideology, whatever form it might take, a repugnance. The speech of New York streets and households soiled them: you could see it in their proud pained meticulous frowns. They were intent on our elevation. Though they were dead set on annihilating Yiddish-derived "dentalization," they could not be said to be anti-Semites, since they were just as set on erasing the tumbling consonants of Virginia Greene's Alexander Avenue Irish Bronx; and besides, in our different styles, we *all* dentalized. Was it, then, the Melting Pot that inspired Trolander, Davis, and Papp? But not one of us was an "immigrant"; we were all fully Americanized, and our parents before us, except for the handful of foreign-born "German refugees." These were marched off to a special Speech Clinic for segregated training; their *r*'s drew Mrs. Davis's eyes toward heaven, and I privately recognized that the refugees were almost all of them hopeless cases. A girl named Hedwig said she *didn't care*, which made me conclude that she was frivolous, trivialized, not serious; wasn't it ignominious enough (like a kind of cheese) to be called "Hedwig"?

Only the refugees were bona fide foreigners. The rest of us were garden-variety subway-riding New Yorkers. Trolander, Davis, and Papp saw us nevertheless as tainted with foreignness, and it was the remnants of that foreignness they meant to wipe away: the last stages of the great turn-of-the-century alien flood. Or perhaps they intended that, like Shaw's Eliza, we should have the wherewithal to rise to a higher station. Yet, looking back on their dress and manner, I do not think Trolander, Davis, and Papp at all sought out or even understood "class"; they were reliably American, and class was nothing they were capable of believing in.

What, then, did these ferrywomen imagine we would find on the farther shore, once we left behind, through artifice and practice, our native speech? Was it a kind of "manners," was it what they might have called "breeding"? They thought of themselves as democratic noblewomen (nor did they suppose this to be a contradiction in terms), and they expected of us, if not the same, then at least a recognition of the category. They trusted in the power of models. They gave us the astonishing maneuvers of their teeth, their tongues, their lungs, and drilled us in imitation of those maneuvers. In the process, they managed—this was their highest feat—to break down embarrassment, to deny the shaming theatricality of the ludicrous. We lost every delicacy and dignity in acting like freaks or fools while trying out the new accent. Contrived consonants began freely to address feigned vowels: a world of parroting and parody. And what came of it all?

What came of it was that they caused us—and here was a category *they* had no recognition of—they caused us to exchange one regionalism for another. New York gave way to Midwest. We were cured of Atlantic Seaboard, a disease that encompassed north, middle, and south; and yet only the middle, and of that middle only New York, was considered to be on the critical list. It was New York that carried the hottest and sickest inflammation. In no other hollow of the country was such an effort mounted, on such a scale, to eliminate regionalism. The South might have specialized in Elocution, but the South was not ashamed of its idiosyncratic vowels; neither was New England; and no one sent missionaries.

Of course this was exactly what our democratic noblewomen were: missionaries. They restored, if not our souls, then surely and emphatically our *r*'s—those *r*'s that are missing in the end syllables of New Yorkers, who call themselves Noo Yawkizz and nowadays worry about muggizz. From Boston to New York to Atlanta, the Easterner is an Eastinna, his mother is a mutha, his father a fahtha, and the most difficult stretch of anything is the hahd paht; and so fawth. But only in New York is the absent *r* —i.e., the absent *aw*—an offense to good mannizz. To be sure, our missionaries did not dream that they imposed a parochialism of their own. And perhaps they were right not to dream it, since by the forties of this century the radio was having its leveling effect, and Midwest speech, colonizing by means of "announcers," had ascended to the rank of standard speech.

Still, only forty years earlier, Henry James, visiting from Eng-

land after a considerable period away, was freshly noticing and
acidly deploring the pervasively conquering *r*:

> . . . the letter, I grant, gets terribly little rest among those great
> masses of our population that strike us, in the boundless West es-
> pecially, as, under some strange impulse received toward conso-
> nantal recovery of balance, making it present even in words from
> which it is absent, bringing it in everywhere as with the small vulgar
> effect of a sort of morose grinding of the back teeth. There are, you
> see, sounds of a mysterious intrinsic meanness, and there are sounds
> of a mysterious intrinsic frankness and sweetness; and I think the
> recurrent note I have indicated—fatherr and motherr and otherr,
> waterr and matterr and scatterr, harrd and barrd, parrt, starrt, and
> (dreadful to say) arrt (the repetition it is that drives home the ugli-
> ness), are signal specimens of what becomes of a custom of utterance
> out of which the principle of taste has dropped.

In 1905, to drop the *r* was to drop, for the cultivated ear, a
principle of taste; but for our democratic noblewomen four decades
on, exactly the reverse was true. James's New York/Boston expectations, reinforced by southern England, assumed that Eastern
American speech, tied as it was to the cultural reign of London,
had a right to rule and to rule out. The history and sociolinguistics
governing this reversal is less pressing to examine than the question
of "standard speech" itself. James thought that "the voice *plus* the
way it is employed" determined "positively the history of the
national character, almost the history of the people." His views
on all this, his alarms and anxieties, he compressed into a fluid
little talk ("The Question of Our Speech") he gave at the Bryn
Mawr College commencement of June 8, 1905—exactly one year
and two days before my mother, nine years old, having passed
through Castle Garden, stood on the corner of Battery Park, waiting to board the horsecar for Madison Street on the Lower East
Side.

James was in great fear of the child waiting for the horsecar.
"Keep in sight," he warned, "the so interesting historical truth
that no language, so far back as our acquaintance with history

goes, has known any such ordeal, any such stress or strain, as was to await the English in this huge new community it was to help, at first, to father and mother. It came *over*, as the phrase is, came over originally without fear and without guile—but to find itself transplanted to spaces it had never dreamed, in its comparative humility, of covering, to conditions it had never dreamed, in its comparative innocence, of meeting." He spoke of English as an "unfriended heroine," "our transported medium, our unrescued Andromeda, our medium of utterance, . . . disjoined from all the associations, the other presences, that had attended her, that had watched for her and with her, that had helped to form her manners and her voice, her taste and her genius."

And if English, orphaned as it was and cut off from its "ancestral circle," did not have enough to contend with in its own immigrant situation, arriving "without fear and without guile" only to be ambushed by "a social and political order that was both without previous precedent and example and incalculably expansive," including also the expansiveness of a diligent public school network and "the mighty maniac" of journalism—if all this was not threatening enough, there was the special danger my nine-year-old mother posed. She represented an unstable new ingredient. She represented violation, a kind of linguistic Armageddon. She stood for disorder and promiscuity. "I am perfectly aware," James said at Bryn Mawr,

> that the common school and the newspaper are influences that shall often have been named to you, exactly, as favorable, as positively and actively contributive, to the prosperity of our idiom; the answer to which is that the matter depends, distinctively, on what is meant by prosperity. It is prosperity, of a sort, that a hundred million people, a few years hence, will be unanimously, loudly—above all loudly, I think!—speaking it, and that, moreover, many of these millions will have been artfully wooed and weaned from the Dutch, from the Spanish, from the German, from the Italian, from the Norse, from the Finnish, from the Yiddish even, strange to say, and (stranger still to say), even from the English, for the sweet sake, or the sublime consciousness, as we may perhaps put it, of speaking,

of talking, for the first time in their lives, *really* at their ease. There are many things our now so profusely important and, as is claimed, quickly assimilated foreign brothers and sisters may do at their ease in this country, and at two minutes' notice, and without asking any one else's leave or taking any circumstance whatever into account —any save an infinite uplifting sense of freedom and facility; but the thing they may best do is play, to their heart's content, with the English language, or, in other words, dump their mountain of promiscuous material into the foundation of the American.

"All the while we sleep," he continued, "the vast contingent of aliens whom we make welcome, and whose main contention, as I say, is that, from the moment of their arrival, they have just as much property in our speech as we have, and just as good a right to do what they choose with it . . . all the while we sleep the innumerable aliens are sitting up (*they* don't sleep!) to work their will on their new inheritance." And he compared the immigrants' use of English to oilcloth—"highly convenient . . . durable, tough, cheap."

James's thesis in his address to his audience of young aristocrats was not precisely focused. On the one hand, in describing the depredations of the innumerable sleepless aliens, in protesting "the common schools and the 'daily paper,' " he appeared to admit defeat—"the forces of looseness are in possession of the field." Yet in asking the graduates to see to the perfection of their own speech, he had, he confessed, no models to offer them. Imitate, he advised—but whom? Parents and teachers were themselves not watchful. "I am at a loss to name you particular and unmistakable, edifying and illuminating groups or classes," he said, and recommended, in the most general way, the hope of "encountering, blessedly, here and there, articulate individuals, torch-bearers, as we may rightly describe them, guardians of the sacred flame."

As it turned out, James not only had no solution; he had not even put the right question. These young women of good family whom he was exhorting to excellence were well situated in society to do exactly what James had described the immigrants as doing:

speaking "*really* at their ease," playing, "to their heart's content, with the English language" in "an infinite uplifting sense of freedom and facility." Whereas the "aliens," hard-pressed by the scramblings of poverty and cultural confusions, had no notion at all of linguistic "freedom and facility," took no witting license with the English tongue, and felt no remotest ownership in the language they hoped merely to earn their wretched bread by. If they did not sleep, it was because of long hours in the sweatshops and similar places of employment; they were no more in a position to "play" with English than they were to acquire bona fide *Mayflower* ancestry. Ease, content, facility—these were not the lot of the unsleeping aliens.

To the young people of Bryn Mawr James could offer nothing more sanguine, nothing less gossamer, than the merest metaphor —"guardians of the sacred flame." Whom then should they imitate but himself, the most "articulate individual" of them all? We have no record of the graduates' response to James's extravagant "later style" as profusely exhibited in this address: whatever it was, they could not have accepted it for standard American. James's English had become, by this time, an invention of his own fashioning, so shaded, so leafy, so imbricated, so brachiate, so filigreed, as to cast a thousand momentary ornamental obscurities, like the effect of the drill-holes in the spiraled stone hair of an imperial Roman portrait bust. He was the most eminent torchbearer in sight, the purest of all possible guardians of the flame—but a model he could not have been for anyone's everyday speech, no more than the Romans talked like the Odes of Horace. Not that he failed to recognize the exigencies of an active language, "a living organism, fed by the very breath of those who employ it, whoever these may happen to be," a language able "to respond, from its core, to the constant appeal of time, perpetually demanding new tricks, new experiments, new amusements." He saw American English as the flexible servant "of those who carry it with them, on their long road, as their specific experience grows larger and more complex, and who need it to help them to meet this expansion." And at the same time he excluded from these widened possibilities its slangy young native speakers and the very immigrants whose educated children would enrich and reanimate the American language (eight decades later we may judge how vividly), as well as master and augment its literature.

Its literature. It is striking beyond anything that James left out, in the course of this lecture, any reference to reading. Certainly it was not overtly his subject. He was concerned with enunciation and with idiom, with syllables, with vowels and consonants, with tone and inflection, with *sound*—but he linked the American voice to such "underlying things" as "proprieties and values, perfect possessions of the educated spirit, clear humanities," as well as "the imparting of a coherent culture." Implicit was his conviction that speech affects literature, as, in the case of native speakers, it inevitably does: naturalism in the dialogue of a novel, say, is itself always a kind of dialect of a particular place and time. But in a newly roiling society of immigrant speakers, James could not see ahead (and why should he have seen ahead? Castle Garden was unprecedented in all of human history) to the idea that a national literature can create a national speech. The immigrants who learned to read learned to speak. Those who only learned to speak did not, in effect, learn to speak.

In supposing the overriding opposite—that quality of speech creates culture, rather than culture quality of speech—James in "The Question of Our Speech" slighted the one formulation most pertinent to his complaints: the uses of literature. Pressing for "civility of utterance," warning against "influences round about us that make for . . . the confused, the ugly, the flat, the thin, the mean, the helpless, that reduce articulation to an easy and ignoble minimum, and so keep it as little distinct as possible from the grunting, the squealing, the barking or roaring of animals," James thought it overwhelmingly an issue of the imitation of oral models, an issue of "the influence of *observation*," above all an issue of manners—"for that," he insisted, "is indissolubly involved." How like Mrs. Olive Birch Davis he is when, at Bryn Mawr, he hopes to inflame his listeners to aspiration! "At first dimly, but then more and more distinctly, you will find yourselves noting, comparing,

preferring, at last positively emulating and imitating." Bryn Mawr,
of course, was the knowing occasion, not the guilty target, of this
admonition—he was speaking of the young voices he had been
hearing in the street and in the parlors of friends, and he ended
with a sacred charge for the graduates themselves: "you may,
sounding the clearer note of intercourse as only women can, become yourselves models and missionaries [sic], perhaps even a little
martyrs, of the good cause."

But why did he address himself to this thesis exclusively in
America? Could he not, even more emphatically, have made the
same declarations, uttered the same dooms, in his adopted England? No doubt it would not have been seemly; no doubt he
would have condemned any appearance of ingratitude toward his
welcoming hosts. All true, but this was hardly the reason the
lecture at Bryn Mawr would not have done for Girton College. In
Britain, regionalisms are the soul of ordinary English speech, and
in James's time more than in our own. Even now one can move
from hamlet to hamlet and hear the vowels chime charmingly with
a different tone in each village. Hull, England, is a city farther
from London in speech—though in distance only 140 miles to the
north—than Hull, Massachusetts, is from San Francisco, 3,000
miles to the west. Of England, it is clear, James had only the
expectations of class, and a single class set the standard for cultivated speech. Back home in America, diversity was without enchantment, and James demanded a uniform sound. He would not
have dreamed of requiring a uniform British sound: English diversity was *English* diversity, earned, native, beaten out over generations of the "ancestral circle"—while American diversity meant
a proliferating concatenation of the innumerable sleepless aliens
and the half-educated slangy young. With regard to England,
James knew whence the standard derived. It was a quality—an
emanation, even—of those who, for generations, had been privileged in their education. As Virginia Woolf acknowledged in connection with another complaint, the standard was Oxbridge. To
raise the question of "our" speech in England would have been a
superfluity: both the question and the answer were self-evident.

In England the question, if anyone bothered to put it at all, was: Who sets the standard? And the answer, if anyone bothered to give it at all, was: Those who have been through the great public schools, those who have been through either of the great pair of ancient universities—in short, those who run things.

This was perhaps what led James, in his American reflections, to trip over the issues, and to miss getting at the better question, the right and pertinent question: *the* question, in fact, concerning American speech. In Britain, and in the smaller America of his boyhood that strained to be a mirror of the cousinly English culture, it remained to the point to ask who sets the standard. And the rejoinder was simple enough: the people at the top. To risk the identical question in the America of 1905, with my mother about to emerge from Castle Garden to stand waiting for the horsecar on the corner of Battery Park, was unavoidably to hurtle to the very answer James most dreaded and then desperately conceded: the people at the bottom.

The right and pertinent question for America was something else. If, in politics, America's Enlightenment cry before the world was to be "a nation of laws, not of men," then it was natural for culture to apply in its own jurisdiction the same measure: unassailable institutions are preferable to models or heroes. To look for aristocratic models for common speech in the America of 1905 was to end exactly where James *did* end: "I am at a loss to name you particular and unmistakably edifying and illuminating groups or classes." It could not be done. As long as James believed—together with Trolander, Davis, and Papp, his immediate though paradoxical heirs: paradoxical because their ideal was democratic and his was the-people-at-the-top—as long as he believed in the premise of "edifying and illuminating" models, his analysis could go nowhere. Or, rather, it could go only into the rhapsody of vaporous hope that is the conclusion of "The Question of Our Speech"—"become yourselves models and missionaries, even a little martyrs, of the good cause." Holy and resplendent words I recognize on the instant, having learned them—especially the injunction to martyrdom—at the feet of Trolander, Davis, and Papp.

No, it was the wrong question for America, this emphasis on *who*; the wrong note for a campus (however homogeneous, however elite) just outside Philadelphia, that Enlightenment citadel, whose cracked though mighty Bell was engraved with a rendering of the majestic Hebrew word *dror*: a word my nine-year-old mother, on her way to Madison Street, would have been able to read in the original, though presumably James could not—a deprivation of literacy my mother might have marked him down for. "All life," James asserted on that brilliant June day (my mother's life was that day still under the yoke of the Czar; the Kishinev pogrom, with its massacre and its maimings, had occurred only two years earlier), "all life comes back to the question of our speech, the medium through which we communicate with each other; for all life comes back to the question of our relations with each other." And: "A care for tone is part of a care for many things besides; for the fact, for the value, of good breeding, above all, as to which tone unites with various other personal, social signs to bear testimony. The idea of good breeding . . . is one of the most precious conquests of civilization, the very core of our social heritage."

Speech, then, was *who*; it was breeding; it was "relations"; it was manners; and manners, in this view, make culture. As a novelist, and particularly as a celebrated practitioner of "the novel of manners" (though to reduce James merely to this is to diminish him radically as a recorder of evil and to silence his full moral genius), it was requisite, it was the soul of vitality itself, for James to analyze in the mode of *who*. But for a social theorist—and in his lecture social theory was what James was pressing toward—it was a failing and an error. The absence of models was not simply an embarrassment; it should have been a hint. It should have hinted at the necessary relinquishment of *who* in favor of *what*: not who appoints the national speech, but what creates the standard.

If, still sticking to his formulation, James had dared to give his private answer, he might have announced: "Young women, I, Henry James, am that august Who who fixes the firmament of our national speech. Follow me, and you follow excellence." But how had this vast substantial Who that was Henry James come to be fashioned? It was no Who *he* followed. It was instead a great cumulative corporeal What, the voluminous and manifold heritage of Literature he had been saturated in since childhood. In short, he *read*: he was a reader, he had always read, reading was not so much his passion or his possession as it was his bread, and not so much his bread as it was the primordial fountain of his life. Ludicrous it is to say of Henry James that he read, he was a reader! As much say of Vesuvius that it erupted, or of Olympus that it kept the gods. But reading—just that, *what is read*—is the whole, the intricate, secret of his exemplum.

The vulgarity of the low press James could see for himself. On the other hand, he had never set foot in an American public school (his education was, to say the least, Americanly untypical), and he had no inkling of any representative curriculum. Nevertheless it was this public but meticulous curriculum that was to set the standard; and it was a curriculum not far different from what James might have found for himself, exploring on his own among his father's shelves.

A year or so after my mother stepped off the horsecar into Madison Street, she was given Sir Walter Scott's "The Lady of the Lake" to read as a school assignment. She never forgot it. She spoke of it all her life. Mastering it was the triumph of her childhood, and though, like every little girl of her generation, she read *Pollyanna*, and in the last months of her eighty-third year every word of Willa Cather, it was "The Lady of the Lake" that enduringly typified achievement, education, culture.

Some seventy-odd years after my mother studied it at P.S. 131 on the Lower East Side, I open "The Lady of the Lake" and take in lines I have never looked on before:

> Not thus, in ancient days of Caledon,
> > Was thy voice mute amid the festal crowd,
> When lay of hopeless love, or glory won,
> > Aroused the fearful, or subdued the proud.
> At each according pause was heard aloud
> > Thine ardent symphony sublime and high!
> Fair dames and crested chiefs attention bowed;

For still the burden of thy minstrelsy
Was Knighthood's dauntless deed, and Beauty's matchless eye.

O wake once more! how rude soe'er the hand
   That ventures o'er thy magic maze to stray;
O wake once more! though scarce my skill command
   Some feeble echoing of thine earlier lay;
Though harsh and faint, and soon to die away,
   And all unworthy of thy nobler strain,
Yet if one heart throb higher at its sway,
   The wizard note has not been touched in vain.
Then silent be no more! Enchantress, wake again!

My mother was an immigrant child, the poorest of the poor.
She had come in steerage; she knew not a word of English when
she stepped off the horsecar into Madison Street; she was one of
the innumerable unsleeping aliens. Her teachers were the entirely
ordinary daughters of the Irish immigration (as my own teachers
still were, a generation on), and had no special genius, and as-
suredly no special training (a certain Miss Walsh was in fact fe-
rociously hostile), for the initiation of a Russian Jewish child into
the astoundingly distant and incomprehensible premises of such
poetry. And yet it was accomplished, and within the briefest
period after the voyage in steerage.

What was accomplished was not merely that my mother
"learned" this sort of poetry—i.e., could read and understand it.
She learned what it represented in the widest sense—not only the
legendary heritage implicit in each and every word and phrase (to
a child from Hlusk, where the wooden sidewalks sank into mud
and the peasants carried water buckets dangling from shoulder
yokes, what was "minstrelsy," what was "Knighthood's dauntless
deed," what on earth was a "wizard note"?), but what it represented
in the American social and tribal code. The quickest means of
stitching all this down is to say that what "The Lady of the Lake"
stood for, in the robes and tapestries of its particular English, was
the received tradition exemplified by Bryn Mawr in 1905, including James's presence there as commencement speaker.

The American standard derived from an American institution: the public school, free, democratic, open, urgent, pressing on the young a program of reading not so much for its "literary value," though this counted too, as for the stamp of Heritage. All this James overlooked. He had no firsthand sense of it. He was himself the grandson of an ambitiously money-making Irish immigrant; but his father, arranging his affluent life as a metaphysician, had separated himself from public institutions—from any practical idea, in fact, of institutions *per se*—and dunked his numerous children in and out of school on two continents, like a nomad in search of the wettest oasis of all. It was hardly a wonder that James, raised in a self-enclosed clan, asserted the ascendancy of manners over institutions, or that he ascribed to personal speech "positively the history of the national character, almost the history of the people," or that he spoke of the "ancestral circle" as if kinship were the only means to transmit that national character and history.

It was as if James, who could imagine nearly everything, had in this instance neglected imagination itself: kinship as construct and covenant, kinship imagined—and what are institutions if not invented kinship circles: society as contract? In the self-generating Enlightenment society of the American founding philosophers, it was uniquely the power of institutions to imagine, to create, kinship and community. The Constitution, itself a kind of covenant or imaginatively established "ancestral circle," created peoplehood out of an idea, and the public schools, begotten and proliferated by that idea, implemented the Constitution; and more than the Constitution. They implemented and transmitted the old cultural mesh. Where there was so much diversity, the institution substituted for the clan, and discovered—through a kind of civic magnetism—that it could transmit, almost as effectively as the kinship clan itself, "the very core of our social heritage."

To name all this the principle of the Melting Pot is not quite right, and overwhelmingly insufficient. The Melting Pot called for imitation. Imagination, which is at the heart of institutionalized covenants, promotes what is intrinsic. I find on my shelves two old textbooks used widely in the "common schools" James deplored. The first is *A Practical English Grammar*, dated 1880, the work of one Albert N. Raub, A.M., Ph.D. ("Author of 'Raub's Readers,' 'Raub's Arithmetics,' 'Plain Educational Talks, Etc.' "). It is a relentless volume, thorough, determined, with no loopholes; every permutation of the language is scrutinized, analyzed, accounted for. It is also a commonplace book replete with morally instructive quotations, some splendidly familiar. Each explanatory chapter is followed by "Remarks," "Cautions," and "Exercises," and every Exercise includes a high-minded hoard of literary Remarks and Cautions. For instance, under Personal Pronouns:

> Though the mills of God grind slowly,
>   yet they grind exceedingly small;
> Though with patience He stands waiting,
>   with exactness grinds He all.

> This above all, to thine own self be true,
> And it must follow, as the night the day,
> Thou canst not then be false to any man.

> These are thy glorious works, Parent of good,
>   Almighty! Thine this universal frame.

> Alas! they had been friends in youth,
> But whispering tongues can poison truth;
> And constancy lives in realms above,
>   And life is thorny, and youth is vain;
> And to be wroth with one we love
>   Doth work like madness on the brain.

So much for Longfellow, Shakespeare, Milton, and Coleridge. But also Addison, Cowper, Pope, Ossian, Scott, Ruskin, Thomson, Wordsworth, Trollope, Gray, Byron, Whittier, Lowell, Holmes, Moore, Collins, Hood, Goldsmith, Bryant, Dickens, Bacon, Franklin, Locke, the Bible—these appear throughout, in the form of addenda to Participles, Parsing, Irregular Verbs, and the rule of the Nominative Independent; in addition, a handful of lost presences: Bushnell, H. Wise, Wayland, Dwight, Blair, Mrs. Welby (nearly the only woman in the lot), and Anon. The *content* of this volume is not its subject matter, neither its syntactic lesson nor its poetic maxims. It is the voice of a language; rather, of language itself, language as texture, gesture, innateness. To read from beginning to end of a schoolbook of this sort is to recognize at once that James had it backwards and upside down: it is not that manners lead culture; it is culture that leads manners. What shapes culture—this is not a tautology or a redundancy—is culture. "Who makes the country?" was the latent question James was prodding and poking, all gingerly; and it was the wrong—because unanswerable—one. "What kind of country shall we have?" was Albert N. Raub's question, and it *was* answerable. The answer lay in the reading given to the children in the schoolhouses: the institutionalization, so to say, of our common speech at its noblest.

My second text is even more striking: *The Etymological Reader*, edited by Epes Sargent and Amasa May, dated 1872. "We here offer to the schools of the United States," begins the Preface, "the first systematic attempt to associate the study of etymology with exercises in reading." What follows is a blitz of "vocabulary," Latin roots, Saxon roots, prefixes, and suffixes, but these quickly subside, and nine tenths of this inventive book is an anthology engaging in its richness, range, and ambition. "Lochinvar" is here; so are the Declaration of Independence and selections from Shakespeare; so is Shelley's "To a Skylark"; so is the whole "Star-Spangled Banner." But also: "Description of a Bee Hunt," "Creation a Continuous Work," "The Sahara," "Anglo-Saxon and Norman French," "Conversation," "Progress of Civilization," "Effects of Machinery," "On the Choice of Books," "Our Indebtedness to the Greeks," "Animal Heat," "Corruptions of Language," "Jerusalem from the Mount of Olives," "On the Act of Habeas Corpus," "Individual Character," "Going Up in a Balloon," and dozens of other essays. Among the writers: Dickens, Macaulay, Wordsworth, Irving, Mark Twain, Emerson, Channing, John Stuart Mill, Carlyle, De Quincey, Tennyson, Mirabeau, and so on and so on.

It would be foolish to consider *The Etymological Reader* merely

charming, a period piece, "Americana"—it is too immediately useful, too uncompromising, and, for the most part, too enduring to
be dismissed with condescension.

> It was one of those heads which Guido has often painted—mild,
> pale, penetrating, free from all commonplace ideas of fat, contented
> ignorance, looking downward upon the earth; it looked forward, but
> looked as if it looked at something beyond this world. How one of
> his order came by it, Heaven above, who let it fall upon a monk's
> shoulders, best knows; but it would have suited a Brahmin, and had
> I met it upon the plains of Hindostan, I had reverenced it.

To come upon Sterne, just like this, all of a sudden, for the first
time, pressed between Southey's sigh ("How beautiful is night!")
and Byron's "And the might of the Gentile, unsmote by the sword,
/ Hath melted like snow in the glance of the Lord"—to come upon
Sterne, just like that, is to come upon an unexpected human fact.
Such textbooks filled vessels more fundamental than the Melting
Pot—blood vessels, one might venture. Virtuous, elevated, striv-
ing and stirring, the best that has been thought and said: thus the
voice of the common schools. A fraction of their offerings had a
heroic, or monumental, quality, on the style perhaps of George
Washington's head. They stood for the power of civics. But the
rest were the purest belles-lettres: and it was belles-lettres that
were expected to be the fountainhead of American civilization,
including civility. Belles-lettres provided style, vocabulary, speech
itself; and also the themes of Victorian seriousness: conscience and
work. Elevated literature was the model for an educated tongue.
Sentences, like conscience and work, were demanding.

What did these demanding sentences do in and for society? First,
they demanded to be studied. Second, they demanded sharpness
and cadence in writing. They promoted, in short, literacy—and
not merely literacy, but a vigorous and manifold recognition of
literature as a *force*. They promoted an educated class. Not a hereditarily educated class, but one that had been introduced to the
initiating and shaping texts early in life, almost like the hereditarily
educated class itself.

All that, we know, is gone. Where once the *Odyssey* was read in the schools, in a jeweled and mandarin translation, Holden Caulfield takes his stand. He is winning and truthful, but he is not demanding. His sentences reach no higher than his gaze. The idea of belles-lettres, when we knock our unaccustomed knees against it, looks archaic and bizarre: rusted away, like an old car chassis. The content of belles-lettres is the property of a segregated caste or the dissipated recollections of the very old.

Belles-lettres in the schools fashioned both speech and the art of punctuation—the sound and the look of nuance. Who spoke well pointed well; who pointed well spoke well. One was the skill of the other. No one now punctuates for nuance—or, rather, whoever punctuates for nuance is "corrected." Copy editors do not know the whole stippled range of the colon or the semicolon, do not know that "O" is not "oh," do not know that not all juxtaposed adjectives are coordinate adjectives; and so forth. The degeneration of punctuation and word-by-word literacy is pandemic among English speakers: this includes most poets and novelists. To glimpse a typical original manuscript undoctored by a copy editor is to suffer a shock at the sight of ignorant imprecision; and to examine a densely literate manuscript after it has passed through the leveling hands of a copy editor is again to suffer a shock at the sight of ignorant imprecision.

In 1930 none of this was so. The relentlessly gradual return of aural culture, beginning with the telephone (a farewell to letter-writing), the radio, the motion picture, and the phonograph, speeded up by the television set, the tape recorder, and lately the video recorder, has by now, after half a century's worth of technology, restored us to the pre-literate status of face-to-face speech. And mass literacy itself is the fixity of no more than a century, starting with the advancing reforms following the industrial revolution—reforms introducing, in England, the notion of severely limited leisure to the classes that formerly had labored with no leisure at all. Into that small new recreational space fell what we now call the "nineteenth-century novel," in both its supreme and its lesser versions. The act of reading—the *work*, in fact, of the act of reading—appeared to complicate and intensify the most ordinary intelligence. The silent physiological translation of letters into sounds, the leaping eye encoding, the transmigration of blotches on a page into the story of, say, Dorothea Brooke, must surely count among the most intricate of biological and transcendent designs. In 1930 the so-called shopgirl, with her pulp romance, is habitually engaged in this electrifying webwork of eye and mind. In 1980 she reverts, via electronics, to the simple speaking face. And then it is all over, by and large, for mass literacy. High literacy has been the province of an elite class since Sumer; there is nothing novel in having a caste of princely readers. But the culture of mass literacy, in its narrow period from 1830 to 1930, was something else: Gutenberg's revolution did not take effect in a popular sense—did not properly begin—until the rise of the middle class at the time, approximately, of the English Reform Act of 1832. Addison's *Spectator*, with its Latin epigraphs, was read by gentlemen, but Dickens was read by nearly everyone. The almost universal habit of reading for recreation or excitement conferred the greatest complexity on the greatest number, and the thinnest sliver of history expressed it: no more than a single century. It flashed by between aural culture and aural culture, no longer-lived than a lightning bug. The world of the VCR is closer to the pre-literate society of traveling mummers than it is to that of the young Scott Fitzgerald's readership in 1920.

When James read out "The Question of Our Speech" in 1905, the era of print supremacy was still in force, unquestioned; the typewriter and the electric light had arrived to strengthen it, and the telephone was greeted only as a convenience, not a substitute. The telephone was particularly welcome—not much was lost that ought not to have been lost in the omission of letters agreeing to meet the 8:42 on Tuesday night on the east platform. Since then, the telephone has abetted more serious losses: exchanges between artists and thinkers; documents of family and business relations; quarrels and cabals among politicians; everything that in the past tended to be preserved for biographers and cultural historians. The advent of the computer used as word processor similarly points toward the wiping out of any *progressive* record of thought; the grain of a life can lie in the illumination of the crossed-out word.

But James, in the remoteness of post-Victorian technology, spoke unshadowed by these threatened disintegrations among the community of the literate; he spoke in the very interior of what seemed then to be a permanently post-aural culture. He read from a manuscript; later that year, Houghton, Mifflin published it together with another lecture, this one far more famous, "The Lesson of Balzac." We cannot hear his voice on a phonograph record, as we can hear his fellow self-exile T. S. Eliot's; and this, it might be said, is another kind of loss. If we cherish photographs of Henry James's extraordinarily striking head with its lantern eyes, we can regret the loss of a filmed interview of the kind that nowadays captures and delivers into the future Norman Mailer and John Updike. The return to an aural culture is, obviously, not *all* a question of loss; only of the most significant loss of all: the widespread nurture by portable print; print as water, and sometimes wine. It was, in its small heyday (we must now begin to say *was*), the most glorious work of the eye-linked brain.

And in the heyday of that glorious work, James made a false analysis. In asking for living models, his analysis belonged to the old aural culture, and he did not imagine its risks. In the old aural culture, speech *was* manner, manner *was* manners, manners *did* teach the tone of the civilized world. In the new aural culture, speech remains manner, manner becomes manners, manners go on teaching the tone of the world. The difference is that the new aural culture, based, as James urged, on emulation, is governed from below. Emulation as a principle cannot control its sources. To seize on only two blatancies: the guerrilla toy of the urban underclass, the huge and hugely loud portable radio—the "ghetto blaster"—is adopted by affluent middle-class white adolescents; so is the locution "Hey, man," which now crosses both class and gender. James worried about the replacement in America of "Yes" by "Yeah" (and further by the comedic "Yep"), but its source was the drawl endemic to the gilt-and-plush parlors of the upper middle class. "Yeah" did not come out of the street; it went into the street.

But it is also fairly certain that the "Yeah"-sayers, whatever their place in society, could not have been strong readers, even given the fissure that lies between reading and the style of one's talk. The more attached one is to the community of readers, the narrower the fissure. In a society where belles-lettres are central to education of the young, what controls speech is the degree of absorption in print. Reading governs speech, governs tone, governs manner and manners and civilization. "It is easier to overlook any question of speech than to trouble about it," James complained, "but then it is also easier to snort or neigh, to growl or 'meaow,' than to articulate and intonate."

And yet he overlooked the primacy of the high act of reading. No one who, in the age of conscience and work, submitted to "The Lady of the Lake," or parsed under the aegis of Albert N. Raub, or sent down a bucket into *The Etymological Reader*, was likely to snort or neigh or emit the cry of the tabby. Agreed, it was a more publicly formal and socially encrusted age than ours, and James was more publicly formal and socially encrusted than many of his contemporaries: he was an old-fashioned gentleman. He had come of age during the Civil War. His clothes were laid out by a manservant. His standard was uncompromising. All the same, he missed how and where his own standard ruled. He failed to discover it in the schoolhouses, to which it had migrated after the attenuation of the old aural culture. To be sure, the school texts, however aspiring, could not promise to the children of the poor, or to the children of the immigrants, or to the children of working men, any hope of a manservant; but they *did* promise a habit of speech, more mobilizing and organizing, even, than a valet. The key to American speech was under James's nose. It was at that very moment being turned in a thousand locks. It was opening gate after gate. Those who could read according to an elevated standard could write sufficiently accomplished sentences, and those who could write such sentences could "articulate and intonate."

"Read, read! Read yourself through all the stages of the masters of the language," James might have exhorted the graduates. In-

stead, he told them to seek "contact and communication, a benef-
icent contagion," in order to "bring about the happy state—the
state of sensibility to tone." It offended him, he confessed, that
there were "forces assembled to make you believe that no form of
speech is provably better than another." Forty years on, Trolander,
Davis, and Papp set their own formidable forces against the forces
of relativism in enunciation. Like James, they were zealous to
impose their own parochialisms. James did not pronounce the *r* in
"mother"; it was, therefore, vulgar to let it be heard. Our Mid-
western teachers *did* pronounce the *r*; it was, therefore, vulgar *not*
to let it be heard. How, then, one concludes, *is* any form of speech
"provably better than another"? In a relativist era, the forces rep-
resenting relativism in enunciation have for the moment won the
argument, it seems; yet James has had his way all the same. With
the exception of the South and parts of the East Coast, there is
very nearly a uniform *vox Americana*. And we have everywhere a
uniform "tone." It is in the streets and in the supermarkets, on
the radio and on television; and it is low, low, low. In music, in
speech, in manner, the upper has learned to imitate the lower.
Cheapened imprecise speech is the triumph of James's tribute to
emulation; it is the only possible legacy that could have come of
the principle of emulation.

Then why did James plead for vocal imitation instead of reading?
He lived in a sea of reading, at the highest tide of literacy, in the
time of the crashing of its billows. He did not dream that the sea
would shrink, that it was impermanent, that we would return,
through the most refined technologies, to the aural culture. He
had had his own dealings with a continuing branch of the aural
culture—the theater. He had written for it as if for a body of
accomplished readers, and it turned on him with contempt. "Forget
not," he warned in the wake of his humiliation as a playwright,
"that you write for the stupid—that is, your maximum of refinement must meet the minimum of intelligence of the audience—
the intelligence, in other words, of the biggest ass it may conceivably contain. It is a most unholy trade!" He was judging, in this
outcry, all those forms that arrange for the verbal to bypass the

eye and enter solely through the ear. The ear is, for subtlety of interpretation, a coarser organ than the eye; it follows that nearly all verbal culture designed for the ear is broader, brighter, larger, louder, simpler, less intimate, more insistent—more *theatrical*—than any page of any book.

For the population in general, the unholy trades—they are now tremendously in the plural, having proliferated—have rendered reading nearly obsolete, except as a source of data and as a means of record-keeping—"warehousing information." For this the computer is an admittedly startling advance over Pharaoh's indefatigably meticulous scribes, notwithstanding the lofty liturgical poetry that adorned the ancient records, offering a tendril of beauty among the granary lists. Pragmatic reading cannot die, of course, but as the experience that feeds *Homo ridens*, reading is already close to moribund. In the new aural culture of America, intellectuals habitually define "film" as "art" in the most solemn sense, as a counterpart of the literary novel, and ridicule survivors of the age of "movies" as naïfs incapable of making the transition from an old form of popular entertainment to a new form of serious expression meriting a sober equation with written art—as if the issue had anything to do with what is inherently complex in the medium, rather than with what is inherently complex in the recipient of the medium. Undoubtedly any movie is more "complicated" than any book; and also more limited by the apparatus of the "real." As James noted, the maker of aural culture brings to his medium a "maximum of refinement"—i.e., he does the best he can with what he has to work with; sometimes he is even Shakespeare. But the job of sitting in a theater or in a movie house or at home in front of a television set is not so reciprocally complex as the wheels-within-wheels job of reading almost anything at all (including the comics). Reading is an act of imaginative conversion. That specks on a paper can turn into tale or philosophy is as deep a marvel as alchemy or wizardry. A secret brush construes phantom portraits. In the proscenium or the VCR everything is imagined *for* one: there is nothing to do but see and hear, and what's there is what is literally there. When film is "poetic," it is almost never because of language, but rather because of the resemblance to paintings or engravings—one thinks of the knight on a horse in a field of flowers in Bergman's *The Virgin Spring*. Where film is most art, it is least a novelty.

The new aural culture is prone to appliance-novelty—a while ago who could have predicted the video recorder or the hand-held miniature television set, and who now knows what variations and inventions lie ahead? At the same time there is a rigidity to the products of the aural culture—like those static Egyptian sculptures, stylistically unaltered for three millennia, that are brilliantly executed but limited in imaginative intent.

In the new aural culture there is no prevalent belles-lettres curriculum to stimulate novel imaginative intent, that "wizard note" of the awakened Enchantress; what there is is replication—not a reverberation or an echo, but a copy. The Back to Basics movement in education, which on the surface looks as if it is calling for revivification of a belles-lettres syllabus, is not so much reactionary as lost in literalism, or *trompe l'oeil*: another example of the replication impulse of the new aural culture, the culture of theater. Only in a *trompe l'oeil* society would it occur to anyone to "bring back the old values" through bringing back the McGuffey Reader—a scenic designer's idea, and still another instance of the muddle encouraged by the notion of "emulation." The celebration of the McGuffey Reader can happen only in an atmosphere where "film," a copyist's medium, is taken as seriously as a book.

A book is not a "medium" at all; it is far spookier than that, one of the few things-in-themselves that we can be sure of, a Platonic form that can inhabit a virtual infinity of experimental incarnations: any idea, any story, any body of poetry, any incantation, in any language. Above all, a book is the riverbank for the river of language. Language without the riverbank is only television talk—a free fall, a loose splash, a spill. And that is what an aural society, following a time of complex literacy, finally admits to: spill and more spill. James had nothing to complain of: he flourished in a period when whoever read well could speak well; the rest was provincialism—or call it, in kindness, regional exclusiveness. Still, the river of language—to cling to the old metaphor—ran most forcefully when confined to the banks that governed its course. But we who come after the hundred-year hegemony of the ordinary reader, we who see around us, in all these heaps of appliances (each one a plausible "electronic miracle"), the dying heaves of the caste-free passion for letters, should know how profoundly—and possibly how irreversibly—the mummers have claimed us.

Sholem Aleichem's Revolution

Yiddish is a direct, spirited, and spiritually alert language that is almost a thousand years old—centuries older than Chaucerian English, and, like the robust speech of Chaucer's pilgrims, expressively rooted in the quotidian lives of ordinary folk. It is hard to be pretentious or elevated in Yiddish and easy to poke fun. Yiddish is especially handy for satire, cynicism, familiarity, abuse, sentimentality, resignation, for a sense of high irony, and for putting people in their place and events in bitter perspective: all the defensive verbal baggage an involuntarily migratory nation is likely to need en route to the next temporary refuge. In its tenderer mien, Yiddish is also capable of a touching conversational intimacy with a consoling and accessible God. If Yiddish lacks cathedral grandeur, there is anyhow the compensation of coziness, of smallness, of a lovingly close, empathic, and embracing Creator who can be appealed to in the diminutive. Yiddish is a household tongue, and God, like other members of the family, is sweetly informal in it.

Published in *The New Yorker*, March 28, 1988

Starting in the early medieval period, the Jews of Europe were rarely allowed a chance to feel at home. Consequently Yiddish developed on the move, evolving out of a mixture of various tenth-century urban German dialects (not exclusively Middle High German, a linguistic misapprehension only recently superseded), and strengthened in its idiosyncrasies by contributions from French, Italian, Slavic, Hebrew, and Aramaic. (The last, the language of the Talmud and of Jesus, was widely in use in the Near East beginning around 300 B.C.E.) Until the end of the eighteenth century, Yiddish was the overwhelming vernacular of European Jewish communities from Amsterdam to Smolensk, from the Baltic to the Balkans, and as far south as Italy. Driven relentlessly eastward by the international brutality of the Crusaders and by the localized brutality of periodic pogroms, the language suffered successive uprootings and took on new morphological influences. In 1492, when Columbus sailed the ocean blue and Ferdinand and Isabella issued their anti-Jewish edict of expulsion, the language of the Spanish Jews—called Judezmo or Ladino—underwent its own upheavals, fleeing the depredations of the Inquisition to Holland, Italy, Turkey, North Africa, and even the New World.

And all the while Yiddish remained a language without a name, or almost so. "Yiddish" means "Jewish," or what Jews speak—but this term became current only toward the close of the nineteenth century. Before then, the everyday speech of Ashkenazi Jews (i.e., Jews without Spanish or Arabic language connections) was designated "Judeo-German," which essentially misrepresented it, since it was steadfastly a language in its own right, with its own regionalisms and dialects. To think of Yiddish (as many German-speakers tend to) merely as a fossilized or corrupted old German dialect would oblige us similarly to think of French as a deformed and slurred vestige of an outlying Latin patois deposited on the Rhône by a defunct Roman colony. But "Judeo-German" at least implied a modicum of dignity; at any rate, it was a scholar's word. The name Jews themselves, intellectuals in particular, habitually clapped on Yiddish was not a name at all; it was, until the miraculous year 1888, an opprobrium: *zhargón*. Gibberish; prattle; a subtongue, something less than a respectably cultivated language. Yiddish was "jargon" to the intellectuals despite its then eleven million speakers (i.e., before the Nazi decimations), despite the profusion of its press, theater, secular educational systems, religious and political movements, and despite its long (though problematical) history of literary productivity.

In 1888—effectively overnight—this contemptuous view of Yiddish was overturned, and by a single powerful pen writing in Yiddish. The pen had a pen name: Sholem Aleichem, a Hebrew salutation that literally means "peace to you" (the familiar Arabic cognate is *salaam aleykum*), and conveys a vigorously affectionate delight in encountering a friend, or someone who can immediately become a friend, if not an instant confidant. Almost no phrase is more common in Yiddish—as common as a handshake. The pseudonym itself declared a revolutionary intention: Yiddish as a literary vehicle was at last to be welcomed, respected, celebrated. The name, like the writer, looked to a program, and Sholem Aleichem was already a prolific author of short stories and feuilletons when, at the age of twenty-nine, he founded a seminal Yiddish literary annual, *Di Yidishe Folksbibliotek* ("The Popular Jewish Library"). The money ran out in a couple of years, and the new periodical vanished. But the revisionist ardor of its first issue alone—an electrifying burst of promulgation and demonstration—permanently changed the fortunes of Yiddish. The despised *zhargón* was all at once removed from scorn and placed in a pantheon of high literary art, complete with a tradition, precursors, genres, a sense of historical development, and uncompromising critical goals—a conscious patrimony that, only the day before, no one had dreamed was there.

It had not been there. The aesthetics of literary self-awareness, a preoccupation with generational classifications, issues of precedent and continuity—all these were fictions, the deliberate invention of Sholem Aleichem himself. It was Sholem Aleichem who, invoking Gogol and Turgenev as models, established the genres and identified a radical precursor: the novelist and critic Sholem Yankev Abramovitsh, who wrote under the nom de plume of

Mendele Moykher-Sforim (Mendele the Book Peddler). In the very hour Sholem Aleichem was naming him the "grandfather" of Yiddish literature, Mendele was no more than fifty-two years old, in mid-career. According to Professor Dan Miron, a leading scholar of Yiddish letters (who reveals all these marvels in his enchanting study, *A Traveler Disguised*), "What was unimaginable in 1885 was taken for granted in 1895. In 1880 Yiddish writers did not suspect that they had a history; by the early 1890s they had already produced one 'classic' writer; before the century ended *The History of Yiddish Literature in the Nineteenth Century* was written in English for American readers by a Harvard instructor." It was, in short, a process of historical mythmaking so rapid and extreme, and so bewitching, that the historians themselves swallowed it whole in no time at all. And Sholem Aleichem was the premier mythmaker and founder of that process.

But why was Yiddish so disreputable that it needed a Sholem Aleichem to fabricate a grand intellectual pedigree for it? Like any other language, it *did* have a genuine history, after all: a living civilization had eaten, slept, wept, laughed, borne babies, earned its bread or failed to, and had, in fact, read and written stories in Yiddish for nearly five centuries. Contempt for Yiddish, moreover, was simultaneously internal and external—Jewish intellectuals as well as Gentiles of every class habitually derided it. The Gentile world despised Yiddish as a marginal tongue because it was spoken by a people deemed marginal by Christendom; that was simple enough. And while it is true that the prejudices of the majority can sometimes manage to leave an unsavory mark on a minority's view of itself, Gentile scorn for Yiddish had almost nothing to do with the contumely Jewish social and intellectual standards reserved for Yiddish. The trouble with Yiddish, from the Jewish standpoint, was that it wasn't Hebrew. Yiddish was the language of exile—temporary, make-do; it belonged to an unfortunate phase of history: an ephemeral if oppressive nightmare only lightened by the unquenchable hope of national restoration. Yiddish was an empty vessel, uncultivated, useless for significant expression and high experience. It was the instrument of women and the ignorant—categories that frequently overlapped.

Hebrew, by contrast, was regarded as synonymous with Jewish reality. Besides being the language of Scripture, of the liturgy, of daily prayer, it was the sole medium of serious life, which could mean one thing only: serious learning. In a society where fundamental literacy was expected of everyone without exception, including women, and where the scholar was situated at the apex of communal distinction, "ignorant" signified insufficient mastery of Hebrew. Everyone, including women—who could recite from the Hebrew prayer book—had some degree of access to Hebrew. A young boy's basic education began with the Pentateuch; if he never acquired much of anything else, he still had that, along with the daily prayer book, the Passover Haggadah, and a smattering of commentary. And of course Yiddish itself, written in the Hebrew alphabet, is peppered with liturgical and biblical allusions, as well as homelier matter in Hebrew—which is why, while a knowledge of Yiddish may assure an understanding of a sentence in German, the reverse is not so likely. From the time of the destruction of the Second Temple in the year 70, Hebrew remained a living language in everyday reading and writing use. It may have suffered severe popular contraction—practically no one *spoke* it—but it never became moribund. My own father, who wrote a rather formal Victorian-style English, would never consider writing in English or Yiddish when he wanted to address a letter to a person of learning—a rabbi he respected, or perhaps the headmaster of a yeshiva: in the world he was reared in (he was born in White Russia in 1892), Hebrew was the only appropriate vehicle for a civilized pen. It took—and gave—the measure of a mind. You might tie your shoelaces in Yiddish, but Hebrew was the avenue of thought and certainly of civility.

When Enlightenment ideas finally spread to the isolated Yiddish-speaking communities of Eastern Europe, they arrived a century late and turned out to have a somewhat different character. Like the Gentile Enlightenment, Haskalah—the name for the Enlightenment movement among Jews—fostered the advancement of secularization and an optimistic program for the improvement of the common people. On the face of it, it might seem that Hebrew would have been left behind in the turmoil of the new liberalization, and that the language of the Bible would at least attenuate in an atmosphere where the claims of piety were thinning out— just as Latin, after the decline of the authority of Christian scholasticism, was gradually compelled to give way to a diversity of vernaculars. In Jewish society exactly the opposite happened: the progress of Haskalah only intensified the superior status of Hebrew and accelerated its secular use. As the temporal more and more replaced the theological (though these phrases don't quite fit the Jewish sense of how spiritual traditions and this-worldliness are intertwined), Hebrew pressed more urgently than ever toward the forefront of intellectual life. Hebrew belles-lettres began to be taken seriously by temperaments that had formerly regarded stories and novels as a species of levity fit only for women and the ignorant—and therefore written exclusively in Yiddish. The first Hebrew novel—*The Love of Zion*, by Abraham Mapu—didn't appear until 1853, but it was very quickly followed by wave after wave of explosively burgeoning literary forms—fiction, essays, poetry. Hebrew composition, which over the last millennium or so had been chiefly employed in scholarly responsa on ethical and juridical issues, was suddenly converted to high imaginative art. Not that original Hebrew literature had never before burst out in European Jewish experience: the majestic poets of medieval Spain had astounded their little historical span with lyrical masterpieces to vie with the Song of Songs; and the experimental poets of Renaissance Italy echoed Petrarch and Dante in Hebrew stanzas.

But the influence—and domination—of Hebrew among nineteenth-century Eastern European Jews was so pronounced that it was presumed the literary stigma attached to Yiddish would never be overcome. And at the same time, a noisy rush of activism expressed in competing currents of idealism, cultural or political, was beginning to awaken a harassed community to the potential of change and renewal. The most ancient of these currents, faithfully reiterated three times a day in the prayer book, refreshed in every season by religious festivals geared to biblical agricultural cycles, seemingly the least political of all in its psychological immanence, was the spirit of national return to Jerusalem. Under the influence of Haskalah, the renascence of literary Hebrew nourished, and was nourished by, this irreducible grain of religio-national aspiration immemorially incorporated in traditional Jew-ish sensibility. The more secularized Hebrew became, and the more dedicated to belles-lettres, the more it found itself, by virtue of its *being* Hebrew, harking back to the old emotional sources—sometimes even while manifestly repudiating them. The Hebrew belles-lettrists might appear to be focusing on modernist issues of craft and style—particularly at the expense of Yiddish, which the Hebraists declared lacked all possibility of style—but the prestige of Hebrew was also the prestige of national consciousness.

This was the cultural situation into which Sholem Aleichem thrust his manifesto for the equal status of Yiddish.

He was born Sholem Rabinovitsh in a town in the Ukraine in 1859, only three years after the abolition of a Czarist conscription scheme for the assimilation of Jewish children, whereby boys were seized at age twelve and subjected to thirty-one years of military confinement. He died in New York in 1916 (three months after the death of Henry James), having been driven there two years before by the upheavals of war and revolution; but he had already fled Russia a decade before that, after living through the ferocious government-sponsored pogroms of 1905. No version or variety of political or social malevolence failed to touch the Jews of Russia, and Sholem Aleichem—whose fame, after all, was that of sprightly comic artist—omitted few of these brutalities from his tales. The comparison with Mark Twain that emerged in Sholem Aleichem's own lifetime was apt: both men kept people laughing even as they probed the darkness—though Sholem Aleichem, for whom cruelty had an explicit habitation and name, never fell prey to a generalized misanthropy of the *Pudd'nhead Wilson* sort.

As a boy, Sholem Aleichem had Pickwickian propensities, and entertained his family with mimicry and comic skits. His writer's gift—reflecting the normal bilingualism of Jewish life—rapidly turned up in both Yiddish and Hebrew. Not long afterward, though, he acquired a third literary language. After a conventional cheder training (Bible and Talmud in a one-room school), he managed to gain admission to a Russian secondary school; the university education that would ordinarily follow was mainly closed to Jews. But his exposure to Russian studies enabled him to get a job as a Russian tutor in a Russified Jewish family of means—he eventually married his young pupil, Olga Loyev—and emphatically opened Russian to him as a literary instrument. Though his earliest serious literary venture of any kind was a novel in imitation of Mapu, called *The Daughter of Zion* and written in Hebrew, his first published articles appeared in Russian, Hebrew, and Yiddish.

When he ultimately settled on Yiddish, he disappointed no one more than his father, a struggling innkeeper who was an enthusiastic disciple of Haskalah, and who had hoped his son would develop into an exclusively Hebrew writer. And much later, after Sholem Aleichem had become virtually an institution, and was celebrated as the soul of Jewish self-understanding wherever Yiddish was spoken, the language that nevertheless prevailed as the mother tongue of his household was not Yiddish but Russian; he raised his children in it. If this suggests itself as a paradox, it also reminds us of Isaac Babel, born thirty-five years after Sholem Aleichem, arrested and silenced by the Soviets in 1939.* Babel too wrote a handful of stories that might be described as revealing the soul of Jewish self-understanding. (One of these, "Shabos Nahamu," with its Hebrew-Yiddish title, could readily pass for a romping fable of Sholem Aleichem's, except for the Chekhovian cadence of its last syllables.) Whether because he chose to write in Russian, or for some other reason, Babel is not usually counted as a Jewish writer. This leads one to imagine what the consequences might have been had Sholem Aleichem, like Babel, committed himself wholly to Russian: it is highly probable that Russian literature might have been augmented by still another dazzling writer. What is certain is that there would have been no Sholem

*Patricia Blake, a Babel scholar, notes that at the time of his arrest Babel was engaged in translating Sholem Aleichem into Russian. The manuscript was confiscated by the NKVD.

Aleichem. To produce a Sholem Aleichem, Yiddish is a sine qua non.

That may appear to be an unremarkable statement. One might just as well say that to produce a Guy de Maupassant, French is a sine qua non; or that to produce a Selma Lagerlöf, Swedish is indispensable. For these writers, though, there was no difference between the legacy of the literary mainstream and the daily language that seemed no more a matter of choice than breathing; for them literature was conducted in the vernacular. But Sholem Aleichem was faced with a cultural redundancy—internal bilingualism—known almost nowhere else in Europe (Ireland, with important differences, comes to mind). Yiddish was the common language of breathing—the people's language—and Hebrew was the language of the elitist literary center. In these circumstances, to choose Yiddish, and to insist that it be taken seriously—that it become, if not *the* literary center, then one at least equally respectable—was a mettlesome and revolutionary act.

In a way, a version of this revolution—a revolution in favor of Yiddish—had already occurred a century before, with the advent of the Hasidic movement: romantic, populist, anti-establishment, increasingly cultlike in its attachment to charismatic teachers. The Hasidic leaders, resenting the dominance of the stringently rationalist intellectualism that held pride of place in Jewish communal life, enlisted the Yiddish-speaking masses against the authority of the learned (where learned always meant learned in Hebrew), and offered instead the lively consolations of an emotional pietism. The movement caught on despite—or maybe because of—the fact that scholarliness was unstintingly prized, far above earning power: a scholar-husband was a great catch, and the bride's father would gladly support him if he could; so, often enough, would the bride. (My Russian grandmother, for instance, the mother of eight, ran a dry goods shop while my grandfather typically spent all his waking hours in the study-house.) The corollary of this, not unexpectedly, was that simple people deficient in learning were looked down on. At its inception, Hasidism was a popular rebellion against this sort of intellectual elitism; it threw off rigor and lavished dance, song, legend, story, merriment, and mysticism (the last too frequently fading into superstitious practice) on ordinary mortals whose psalms and prayers were in Hebrew but whose grammar was at best lame.

While there lurked in Hasidism a kind of precedent for an unashamed turn to the Yiddish tale—including at least one fabulist of Kafka-like artistry—Sholem Aleichem's revolution had another source. Like the belletristic passions of the Hebraists, it belonged to the Enlightenment. For the Hasidim, stories told in Yiddish were the appurtenances of a fervent piety; for Sholem Aleichem, they were vessels of a conscious literary art. Hasidism concentrated on devoutness and turned its back on modernism. Haskalah, with its hugely sophisticated modernist aesthetics, had little tolerance for Hasidic revivalism (though it later made literary capital of it). And yet the objectives of the two movements, the popular and the elevated, met in Sholem Aleichem. He had in common with the Hasidic impulse a tenderness toward plain folk and the ambition to address the human heart unassumingly and directly, in its everyday tongue. And he had, through the refinements of Haskalah, all the complexities of high literary seriousness and what we nowadays call the strategies of the text. This combination of irreconcilables—a broad leniency and a channeled pointedness—may be what fashioned him into the master of irony we know as Sholem Aleichem.

Of course we do not really know him—not in English anyhow, and with the passing of the decades since the Nazi extirpation of Yiddish-speaking European civilization, fewer and fewer native readers of literary Yiddish are left. For Americans, Sholem Aleichem has always been no more than a rumor, or two or three rumors, all of them misleading. First there is the rumor of permanent inaccessibility because of the "special flavor" of Yiddish itself—its unfamiliar cultural premises and idiomatic uniqueness. But every language is untranslatable in precisely that sense; Robert Frost's mot—poetry is what gets lost in translation—is famous enough, and the Hebrew poet Bialik compared translation to kissing through a handkerchief. Yiddish is as amenable to translation as any other language—which may mean, despite certain glorious exceptions, not very. As for the historical and cultural idiosyncrasies inherent in Yiddish, they are not especially difficult or esoteric, and for the most part require about as much background as, say, managing to figure out what a name day is in Chekhov. If there should be any more trouble than that, the impairment will be in the unaccoutered contemporary reader, not in the passage: Sholem Aleichem is no more disadvantaging than Milton might be to anyone who comes to him innocent of biblical referents. Even so, saturated in allusiveness, Sholem Aleichem is a thousand times closer to Dickens and Mark Twain and Will Rogers than he can possibly be to more encumbered figures; he was a popular presence, and stupendously so. His lectures and readings were mobbed; he was a household friend; he was cherished as a family valuable. His fiftieth birthday was a public event, and at his death hundreds of thousands filled the streets as his cortege wound through the Bronx and Harlem, down to the Lower East Side and into Brooklyn for the burial.

And still he was not what another rumor makes him out to be: simpleminded, sentimental, peasantlike, old-countryish, naive, pre-modern—the occasion of a nostalgia for a sweeter time, pogroms notwithstanding. It would be easy to blame *Fiddler on the Roof* for these distortions, but the Broadway musical—to which all those adjectives *do* apply, plus slickness—didn't arrive until 1964, and Sholem Aleichem had been misrepresented in this way long, long before. In fact, these well-established misconceptions may have been the inspiration for the emptied-out prettified romantic vulgarization (the Yiddish word for it is *shund*) typified by the musical's book and lyrics: exactly the sort of *shund* Sholem Aleichem, in seeking new literary standards for Yiddish, had battled against from the start. Whatever its success as a celebrated musical, the chief non-theatrical accomplishment of *Fiddler on the Roof* has been to reduce the reputation of a literary master to the very thing he repudiated.

That the sophisticated chronicler of a society in transition should be misconstrued as a genial rustic is something worse than a literary embarrassment. Dickens is not interchangeable with Sam Weller, or Mark Twain with Aunt Polly, or Sholem Aleichem with Tevye. (And even the Tevye we think we know isn't the Tevye on the page.) This quandary of misperceived reputation may possibly stem from the garbled attitudes of some of the Yiddish-speaking immigrants' descendants, who inherited a culture—failed to inherit it, rather—only in its most debilitated hour, when it was nearly over and about to give up the ghost. The process of attenuation through competing influences had already commenced in the Jewish villages of Eastern Europe (and was to become Sholem Aleichem's great subject). In the rush to Americanization, the immigrants, zealously setting out to shake off the village ways they had brought with them, ended by encouraging amnesia of the central motifs and texts of their civilization. A certain text orientation remained, to be sure, which their American-born successors would learn to bring to bear on Whitman and James and Emerson and Faulkner, not to mention Bloomsbury; but the more intrinsic themes of Jewish conceptual life came to be understood only feebly, vestigially, when, substantially diluted by the new culture, they were almost beyond recognition, or were disappearing altogether. Among the immigrants' children and grandchildren, the misshapen shard was mainly taken for the original cup. And generations that in the old country had been vividly and characteristically distinct from the surrounding peasant society were themselves dismissed as peasants by their "modern" offspring—university-educated, perhaps, but tone-deaf to history.

Now, toward the end of the twentieth century—with a startling abundance that seems close to mysterious—we are witnessing a conscientious push toward a kind of restitution. Something there is that wants us finally to see—to see fairly, accurately, richly—into the substance of Yiddish prose and poetry, even if necessarily through the seven veils of translation. The buzz of anthologists hopeful of gaining attention for Yiddish has always been with us, but a worshipful air of do-goodism, whether hearty or wistful or polemical, frequently trails these votary efforts. A serious critical focus was inaugurated more than thirty years ago by Irving Howe and his then-collaborator, the late Yiddish poet Eliezer Greenberg, with their thick pair of "Treasuries"—collections of Yiddish stories and poems enhanced by first-rate introductions. These were succeeded in 1972 by the Howe-Greenberg *Voices from the Yiddish*, a compilation of literary and historical essays, memoirs, and diaries, and again in 1974 by selections from the tales of I. L. Peretz, one of the three classic writers of the Yiddish narrative. (Mendele and Sholem Aleichem are the others.) The last two or three years, however, have brought about an eruption—if this word is too strong, "efflorescence" is not nearly strong enough—of dedicated translation: *My Mother's Sabbath Days*, a memoir by Chaim Grade, translated by Chana Kleinerman Goldstein and Inna Hecht Grade; the extant parts of *The Family Mashber*, an extraordinary work long quiescent in the Soviet Union, by Der Nister ("The Hidden One," the pen name of Pinkhas Kahanovitsh, who died in a Soviet prison in 1950), translated by Leonard Wolf; *American Yiddish Poetry*, the first of a series of scholarly anthologies projected by Benjamin and Barbara Harshav and designed to support the thesis that poetry written in Yiddish, composed on American soil and expressive of American experience, counts significantly as American poetry; the splendid new *Penguin Book of Modern Yiddish Verse*, a landmark volume brilliantly edited and introduced by Irving Howe, Ruth R. Wisse, and Khone Shmeruk; *In the Storm* and *The Nightingale*, novels by Sholem Aleichem, lucidly translated by Aliza Shevrin; Richard J. Fein's devoted rendering of the poetry of Jacob Glatstein, and Ruth Whitman's of Abraham Sutzkever; and doubtless others that have escaped me. One result of all this publishing activity is that Isaac Bashevis Singer, the sole Yiddish-language Nobel winner and the only Yiddish writer familiar in any substantial degree to American readers, can finally be seen as one figure among a multitude of others in a diverse, complex, and turbulent community of letters. Too often—lacking an appropriate cultural horizon and seemingly without an ancestry—Singer has had the look in English of an isolated hermit of language fallen out of a silent congregation and standing strangely apart. The current stir of industry among translators begins at last to hint at the range and amplitude of modern Yiddish literature.

All these freshly revealed novelists and poets are, in one respect or another, the heirs of Sholem Aleichem, and if there is a single work among those now emerging in English that is the herald and signature of the rest, it is, unsurprisingly, Sholem Aleichem's *Tevye the Dairyman and the Railroad Stories*, issued under the auspices of the newly organized Library of Yiddish Classics, of which Professor Ruth R. Wisse is the series editor. The translator, Hillel Halkin, an Israeli born and reared in the United States, an accomplished translator from Hebrew here tackling Yiddish for the first time, has supplied a superb historical introduction and a clarifying biblical glossary. If it is true that one need not be familiar with Wordsworth, say, before starting on Marianne Moore or the nature prose of Edward Hoagland, then it is just as true that one need not have assimilated Sholem Aleichem before entering the fiction of Chaim Grade or the poetry of Jacob Glatstein; but in both cases it's not a bad idea. Sholem Aleichem provides, in ways weblike and plain, the exegetical groundwork for his literary successors: to race along behind his footsteps brings one quickly and intensely into a society, an atmosphere, a predicament, and, more than anything else, a *voice*. The voice is monologic, partly out of deepest intimacy, a sense of tête-à-tête (with God or the reader), and partly out of verbal ingenuity, comedy, theatricality—even the sweep of aria. "While the crowd laughed, clapped, and frolicked, he wept unseen" is a line from an early version of an epitaph Sholem Aleichem wrote for himself; *Pagliacci* was brand-new in 1892, and its imagery of the clown in pain, trite for us, struck hard at the inventor of Tevye. (An oddity of resemblance: the late Gershom Scholem, the monumental scholar of Jewish mysticism, also identified himself with the idea of a clown.)

The eight Tevye stories are without doubt the nucleus of any understanding of how Yiddish leaped into world literature a hundred years ago (even though world literature may not have taken note of it, then or since). Professor Miron speaks of "the homiletic-sentimental streak" in Yiddish fiction before Mendele and Sholem Aleichem: "definitely antiartistic, inimical to irony, to conscious structural artistry, to the idea of literary technique, to stylistic perfection, and favorable to moralistic sermonizing, to unbridled emotionalism, and to stylistic sloppiness." Tevye stands for everything antithetical to such a catalogue. What one notices first is not the comedy—because the comedy is what Sholem Aleichem is famous for, the comedy is what is expected—but the shock of darkness. Poverty and persecution: while not even Sholem Aleichem can make these funny, he can satirize their reasons for being, or else he can set against them the standard and example of Tevye (as Mark Twain does with Huck Finn). Tevye is not any sort of scholar, this goes without saying: he is a *milkhiger*, meaning that he owns a cow; "dairyman" is too exalted a word for the owner of a cow, a horse, and a wagon. But he is not a fool, he is certainly not a peasant, and he is by no means the malaprop he is reputed to be. Tevye is intelligent; more, he is loving, witty, virtuous, generous, open, unwilling to sacrifice human feeling to grandiose aims—and all without a grain of heroism or sentimentality. He is never optimistic—he is too much at home with the worst that can happen. And he is never wiped out by despair—he is too much at home with Scripture and with the knowledge of frailty, muta-bility, mortality. When his wife, Golde, dies, he quotes from the morning prayer—"What are we and what is our life?"; and also from Ecclesiastes—"Let us hear the conclusion of the whole mat-ter: fear God and keep His commandments, for that is the whole of man."

Tevye's play with sources, biblical and liturgical, is the enchantment—and brevity—of his wit. (Halkin's glossary insures that nearly all of it is gratifyingly at our fingertips.) Though his citations are mostly designed for comical juxtaposition—"And it came to pass," he will chant, with biblical sonorousness, about an ordinary wagon ride from Yehupetz to Boiberik—now and then a passage is straightforwardly plumbed, and then the glancingness of Tevye's brush stroke only abets the resonance of the verse. That sentence from Ecclesiastes, for instance: Tevye doesn't recite it in its entirety. What he actually says is *"ki zeh koyl ha'odom,"* "for that is the whole of man"—and the six scant Hebrew syllables instantly call up, for Tevye and his readers, the full quotation, the tremor of memory aroused by its ancestral uses, the tone and heft of the surrounding passages. Again it is worth keeping in mind that Tevye is not to be regarded as an educated man: he is a peddler of milk and cheese. And still he has a mastery of a plenitude of texts that enables him to send them aloft like experimental kites, twisting their lines as they sail. By contrast, it would be unimaginable for a rustic in a novel by Thomas Hardy (Sholem Aleichem's contemporary, who outlived him by more than a decade) to have memorized a representative handful of Shakespeare's plays from earliest childhood, and to have the habit of liberally quoting from one or the other of these dozens and dozens of times, not only accurately and aptly but stingingly, pointedly, absurdly, and always to an immediate purpose; we would reject such a character as madly idiosyncratic if not wholly implausible. Country people don't get *Macbeth* or *Timon of Athens* by heart, if they are literate at all. And yet Tevye is a vivacious, persuasive creature, warm with the blood of reality. In his world it is not only plausible, it is not unusual, for a milkman or a carpenter to know the Pentateuch and the Psalms inside out, as well as considerable other scriptural and rabbinic territory, and to have the daily and holiday prayer books—no slender volumes, these—backwards and forwards. Tevye's cosmos is verbal. Biblical phrases are as palpable to him as his old horse. When he wants to remark that he has no secrets, he tosses in a fragment from Genesis: "And the Lord said, Shall I hide from Abraham that thing which I do?" When his only cow dies on him, he invokes a Psalm: "The sorrows of death compassed me, and the pains of hell got hold upon me; I found trouble and sorrow." When his daughter Shprintze is being courted by an unsuitable young man, he draws from the Song of Songs: "a lily among thorns." Chaffing a utopian socialist, he turns to a rabbinic tractate, the Ethics of the Fathers, for its illumination of a type of artlessness: "What's mine is yours and what's yours is mine." It is all done with feather-light economy; he drops in only two or three words of the verse in question—an elegant minimalism—confident that his audience will recognize the source and fill in the rest. Or perhaps sometimes not so confident. Tevye's quotations, Halkin comments, "depending on the situation and the person he is talking to, can serve any conceivable purpose: to impress, to inform, to amuse, to intimidate, to comfort, to scold, to ridicule, to show off, to avoid, to put down, to stake a claim of equality or create a mood of intimacy." And he is not above "deliberately inventing, confusing, or misattributing a quote," Halkin continues, "in order to mock an ignoramus who will never know the difference, thus scoring a little private triumph of which he himself is the sole witness."

These virtuoso dartings of language—the prestidigitator's flash from biblical eloquence to its mundane applicability—have a cavorting brilliance reminiscent of the tricks and coruscations of *Finnegans Wake*, where sentences are also put under the pressure of multiple reverberations. Or think of Harold Bloom's thesis of "misprision," whereby an influential resource is usurped for purposeful "misinterpretation," engendering new life in a new text. While these macaronic comparisons—Tevye in the company of James Joyce and Harold Bloom!—may have the selfsame farcical impact as Tevye's own juxtapositions, they serve the point: which is that Sholem Aleichem's Tevye is about as far from the mind, tone, temperament, and language of either folk art or *Fiddler*-type show biz as Boiberik is from Patagonia. Tevye is the stylistic invention of a self-conscious verbal artist, and if he stands for, and speaks for, the folk, that is the consequence of the artist's power. Tevye's manner emerges from the wit and genius of Sholem Aleichem.

Tevye's matter, however—his good and bad luck, his daily travail and occasional victory, the events in his family and in his village and in the next village—belongs unalloyedly to the folk. What happens to Tevye is what is happening to all Jews in the Russian Pale of Settlement; his tales are as political as they are individual, and it is entirely pertinent that Halkin provides a list of government-instigated depredations against Russian Jews from 1881 to 1904, including numbers of pogroms, blood libel charges, restrictions, expulsions, closed towns and cities, special taxes, identity passes, quotas, and other oppressive and humiliating measures. Tevye's life (and the lives of the characters in "The Railroad Stories") is assaulted by them all.

Tevye starts off, in the first of the eight tales, gently enough, with a generous ladling of burlesque. Ten years ago, he recounts in "Tevye Strikes It Rich," "I was such a miserable beggar that rags were too good for me." Unexpectedly he and his nag stumble into an act of slapstick kindness, he is rewarded with a cow, and his career as a *milkhiger* is launched. In the second story, "Tevye Blows a Small Fortune," he is taken in by a con man, a Jew even poorer than himself; when he catches up with the swindler, who by then has lost everything and looks it, Tevye ends by forgiving him and blaming himself. "The Lord giveth and the Lord taketh away," he quotes from Job. But with the third story, "Today's Children," and the remaining five, social and cultural disintegrations begin to rule the narrative. Against the stiff precedents of arranged marriage, Tevye's daughter Tsaytl and a poor young tailor decide to marry for love. Tevye accedes, but he is discontent on three strong counts: custom has been violated and the world turned upside down; Tsaytl has rejected an older widower of some means, a butcher in whose household there will always be enough to eat; and, foremost, Tevye himself is a textual snob with aristocratic aspirations who would like to claim a learned son-in-law. Neither the butcher nor the tailor is capable of the nuanced study of *di kleyne pintelakh*, "the fine points." Still, Tevye defends his daughter's autonomy for the sake of her happiness, despite his certainty that she will go hungry. "What do you have against her that you want to marry her?" he teases the young tailor. In "Hodl," a story that extends the theme of social decomposition, Tevye's daughter by that name also makes her own marital choice—a student revolutionary, a socialist intellectual who is arrested and sent to Siberia. Hodl insists on following him into exile, and when Tevye has driven her in his wagon to the railroad station, he closes the tale in sardonic melancholy: "Let's talk about something more cheerful. Have you heard any news of the cholera in Odessa?"

But the truly unthinkable is yet to come: in "Chava," Tevye's most rebellious daughter elopes with Chvedka, an educated Gentile village boy (a social rarity in himself), and Tevye is torn by anguish and terror. Chava has not only cut the thread of religious and historic continuity, she has joined up with the persecutors. The village priest takes charge of her because, he says, "we Christians have your good in mind," and Tevye cries: ". . . it would have been kinder to poison me or put a bullet in my head. If you're really such a good friend of mine, do me a favor: leave my daughter alone!" In Tevye's universe the loss of a daughter to Christianity—which for him has never shown anything but a murderous face—is the nadir of tragedy; he sobs for her as for a kidnapped child. (*Fiddler on the Roof* conspicuously Americanizes these perceptions. When a pogrom is threatened, Chava reappears with her suitably liberal and pluralist-minded husband, who announces in solidarity, "We cannot stay among people who can do such things to others," and even throws in a post-Holocaust declaration against Gentile "silence." But Sholem Aleichem's Chava returns "to her father and her God," chastened, remorseful, and without Chvedka.) In "Shprintze," the daughter of the sixth tale—her name, by the way, is more decorous than it sounds, deriving from the Italian *speranza*—is jilted by a well-off young rattlebrain who is fond of horses, and drowns herself. Beilke, the daughter of "Tevye Leaves for the Land of Israel," marries a coarse parvenu who, ashamed of a "cheesemonger" father-in-law, wants to pay Tevye off to get him out of the way, even offering him the fulfillment of a dream —a ticket to Palestine. Shprintze and Beilke are the center of "class" stories: as traditional influences lose hold, position based on material possessions begins to count over the authority of intellectual accomplishment, marking a growing leniency toward Gentile ways (typified by Shprintze's feckless suitor's preoccupation with "horses, fishing, and bicycles"). The aristocracy of learning—the essential principle and pillar of shtetl life—is breaking down; the mores of the outer society are creeping, even streaming, in.

In the final narrative, "Lekh-Lekho" (the opening words of God's command to Abraham: "Get thee out of thy country"), everything has come apart. Golde, Tevye's wife, the pragmatic foil for his idealism, is dead. Beilke and her husband have lost their money and are now laboring in the sweatshops of America. Tsaytl's husband, the young tailor, is struck down by consumption; and the hope of Palestine vanishes for Tevye as he takes in his impoverished daughter and her orphans. On top of all this, it is the time of the Beilis blood libel trial—a Jew accused, as late as 1911, of killing a Christian child for its blood. (This grisly anti-Semitic fantasy turns up as far back as Chaucer's "Prioress's Tale.") Tevye's neighbors, after a meeting of the village council, are preparing for a pogrom. "Since you Jews have been beaten up everywhere, why let you get away with it here?" argues Ivan Paparilo, the village elder. "We just aren't certain what kind of pogrom to have. Should we just smash your windows, should we tear up your pillows and blankets and scatter all the feathers, or should we also burn down your house and barn with everything in them?" To which Tevye replies: "If that's what you've decided, who am I to object? You must have good reasons for thinking that Tevye deserves to see his life go up in smoke. . . . You do know that there's a God above, don't you? Mind you, I'm not talking about my God or your God—I'm talking about the God of us all. . . . It may very well be that He wants you to punish me for nothing at all. But the opposite may also be true. . . ." Ultimately the villagers are talked out of the pogrom—they want it, they explain, only to save face with the towns that have already had one. Instead, all the Jews in the village—among them Tevye's family, including the returned Chava—are expelled by order of the provincial governor; and there the Tevye tales end. "Anyone can be a goy," Tevye concludes, "but a Jew must be born one. . . . it's a lucky thing I was, then, because otherwise how would I ever know what it's like to be homeless and wander all over the world without resting my head on the same pillow two nights running?"

Thus the somber matter of Sholem Aleichem's comedy. Tevye's dicta run all through it: what he thinks about God ("Why doesn't He do something? Why doesn't He say something?"), about wickedness ("My problem was men. Why did they have to be so bad when they could just as well have been good?"), about the goals of life ("to do a little good in His world before you die—to give a bit of money to charity, to take someone needy under your wing, even to sit down with educated Jews and study some Torah"), about the situation in Russia ("pogroms in Kishinev, riots, troubles, the new Constantution* [Constitution] . . . God wanted to do us Jews a favor and so He sent us a new catastrophe, a Constantution"), about education ("I'd sooner eat a buttered pig than sit down to a meal with an illiterate. A Jew who can't read a Jewish book is a hundred times worse than a sinner"), about reserve ("secretive people annoy me"), about opportunity ("A cow can sooner jump over a roof than a Jew get into a Russian university! . . . they guard their schools from us like a bowl of cream from a cat"), about faith and resignation ("A Jew has to hope. So what if things couldn't be worse? That's why there are Jews in the world!"), about what to do with money if one ever got any ("make a contribution to charity that would be the envy of any rich Jew"), about ignorance, love, decency, poverty, misery, anti-Semitism, and the tardiness of the Messiah.

"The Railroad Stories," the second half of the Halkin volume, are similar in their use of a monologic narrator, and certainly in their cheerless subject matter. The storyteller of "Baranovich Station" sums up what Jews traveling by train—men scrambling for a living—talk about: "From the Revolution we passed to the Constitution, and from the Constitution it was but a short step to the pogroms, the massacres of Jews, the new anti-Semitic legislation, the expulsion from the villages, the mass flight to America, and all the other trials and tribulations that you hear about these fine days: bankruptcies, expropriations, military emergencies, executions, starvation, cholera, Perushkevich [the founder of the anti-Semitic Black Hundreds] . . ." If we did not absolutely grasp it before, we can profoundly recognize it now: Sholem Aleichem's is a literature of crisis.

And yet "The Railroad Stories," in their slightness and vitality and scattershot abundance—there are twenty of them—strike with a comic sharpness that to my mind exceeds even the effervescent artistry of the Tevye tales. Tevye's voice is elastic, simultaneously

---

*Possibly a pun on Konstantin Petrovich Pobedonostsev, an influential anti-Semite of the time. (I am indebted to Abraham J. Karp for this insight.)

innocent and knowing, never short on acuteness of energy or observation or ironic fervor; but "The Railroad Stories," perhaps
because they are largely unfamiliar to us and have never been
contaminated by reductiveness, yield the plain shock of their form.
Their form is all plotless trajectory: one doesn't apprehend the
mark until after the mark has been hit. To come on these stories
with no inkling of their existence beforehand (I imagine this will
be the experience of numbers of readers) is to understand what it
is to marvel at form—or formlessness—in the hands of literary
genius. There are pronounced resemblances to early Chekhov and
to Babel and Gorky, as well as a recognizable source—the casual
sketch that is the outgrowth of the feuilleton, here strengthened
and darkened by denser resonances. Nevertheless the landscape is
for the most part uniquely Sholem Aleichem's, a Russia not easily
duplicated even by the sympathetic Chekhov, who in his letters
could now and then toss off an anti-Semitic crack as lightly as a
shrug. The most Chekhovian of these stories, "Eighteen from
Pereshchepena"—a vignette of comic misunderstanding that,
when untangled, is seen to be tragic—appears at first to be about
the quota system in schools, but actually turns on the dread of
forced military service: the eighteen Jewish youths "taken" from
the town of Pereshchepena are revealed to be unlucky conscripts,
not lucky students. "The Wedding That Came Without Its Band"
lustily caricatures a pogrom that doesn't come off: a trainload of
hooligans, "in full battle gear, too, with clubs, and tar," get so
drunk—"the conductor and the stoker and even the policeman"
—that they are left behind by the locomotive intended to carry
them to their prey. In "The Miracle of Hoshana Rabbah," a ven-
turesome Jew named Berl and an anti-Semitic priest find themselves improbably but perilously alone together aboard a runaway
engine; the priest, exasperated with Berl, threatens to push him
off. "Just look at the difference, Father, between you and me,"
says Berl, as the engine hurtles wildly on. "I'm doing my best to
stop this locomotive, because I'm trying to save us both, and all
you can think of is throwing me out of it—in other words, of
murdering your fellow man!" An antic moral fable, wherein the

priest is shamed and tamed. But there are plenty of Jewish rascals too—con men and cardsharps and thieves, and a pimp and a cowardly apostate and even an insurance arsonist; and desolate Jews —a teen-age suicide, a desperate father who pursues a Gentile "professor of medicine" to beg him to tend his dying boy, Jews without residence permits who risk arrest by sneaking into town to see a doctor.

All these characters, whether avoiding or perpetrating pogroms, whether hostile or farcical or pathetic or paradoxical, are flushed with the rosiness of comedy. Comedy, the product of ridicule, is too brittle a mode in the absence of compassion, and too soppy a mode in the absence of briskness. Sholem Aleichem is always brisk and always ready to display just enough (sparing) kindliness to keep the tone on the far side of soppiness. Here he is, in "Third Class," matter-of-fact without coldness, satiric without meanness, loving without mawkishness:

> When you go third class and wake up in the morning to discover that you've left your tefillin and your prayer shawl at home, there isn't any cause for alarm—you only need to ask and you'll be given someone else's, along with whatever else you require. All that's expected of you in return, once you're done praying, is to open your suitcase and display your own wares. Vodka, cake, a hard-boiled egg, a drumstick, a piece of fish—it's all grist for the mill. Perhaps you have an apple, an orange, a piece of strudel? Out with it, no need to be ashamed! Everyone will be glad to share it with you, no one stands on ceremony here. . . . Before long each of us not only knows all about the others' troubles, he knows about every trial and tribulation that ever befell a Jew anywhere. It's enough to warm the cockles of your heart!

The close-knittedness—or huddling, or nestling—of frequently threatened poor Jews, collectively and individually powerless, who bloom in the fond and comradely safety of fellow Jews on a train; the caustic notion of adversity as one's oldest intimate; trials and tribulations that nevertheless warm the cockles—this is Sholem Aleichem defining, so to speak, the connotations of his nom de plume. That these ironies can rise so pungently from the translated page testifies to how clear and broad an opening Hillel Halkin has bored into the original, where psychological sighs and skeptical gestures are more slender than a hair, or else hidden—a grain here, a grain there—in the crannies of language. A translator's triumph occurs when the reader comes away from the text in the security of having been given a reasonable measure of access. Halkin now and then achieves much more than the merely reasonable—a true bridge across languages, happy moments like this: "Menachem Mendel was his name: a wheeler, a dealer, a schemer, a dreamer, a bag of hot air." Or this: "He called him a scoundrel, a degenerate, a know-nothing, a leech, a bloodsucker, a fiend, a traitor, a disgrace to the Jewish people." Such jubilant and exuberant flights let us know without question that we have been catapulted right inside what Maurice Samuel once called "the world of Sholem Aleichem."

But even where there is generous overall access, there can be problems and irritations. Especially with Sholem Aleichem, tone is everything. Halkin's work, stemming perhaps from his frank belief in "untranslatabilities," is too often jarred by sudden clangs that do violence to both tongues, bringing on startling distractions in the English while derailing our expectations of the Yiddish. Either we are in Sholem Aleichem's milieu or we are not—that is the crux. To transmute Sholem Aleichem's easy idiomatic language into familiar slang is not necessarily a bad or inept solution; it requires of the translator a facile and supple ear, alert to the equation of idioms in two cultures. And it isn't that Hillel Halkin lacks such an ear; just the opposite. What he lacks, I am afraid, is an instinct for what is apropos. American street talk is preposterous in the mouths of people in a forest outside Yehupetz on the way to Boiberik—and the more skillfully and lavishly these relaxed Americanisms are deployed, the more preposterous they seem. "He looks at me like the dumb bunny he is," "I blew in this morning," "It drives me up the wall," "holy suffering catfish!"— absurd locutions for poor Jews in a Russian railway carriage at the turn of the century, especially in the company of the occasional British "quite" and a stilted "A black plague take them all" (a stock imprecation that in Yiddish stings without sounding rococo). And what are we to do with a Tevye who is "bushed," who downs his brandy with "Cheers!" (even *Fiddler* stuck by *l'khayim*), who tells someone, "You're off your trolley"? With ripe improbability the Jews on the train say "the gospel truth," "doesn't that beat all for low-downness," "tried to pin such a bum rap on me," "you're all bollixed up," "some meatball he was," "a federal case," and, painfully, for dancing, "everyone cut the rug up." Somewhere there is an agonizing 1940s "swell." Under such an assault, tone collapses and imagination dies.

But these are phrases snatched out of context. Here, by contrast, is a bit of dialogue between Tevye and his daughter Chava concerning Chvedka, the young Gentile she will eventually run off with:

> "Well, then," I say, "what sort of person is he? Perhaps you could enlighten me."
>
> "Even if I told you," she says, "you wouldn't understand. Chvedka is a second Gorky."
>
> "A second Gorky?" I say. "And who, pray tell, was the first?"
>
> "Gorky," she says, "is only just about the most important man alive."
>
> "Is he?" I say. "And just where does he live, this Mr. Important of yours? What's his act and what makes him such a big deal?"

In the Yiddish, Tevye's bitterness is less elaborately spoken, and effectively more cutting. Instead of "Perhaps you could enlighten me," Tevye comes back with a curt "Let's hear," all the more biting for its brevity. "Pray tell," absent in the original, is too fancy; Tevye grunts out his sardonic helplessness in a single fricative, a *zhe* attached to the sentence's opening word. This *zhe*, in no way portable into English, is nonetheless rawly expressive, and deserves better than the tinkle of Halkin's "Pray tell." But the real blow to Tevye's language (and his moral cosmos) is struck in the last line quoted above, which, in the light of the Yiddish original, is insupportably charmless and hollow—lingo far too carelessly parochial to reflect Tevye's sufferings in a pharaonic

Russia. Agreed, the original is intimidating. *"Vu zitst er, der tane dayner, vos iz zayn gesheft un vos far a droshe hot er gedarshnt?"* Literally, "Where does he sit, that *tane* of yours, how does he get his living, and what kind of a *droshe* has he preached?" A *tane* is one of the classical scholastics known as *tannaim*, whose hermeneutics appear in the Mishnah, a collection of sixty-three tractates of law and ethics that constitute the foundation of the Talmud; a *droshe* is a commentary, often formidably allusive, prepared by a serious student of homiletics. For Tevye to compare a Russian peasant boy, whose father he judges to be a swineherd and a drunk, with the most influential sages of antiquity is bruising sarcasm—and not only because Chvedka's family outlook is so remote from the impassioned patrimony of Jewish learning.

More appositely, Tevye is making the point that the Gorky he has never heard of stands as a mote in relation to that patrimony. From Tevye's perspective—and his perspective always includes historical memory, with its emphasis on survival and continuity —Chava, in pursuing Chvedka, is venturing into the transgressions of spiritual self-erasure; Tevye is altogether untouched by that cosmopolitan Western liberalism that will overwhelmingly claim his deracinated descendants. In half a moment, the dialogue has moved from the joke of "a second Gorky" to the outcry of a crumbling tradition wherein a secular Russian author is starting to assume major cultural authority for Jews. However difficult it may be for a translator to convey all this—so complex and hurtful a knot of social and emotional attitudes ingeniously trapped in a two-syllable word—it is certain that Halkin's "this Mr. Important of yours," with its unerring echoes of old radio programs (Molly Goldberg, Fred Allen's Mrs. Nussbaum), has not begun to achieve a solution.

Even so, given its strengths, this volume is likely to serve as the indispensable Sholem Aleichem for some time to come.

A Translator's Monologue

I should like to arrive at some general propositions about translating poetry. There are three points to remember about these propositions: first, they are important; second, they are useful; and third, they are false.

It is their falseness I want to consider above all. Everyone knows the legend of how the Septuagint—the oldest Greek version of the Hebrew Bible—came to be written: seventy sages, we are told, entered seventy separate chambers, and emerged with seventy copies of an identical text.

This is of course a false tale: but its falseness teaches us something significant about how to look at a translated text. If a translation seems flawless, we take it to be authoritative; if it is authoritative, we trust its importance; if we can trust its importance, we know it will be useful. And by "useful" I mean that a translation can serve as a lens into the underground life of another culture.

Translation is not only feasible but inescapable—good transla-

Published in *Prooftexts*, vol. 3 (Baltimore: Johns Hopkins University Press, 1983), pp. 1–8.

tion, exact translation, superb translation: the entire carrying over from one language to another, from one society to another. But in order to believe in the real possibility of translation, the translator must believe in certain impossible theses. These are, as I have said, important, useful, and false.

The first false idea is the most indispensable. It is simply that the poem is not "translated," but uncovered. The seventy sages were able to go into seventy different rooms and come out with a single text because that single text was already *there*. It had only to be found.

In the same way, just as the poem already exists, so does the right, faithful, and true translation already exist, needing only to be uncovered. The translated poem is inherent in the new language. It must be hewn out of the new language as (to turn to a strong but familiar image) a figure locked in the recalcitrant rock is hewn out and revealed.

This commanding proposition, which is both Platonic and false, is also important and useful.

It is important because without this belief a translation can never be seen as a thing achieved, concluded, finished; it will be regarded as merely a try in a series of tries, as an approach, an attempt, an approximation, a probability, a "version" selected out of a myriad of other versions.

But when we read a poem in translation, we want to feel we are reading the poem itself. We do not want to feel suspicious or unsure. We want to hand ourselves over to the *given*-ness of the poem, and to rest in the authority of its being.

Another way of putting this is to say that a translation must be complete, and must be felt to be complete.

A translation that is tentative or "interim" is useless to the reader. For the translator it is like sewing with a thread that has no knot.

There is another purpose in believing in the false proposition that a translation of a poem pre-exists. It touches on the mutual obligations of translator and poem. Is the translator the poem's tenant or its landlord? If the translator is the poem's tenant, the translator is obligated to the poem for its heat. If the translator is the poem's landlord, the poem is obligated to the translator for its shape. Now at this point one must stop and think sympathetically of the poet, the maker of the original poem in its original language. Does the poet want to share ownership of the poem with the translator? When we read some of the Russian emigrant writers, say, commenting nastily on the inadequacies of their translators, we can see that often enough the poet demands that translation not be independently equivalent or parallel, but subordinate and slavish.

But the relation of the poem to its translation is not that of an object to its shadow, nor even that of an object to its reflection in a mirror. What that relation really is, I will define in a moment.

To understand the relation of the translator to the poem, one must understand the relation of the translator to the original poet.

Now if the notion that the poem-in-translation pre-exists and must be uncovered is my first false but necessary proposition, my second false but necessary proposition is this: *Craft becomes becoming.* By this I intend that the translator should feel himself or herself to *be* the poet, reborn into another language. Though the thesis is magical, the process is not: it is gradual. First the translator begins, bit by bit, to discover the poet's verbal and ideational habits; then, little by little, the translator acquires the poet's obsessions. Next the translator is able to take in the ruling obsession of each single poem. Next the translator is certain he or she *inhabits* the poet, walking up and down inside the maze of the poet's convictions, conditions, tics, and itches. And then at last the translator turns into the poet. Not that the translator has "merged" with the poet; but the one has genuinely become the other.

As with the translator, so with the translation. The poem's translation is not the poem's shadow or reflection. The poem and its translation are two separate artifacts, each equal to the other; and not only "equal" in the sense of being "alike," but each having become the other.

We should be able to put two poems before a reader, the original and its translation, and say, "Here are two poems. They are the same poem. Which was translated from the other?" A better question would be: "Which was written first?" —As if the poem pre-existed not only in translation for the translator, but in conception for the poet; and as if both the poet and the translator had transcribed from the same source, one in one language, the other in another language.

The only justification for translation is the promise that when you hear the poem in translation, you hear the poem itself.

Perhaps it would be helpful if I paused here to summarize my three false propositions, if only to show even more emphatically how false they really are:

First, that the poem in translation is already there, hidden in the language of translation, waiting to be let out, an imperative, imminent, immanent, immutable form ready for release, and, when released, instantly recognizable as both primary and authentic.

Second, that the translator, in becoming the poet, assumes all the authority of the poet over the poem.

Third, that the translation of the poem *is* the poem, as much as the poem itself.

Now here is a summary of the ways in which these falsehoods are important and useful for the translator:

One. If you do not believe the poem-in-translation is already there, you will never find it.

Two. If you do not believe that you have full authority over the poem, its form and its meaning, you will have no authority over it.

Three. If you do not believe you can achieve the poem itself, you will be in possession only of a fuzzy shadow and a cracked mirror.

Now you will protest that all these falsehoods and their fine corollaries are only an apparatus to give courage to the fainthearted translator; and I agree; and the moment I agree, my apparatus collapses, and I am left cowering before the poet and the poem.

I am left cowering especially before the Yiddish poem. Most of the time it is no more difficult to translate from Yiddish into English than from French into German; but those times when it *is* more difficult, it is so much more difficult that the translator despairs. French to German, or German to Italian, or Italian to Russian, brings with it a consistency of theology, hence of culture, hence of role and artifact. But Yiddish to English means a crossing-over from Jewish concepts to Christian concepts, or at best to a secularized sensibility. And whereas prose, whether essay or fiction, can give us a glossary or footnotes, an explanatory parenthesis or an extended paraphrase, the poem is relentless in requiring an equivalent word or phrase, compacted within the compass of three syllables or half a line.

What good *then* are Ideal Passions about the Power of the Pre-Existent Poem?

A translator at work is embrangled—a word derived from *brawl* and *wrangle*—in a thousand questions of diction, gait, suggestion, as opposed to transcription of meter and line length, tonal renderings, fidelity versus sacrifice, transmutation of form; head-cracking marvels and experiments of craft.

What use *then* are Ideal Passions about the Power of the Pre-Existent Poem?

I have found in an old box in the attic a great helter-skelter heap of papers. In sorting them out, I came upon twenty-two sheets relating to a single line of a single poem. These twenty-two pages are the ones that turned up; for all I know, there may have been many more. The line was the first line, and also the title, of a poem by Dovid Einhorn: *geshtorbn der letster bal-tfile*—"the last *bal-tfile* is dead." And if I fail at this moment to translate *bal-tfile*, the reason for it will soon be clear.

The Einhorn poem was among the earliest in the various groups of poems I had translated as a contributor to an anthology of Yiddish poetry, and I came to it as a novice. One of my many errors at that time was to see the translator as a being in thrall to the editor. If the editor offered a suggestion, I took it as an irreversible command. But meanwhile, behind the scenes, I developed a kind of translator's cunning. It wasn't the cunning of brains; I couldn't outwit the editor, who was smarter than I was. But I could outcry him. So, in letter after letter, I raised clamorous laments, I pleaded, I implored, I whined and I wheedled. And as I wheedled the editor toward what I conceived to be the poem's needs, I discovered at last that the poem, all on its own, could make unreasonable demands: for example, it was the poem's assumption that, quite apart from the translator's being in thrall to the editor, English ought to be in thrall to the poem. Or, in other words, that a pretty good, workable English equivalent was all that was requisite, rather than an exactly nuanced representation.

Very gradually, through a series of feverish letters, the line evolved—from the editor's suggested line, to the poem's "English equivalent" line, to that stage where the translator was ready to assume moral authority over the poem. In the final stage the translated line became, not a line of a translated poem, but the line of a *poem*.

The original contained the word "Shekhina," which presents no difficulty to the English reader. It is a word both in the English dictionary and in the vocabulary of Western philosophy. But the perplexity lay in the term *bal-tfile*. For *bal-tfile* the editor proposed "prayer leader."

I dispatched the following moan:

> If it has to be "prayer leader," it has to be "prayer leader." Only this: my spirit drops at the thought of that thin phrase. I have been trying all week with real despair to get at some *oblique* way of suggesting the role without naming it. The chief trouble with "prayer leader" is that it isn't poetry. I've tried it on the line and it looks grotesque: "The last prayer leader is dead." It trivializes an awesome idea. It lacks even the smallest redolence of the original. It's empty-sounding. To one who knows nothing of synagogue practice, it illumines nothing; to one who knows everything, it points to nothing—who will guess *bal-tfile* from "prayer leader"? Isn't this a case of "correct" translation resulting in falseness, in violation? "The last prayer leader is dead" sounds to me exactly as fake, as flat, and as silly as an equally data-ridden term would sound, e.g., "The last underpaid secondary cantor is dead." It moves the poem out of majesty and into personnel. But for the moment I can offer only wails, no solutions.

That was written in April. In August, I find another letter still embroiled in *geshtorbn der letster bal-tfile*. Apparently I had just discarded the phrase "singer in the pulpit."

"Singer in the pulpit" [I wrote], though metrically nice (which is why it lured me), wears churchly robes, and is hardly *bal-tfile*. "Singer before the Ark" came next—at least it describes a synagogue—but the *bal-tfile* is usually not much of a singer, and used in the line it has too many accented syllables anyhow. "Reader of the Law" would suggest that the original is *bal-krie* rather than *bal-tfile*. You will say that the obvious thing to settle on, then, is "prayer leader," which is accurate and neutral enough to come out not entirely Quakerish or Christian Scientist. But it is too bland, I think, just *because* of its neutrality, so I have taken the risk and stayed with "reader of the Law." It is, as "translation," wrong, but in English it is more right than any other alternative. Or so it seems to me now.

To someone not familiar with synagogue practice and personnel, "reader of the Law" is completely in context and holds the poem together. And this would also be true of one familiar with the synagogue, even though he might think *bal-krie*. If he *does* think that (though a reader of a poem should stick with the poem, and not try to translate back in his head), not an iota of violence is done to the poem anyhow.

(Einhorn's shade rises before me and says, "Well, as a matter of fact, I was going to say *bal-krie*, and it was only an accident I said *bal-tfile*.")

At this juncture in the struggle, you observe, I was at that second stage of error where I believed not that the poem is a law over the translator—that would mean "prayer leader"—but that the poem is a law over English, that what is suitable in English will have to do, no matter how mistaken in substance. I was unsympathetic to the poet and was quite willing to call up the poet's ghost in order to get his approval for a workable English, even if it made him recast his poem. When I insisted to the editor that "not an iota of violence is done to the poem," I was clearly an advocate of doing violence. That was August. In September the editor answered as follows:

I agree that "prayer leader" is no good.

So what had I accomplished? I had wheedled him out of one mistake into a new mistake, this one of my own coinage.

By the next month we were skirting *bal-tfile*, letting it lie fallow, and were now embrangled in the word "dolor."

I had rendered a stanza this way:

> And soundless on the steps of the Ark
> the abandoned Shekhina rests,
> her head bowed down in dolor,
> black as night her dress.

The editor wanted "Jewish Spirit" instead of "Shekhina"; he wanted "grief" instead of "dolor."

I answered:

As for "Jewish Spirit," isn't the Shekhina here a concrete figure, like Heine's occasional Virgin? The poet *will* have his Astarte, no matter what. To keep faith with the ballad-feel of the poem, I've indulged in an old ballad-word, dolor.

Apparently I managed to wheedle out "Shekhina," but not "dolor," because my next letter is still at work.

I guess I did choose "dolor" for its archaic feel, so you mustn't object that it's archaic; I meant to reinforce the ballad-quality. But if you prefer another word, I can part with "dolor." What would you think, though, of "sorrow" instead of "grief"? Like "dolor," "sorrow" carries out all those open vowels of the rest of the line: "head," "bowed," "down," whereas "grief" bites the line off rather too quickly, almost as though the stanza were ready to end too soon. Do let your own preference rule, however.

So he let me keep "sorrow."

Very soon afterward, though, we were back at *bal-tfile*. Now I was writing hopelessly:

So what's to be done? Capitulate to literalness, and remove the phrase from poetry and into data? One last-ditch idea, which I throw down on the page in desperation: how about a still more reckless literalness? How about a direct and wholesale translation from the original, how about "master of prayer"? At least it sounds suitably ancient, at least it doesn't sound Protestant. It has rather a Buberian dignity, a bit of authority, a drop of majesty: "The last master of prayer is dead." It comes out, if not poetry, a bit closer to poetry. But what I put under the head of dignity, authority, and majesty (not that the person of the *bal-tfile* has all that; it's the liturgy I'm thinking of)—what I put under that head, you may pronounce pretentious.

Well, if it has to be "prayer leader," it has to be "prayer leader."

Nearly a year later—but I have no documents to show how this came about—I had abandoned the ordeal of the imprecise precision, I had abandoned my trust in English as offering a solution of workable equivalence, and the opening stanza read as follows:

> The last to sing before the Ark is dead.
> Padlocks hang in the house of the Jews.
> The windows are boarded, and shadows
> huddle in shame in the pews.

"Pews" seems to me now very bad. But what of "The last to sing before the Ark is dead"? Will that do for *geshtorbn der letster bal-tfile*? Has the Pre-Existent Poem been uncovered? If seventy translators went into seventy separate rooms, would they all come out word-for-word with this very line? Or would they all come out with "prayer leader"?

What I did not understand then was that I was not wheedling the editor, but educating myself; that I was not exhorting the editor, but beginning dimly to perceive the terrible complexities of the craft of translation. My trials with *geshtorbn der letster bal-tfile* reveal the problem of translation at its most elementary and primitive stages—a tyro's tale. For a long time I did not comprehend that a translator, though continuing to quail before the idea of translation, must nevertheless not be afraid of the poem that awaits; that the translator must dare to be equal master of the poem together with the poet. I did not sympathize with Einhorn because I did not yet know that I was obliged to become Einhorn. I did not have authority over the poem because I did not believe that it was already there; I thought I had to jerry-build it myself, in various makeshift ways. I did not yet see that the poem had a blueprint of its own, a meticulous blueprint as singular as the whorl on a fingertip; and that what I had to do was not look for the ink to reproduce the print, but look for the inexorable lines of the print itself.

By the time I had acquired some experience—by then I was concentrating on the poet H. Leivick—I had learned to trust the doctrine of the Pre-Existent Poem, I was a believer, it seemed to me I was becoming Leivick. With a poem called *Tate-legende* I was surely Leivick, and one of my letters to the editor records how that extraordinary realization opened itself out:

> Meanwhile, as you suggested, I've gone ahead with *Tate-legende* [Father-Legend]. An extremely affecting poem, clear-eyed, sinuous, unsentimental. I toiled over it with a kind of calculating joy—I have about sixteen pages of crowded work-sheets, filled with calculated alternatives: I imagine I keep saying "calculate" because I took risks here and there to seize the tone. I am just now too much devoted to the poem to tell whether it all works; but you will tell me that.
>
> One very, very still night, coming to the words *yingl du mayner, yingl du mayner, / ikh bin dayn tate der roiter* [oh my child, my child, I am your red-haired father], I all at once felt Leivick's father's ghost enter me. Through the ribs and throat.

You can hear in that last paragraph how "calculation" and "risk" suddenly fly away, replaced by becoming.

S. Y. Agnon and the
First Religion

Shmuel Yosef Agnon, the 1966 Nobel winner for literature, was born one hundred years ago, in Galicia, Poland, and died in Jerusalem in 1970. Not long after his death, I wrote a story about Agnon, a kind of parable that meant to toy with the overweening scramble of writers for reputation and the halo of renown. It was called "Usurpation" and never mentioned Agnon by name. Instead, I pretended he was still alive, not yet a laureate: "It happens that there lives in Jerusalem a writer who one day will win the most immense literary prize on the planet." I referred to this writer as "the old man," or else as "the old writer of Jerusalem"—but all the while it was Agnon I not so secretly had in mind; and I even included in my story, as a solid and unmistakable clue, one of his shorter fables: about why the Messiah tarries.

To tell the truth, this midrashic brevity (God knows where I came upon it) was the only work of Agnon's I had ever read. Nothing could have tempted me to look more extensively into Agnon, not even the invention of a story about him: enchanted

---

Published in *Commentary*, December 1988

by the dazzlements his great name gave off, my story was nevertheless substantially blind to the illuminations of his pen. I could scarcely blame myself for this. For decades, Agnon scholars (and Agnon is a literary industry) have insisted that it is no use trying to get at Agnon in any language other than the original. The idea of Agnon in translation has been repeatedly disparaged; he has been declared inaccessible to the uninitiated even beyond the usual truisms concerning the practical difficulties of translation. His scriptural and Talmudic resonances and nuances, his historical and textual layers, his allusive and elusive echoings and patternings, are so marvelously multiform, dense, and imbricated that he is daunting even to the most sophisticated Hebrew readers. What, then, can a poor non-Hebraist possibly make of an Agnonic masterwork when, willy-nilly, it is stripped of a quarter or a half of its texture and its substance, when the brilliant leaves are shaken off the spare, bare, naked-toed trunk? A writer in monolingual America, confined to writing and reading wholly in English, will clearly have no Agnon other than the Agnon who has been Englished. If the prodigal Agnon can be present only in Hebrew, to read him in any other tongue is to be condemned to paucity. The Hebrew prince is an English-language pauper.

So, drawn almost exclusively to the lustiness of literary blue blood, unwilling to see it ransacked and pauperized, it is no wonder that I have kept my distance from the translated Agnon.

But Agnon himself has a different idea of translation and its possibilities. The story that illustrates Agnon's position is both extremely famous and consummately sly—a sort of play, or paradigm, or Oscar Wildean joke. Saul Bellow tells the joke on himself in his Introduction to *Great Jewish Short Stories*, a popular paperback anthology he edited in 1963, some years before either writer had captured the Nobel Prize.

In Jerusalem several years ago, I had an amusing and enlightening conversation with the dean of Hebrew writers, S. Y. Agnon. This spare old man, whose face has a remarkably youthful color, received me in his house, not far from the barbed wire entanglements that divide the city, and while we were drinking tea, he asked me if any of my books had been translated into Hebrew. If they had not been, I had better see to it immediately, because, he said, they would survive only in the Holy Tongue. His advice I assume was only half serious. This was his witty way of calling my attention to a curious situation. I cited Heinrich Heine as an example of a poet who had done rather well in German. "Ah," said Mr. Agnon, "we have him beautifully translated into Hebrew. He is safe."

Now the "curious situation" Bellow alludes to is the fact (as he comments a moment later) that "Jews have been writing in languages other than Hebrew for two thousand years." No one could have been more aware of this variety of language experience than Agnon—which is why Bellow understood Agnon's remark to be "only half serious." But there are two entirely serious elements to take note of in Agnon's response. The first is his apparent confidence in the power of "beautiful translation." A case can be made that Heine, too, with all *his* strata of sources, from medieval ballads to chivalric romances to French satire, will not readily yield to successful translation—perhaps even less so than Agnon, because a poet is always more resistant to translation than a writer of prose, however complex the prose. And yet Agnon does not doubt that "we have him," that Heine can be genuinely Heine even in a language as distant from German, and as alien to European literary styles, as Hebrew. All the same, it is not the translator's skill, much as Agnon seems willing to trust in it, that preserves Heine for Agnon. It is Heine's "return," so to speak, as a Jewish poet, to the sacred precincts of the Land of Israel—his return via the Holy Tongue. For Agnon it may be that Heine in German is less fully Heine than he is in Hebrew: to be "safe" is to have entered into the influences of holiness; redemption is signified by the reversal of exile. Whatever happens outside the Land of Israel, whatever ensues in the other languages of the earth, is, to be sure, saturated in its own belongingness, and may indeed be alluring, and without question "counts" in the world of phenomena; but counts differently, because it is outside the historic circle of redemption that only the Land possesses. The world beyond the

Land, however gratifying or seductive, is flavored with the flavor of exile.

At first glance Agnon's witticism "He is safe" appears to be in praise of translation as a relatively easy triumph of possibility— but only, it seems, if the text in question is drawn from the tongues of exile into the redemptiveness of Hebrew. Presumably translation *out* of Hebrew would be considered not so much a linguistic as a metaphysical lessening. Or else, since the original continues to stand, Agnon Englished would strike Agnon as irrelevant. The calculated remark "He is safe" is a joke that recognizes, after all, the chanciness of translation, that will in fact *not* guarantee that all translation "saves"; and it is this contradiction that makes the joke, since the redemptiveness of translation can work in one direction only. A flawed rendering of Heine into Hebrew may nevertheless partake of redemption; a brilliant rendering of Agnon into English backslides into the perilous flavors of exile.

And that is the second serious point. When you reverse the direction—when translation becomes *yeridah* (descent from the heights of Jerusalem; desertion) rather than *aliyah* (ascent to the sublime; return)—the witticism collapses, a different tone takes hold, and a chink opens into dread, into the regions of the unsafe, of the irrational, into the dark places of alien myth, of luring mermaid and moon-dazed mountain nymph, of Pan and unbridled Eros. The Lorelei will chant her deadly strains out of the bosom of the Rhine, but never out of Lake Kinneret (the Hebrew name for the Sea of Galilee). And Saul Bellow's domesticized metaphysical anecdote—Agnon drinking tea and speculating about Heine's salvation—becomes a parable that, when set to run in reverse, can turn into a tale of baleful exilic potency. Imagine, for instance, that it is not the Land of Israel that is the magnet, but all the lands beyond. Imagine that the longing of heroic temperaments is for exile rather than for redemption. Imagine everything seen upside down and inside out: a yearning for abroad instead of for Jerusalem; a pilgrimage in search of holy talismans that leads away from the Land toward half-pagan scenes. Imagine a sacred tongue that is not Hebrew. Imagine an Exodus undertaken for the sake of returning to the wilderness. Imagine trading the majestic hymns of Scripture for wild incantations and magical ululations. Imagine the Land of Israel as a site of drought and dearth and death and crumbling parapets and squatters and muteness, while faraway countries flow with rivers and songs and color and grace and beauty and joy.

All these ominous reversals of "He is safe," Agnon has already made; he has made them in a work of fiction. If the Land of Israel assures immortality for Jewish poets, the corollary must be that exile can shore up only the short term, the brief lease, until the final slide into oblivion. But what of the opposite proposition? The proposition that the old, old myths, the legends that precede Sinai by a millennium and more, the fables that continue to girdle and enthrall the world, will outlive all? The proposition that compared to the loud song of the Lorelei, out of whose strong throat beat the hypnotic wing-whirrs of a hundred birds, the biblical Hannah's murmured prayer—unaesthetic, humble, almost not there—falls into insignificance?

Such a proposition may be an unlikely meditation for the pen of the "old writer of Jerusalem," "the dean of Hebrew writers," who in 1950, when he delivered up the tale called *Edo and Enam*, had reached the lively age of sixty-two; sixteen years later we see him flying to Sweden, exultant in a yarmulke. Does the pious yarmulke contradict the tale? The tale may be said to hang on the case of the translation into Hebrew of a pair of newly discovered ancient languages; and yet no redemption will come of it. Heine's "Die Lorelei," a song about death through allurement, is transmuted into a Hebrew ballad, and is thereby deemed "safe." But the Enamite Hymns carry, and carry out, the real power of death by allurement: they are all peril. Transported to the Land of Israel they have the capacity to kill, though they too are "beautifully translated" into the Holy Tongue.

Their devoted translator is Dr. Ginath, a scholar without a yarmulke, a wholly secularized scientific philologist and ethnographer, who will go to any length to get hold of lost languages: once, for example, he posed as a mystical holy man from Jerusalem,

"Hacham Gideon," in order to pry out the secret tongue of the living vestige of the tribe of Gad. "These days," remarks the narrator of *Edo and Enam*, "it is as if the earth had opened up and brought forth all that the first ages of man stored away. Has not Ginath discovered things that were concealed for thousands of years, the Edo language and the Enamite Hymns?" Dr. Ginath is the author of "Ninety-nine Words of the Edo Language," and also of an Edo grammar; but

> the Enamite Hymns were more: they were not only a new-found link in a chain that bound the beginnings of recorded history to the ages before, but—in themselves—splendid and incisive poetry. Not for nothing, then, did the greatest scholars come to grips with them, and those who at first had doubted that they were authentic Enamite texts began to compose commentaries on them. One thing, however, surprised. . . . All these scholars affirmed that the gods of Enam and their priests were male; how was it that they did not catch in the hymns the cadence of a woman's song?

"I could hear," continues the narrator, "a kind of echo from my very depths . . . ; ever since the day I had first read the Enamite Hymns that echo had resounded. It was a reverberation of a primal song passed on from the first hour of history through endless generations."

That "cadence of a woman's song" belongs to the autochthonous enchantresses, among them the Lorelei; it is the voice of the intoxicated sibyls who speak for what we may call the First Religion, which is the poetry of Eros and nature, of dryad and nymph and oread, of the sacred maidens whose insubstantial temples are the sea, the rivers, the forests, the meadows and the hills. In *Edo and Enam*, Agnon experiments with importing the hymns of this First Religion into the Land of Israel, into the marrow of Jerusalem itself, where such hymns cannot flourish, where they will grow lethal; and he also imports the singer of the hymns, the enchantress Gemulah, who, when she sang in her native realm, "stirred the heart like . . . the bird Grofith, whose song is sweeter than that of any creature on earth."

Gemulah is from a distant mountainous region, though her people originally lived among springs. According to their tradition, they derive from Gad, which once received a biblical blessing for "enlargement." As warriors, they "advanced into the lands of the Gentiles, for they misconceived the text" of the blessing—"they did not know that the blessing refers only to the time when they lived in the Land of Israel, not to their exile in the lands of other peoples." But it is exile itself they have misconceived; they take it for eternity, and have succumbed to the First Religion. While at least formally they maintain their ancestral hope for the return to Jerusalem, and while Gemulah's father, a learned elder of the tribe, is still able to read to the people from the Midrash and the Jerusalem Targum, "which they have in its complete text, and which he translated into their language," the Gadites are by now profoundly separated. Their speech is unlike any other. In fulfillment of their name, Gad, or Luck, they depend on the stars and deal in charms and talismans and magical texts. Though they continue to circumcise their sons, their alien funeral rites are observed "with songs and dances full of dread and wonder." Gemulah herself is "accomplished in all their songs, those that they had once sung . . . by the springs and also those of the mountains." Gemulah's father hands on to her a "secret knowledge laid up by his ancestors," as well as an arcane private language, an antic invention that separates them even from Gad itself; they are a pair of oracles and sorcerers. In order to "learn from the eagles how they renew their youth," Gemulah's father ascends into the mountains, where he is attacked and devoured by an eagle. Following a long mourning, Gemulah is taken by her bridegroom to the Land of Israel, to the city of Jerusalem, where she sickens and falls mute. The First Religion, woven out of filaments of purest nature poetry, is silenced in the domain of monotheism.

A dumbstruck Lorelei, a somnambulist who "walks wherever the moon leads her," like a mermaid drawn by the tides, Gemulah at last becomes equal to the letters of her name when their positions are set free to recombine: a female golem. And indeed at the tale's opening we are privy to some banter about just such a creature—

"Wasn't it you who said Dr. Ginath had created a girl for himself?"—and we hear Ibn Gabirol invoked, the Hebrew poet of medieval Spain who is said to have carpentered a woman out of wood.

Gemulah's bridegroom is Gavriel Gamzu, a man in a yarmulke, a dealer in rare books and manuscripts. He began as an ordinary yeshiva student, but discovered himself in thrall to "intrinsic beauty," hence to poetry. In youth once, intending to purchase a copy of the *Shulkhan Arukh*, a compendium of laws, he emptied his pockets for the sake of an exotic *divan* of pure verse. "Because he was so fastened to poetry, he came unfastened at the yeshiva," and was driven to wander the world in search of the ravishments of anonymous hymns. The lure of primeval song has brought him to Gemulah's country. A sandstorm in that region, however, leaves him blind in one eye, perhaps as a divine judgment for preferring intrinsic beauty to the discipline of the codes of conduct. From now on his vision is halved, strangely narrowed. Wearing his yarmulke, he lectures against "read[ing] the Law beyond the text," and keeps a stern eye out for "those Bible critics who turn the words of the living God upside down"; but the next instant this one and only eye abandons piety and fixes on the holiness of poets, whose "hallowed hands" have the power to save from the demons of hell. It appears that intrinsic beauty and the Law cannot rest together in peace within the range of a single eye, and may not wed and live together under a roof in Jerusalem. The bewitchment-seeking spirit of Gavriel Gamzu is for the moment more at home away from home, in the lands of exile. Only there do enchantments thrive unrestrained.

Consequently Gamzu's pursuit of rapture can be fulfilled only outside the Land of Israel, in separated communities compromised by long periods of exile. If the uncanniness of Gemulah's song electrifies him into seizing her as his bride, it is not Gadite poetry alone that stirs Gamzu. In his incessant travels he has happened on other deposits of wondrous lyricism—for instance, exilic Jews whose forefathers were young men driven from Jerusalem by Nebuchadnezzar. Riding on millstones, they were carried aloft to their rescue in the isolation of a mysterious new settlement, where "they saw maidens coming up from the sea," and married them; and not long afterward they "forgot Jerusalem." When Ezra summons them to be restored to the Land of Israel, they hang back. Like the Gadites, they mistake exile for permanence. This lost society, the children of mermaids, develops rites and songs over the generations that deviate signally from the practices of Israel. The close presence of women in their synagogue and the singing of unfamiliar hymns of startling sweetness derive, no doubt, from the habits of their ancestresses the sea-maidens.

In delineating these legendary distant tribes sunk in attrition and dilution, can Agnon have had in mind the real precedent of the Jews of Elephantine? A community founded on an island in the Nile by Jewish mercenaries under Persian governance, even after Ezra's return to Jerusalem in the fifth century B.C.E. they defied the ban on multiple temples and insisted on erecting a separate and rival edifice. The Elephantine Papyri testify to the strong position of women among them: bridegrooms had to provide dowries, for example. But the statuary that crept into their temple architecture, and the customs that invaded their practice, including the outright worship of goddesses, severely divided the Elephantinians from the mainstream, and they disappeared into the belly of exile, leaving behind a mere archaeological vapor. In *Edo and Enam*, Agnon condenses the vapor of wayward paganized Jews into the honeyed elixir of Gamzu's hymns—but when the hymns are introduced into the place where the Temple once stood, havoc rules, and Jerusalem begins to unbuild.

Consider the condition of Jerusalem when Gamzu brings into the city his wife, Gemulah, and her father's talismans—mystical leaves, at first sight colorful, then drained of color, on which certain charms are inscribed. These leaves, long buried in a jar in a cave beneath a mountain crag in Gemulah's country, were given to Gamzu by Gemulah's father; they have the power to retrieve her when she escapes to sleepwalk under a full moon, a malady that occurs chiefly when she is away from her native surroundings. When the charms, in the company of the now-ailing Gemulah, settle into Jerusalem, their influence sets off a rash of departures, a rush back down into exile, an explosion of *yeridah*, signifying a descent from lawful holiness. The narrator's wife and children have left Jerusalem for another town; we are not told why. Gerda and Gerhard Greifenbach, who rent part of their house to the scholarly Dr. Ginath, are yearning for foreign lands, and are about to go on a tour. They are described as "dark and distracted," restless and discontent; it is likely that they suffer from the exilic emanations of the two mystical leaves in their possession, gifts from the itinerant Dr. Ginath—perhaps Ginath found them in a bundle of manuscripts purchased from Gamzu; or perhaps he obtained them in Gemulah's country while impersonating Gideon, the Jerusalem Hacham. The Greifenbachs' house is itself tainted by exilic flaws. It was once inhabited by a quarrelsome sectarian from Germany, who ended by abandoning Jerusalem; and again by a couple named Gnadenbrod: the wife refused to live in Jerusalem, and they re-entered exile in Glasgow—immediately after which an earthquake undermined the house and permanently weakened the roof.

Gemulah's presence insinuates exile into the everyday life of Jerusalem, if exile is understood to mean deterioration, peril, and loss. The water supply dries up in tanks, pipes, and taps. Angry Arabs appear out of nowhere to stab young lovers. The city is overrun with housebreakers and squatters. In the general homelessness, newlyweds find it impossible to live together under one roof. All this happens when Gemulah is loosed from her sickbed into Jerusalem, somnambulant, released from muteness only to sing her magical song, *yiddal, yiddal, yiddal, vah, pah, mah*. The body of the city is there, but only as a shell: the spirit of peace is gone from it. Jerusalem itself becomes a kind of golem—which may account for the prevalence of the letter *g*—*gimel*—in all the names of the tale, Gemulah's among them, since *gimel* too is an anagram for golem. In the last scenes we see Gamzu himself turned into a golem at the sound of Gemulah's private language, the language belonging only to herself and her sorcerer father. Reminiscent of the mystical leaves that initially show brilliant colors and then grow brown as earth, "suddenly the colors began to change in Gamzu's face, until at last all color left it, and there remained only a pale cast that gradually darkened, leaving his features like formless clay." Yet when Gamzu first hears Gemulah's voice, on a mountaintop in her own country, he is entranced: Gemulah stands before him as "one of the twelve constellations of the Zodiac, and none other than the constellation Virgo." She is an oracle, one of the minor divinities of the First Religion, an enchantress, an alien nymph displaced.

And it is displacement that governs the imaginings of *Edo and Enam*. Displacement—the grim principle of exile—is what distinguishes Agnon's fictive commentary on the First Religion from, say, the visionary work of the Sicilian Giuseppe di Lampedusa or the Swedish Pär Lagerkvist, each of whom has written a remarkable modernist novella on the subject of the primal enchantress—or, perhaps, on the theme of ecstatic beauty. The First Religion knows nothing of exile; all the world is home to all the divinities, who flower in forest or sea. Lampedusa's enchantress in "The Professor and the Mermaid" is Lighea, "daughter of Calliope," a mermaid or siren who appears to a student of ancient Greek and couples with him, hoping to lure him to oblivion. Like her mother the muse of poetry, in the name of rapture she urges the erasure of all distinctions: "ignorant of all culture, unaware of all wisdom, contemptuous of any moral inhibitions, she belonged, even so, to the fountainhead of all culture, of all wisdom, of all ethics, and could express this primigenial superiority of hers in terms of rugged beauty. 'I am everything [she chants] because I am simply the current of life, with its detail eliminated.' " Lagerkvist's parable, *The Sibyl*, has a Christian lining, and offers a darker view of the ecstatic: all the same, the oracle's power of annihilation (and self-annihilation) is unmistakable, and her utterances in the pit at the temple of Delhi are, like Gemulah's, in a recondite tongue never before heard by mortal ears: "I began to hiss forth dreadful, anguished sounds, utterly strange to me, and my lips moved without my will; it was not I who was doing this. And I heard shrieks, loud shrieks; I didn't understand them, they were quite unintel-

ligible, yet it was I who uttered them. They issued from my gaping
mouth. . . . Not long afterward it happened that I was carried out
of the oracle pit unconscious, violated by [the] god. . . . my ecstasy, my frenzy, was measureless. . . . I smelled a sour stench of
goat; and the god in the shape of the black goat, his sacred beast
in the cave of the oracle, threw itself upon me and assuaged itself
and me in a love act in which pain, evil, and voluptuousness were
mingled."*

The siren and the sibyl, potent representatives of the First Religion, swallow up all things—every achievement, every desire,
every idea—into the poetry of ecstatic obliteration, Eros joined
with degradation and death. Gemulah's bewitchment of Gamzu
is no different, though Agnon's voice, like Gemulah's, is airier:

> Because songs are conjoined, they are linked up with one another,
> the songs of the springs with the songs of high mountains, and those
> of high mountains with the songs of the birds of the air. And among
> these birds there is one whose name is Grofith; when its hour comes
> to leave the world, it looks up to the clouds and raises its voice in
> song; and when its song is ended, it departs from the world. All
> these songs are linked together in the language of Gemulah. Had
> she uttered that song of Grofith, her soul would have departed from
> her, and she would have died.

Yet finally Gamzu opposes Gemulah's sorcery in a way imagination
will never dream of opposing the siren's song or the oracle's cry:
he puts his hand over Gemulah's mouth to save her from singing
the notes of Grofith, the poetry of ecstatic frenzy, which can kill.
It is the hand of anti-myth. Who, in the gossamer realms of the
First Religion, dares to stop the mouths of Delphic sibyls or glittering mermaids?

And still Gemulah dies. She dies for magic, for voluptuous
longing, for ecstasy; she dies singing the song of the bird Grofith
after all, bidden to do so by Dr. Ginath, whom she takes to be
the Jerusalem Hacham, the magus who once sojourned in her
country. As an act of science, the philologist Ginath transcribes

---

*A longer extract from this same passage may be found on page 272.

the strange syllables of her mysterious language; but Gemulah has
no science; she is the antithesis of science. Spellbound under the
moon, she walks on the roof of Ginath's part of the Greifenbachs'
house—the very roof weakened long ago by an earthquake that
came as a judgment upon those who abandon Jerusalem to run
after exile. Ginath pursues her, and together they fall to their
deaths.

Scanning the obituary notices in the newspaper, the narrator
happens on a curious misprint: the announcement of the death of
a Dr. Gilath. The letter *l* has been substituted for the letter *n*.
Agnon's Hebrew readers can readily guess the reason. "Ginath"
(which means "garden") suggests the garden of esoteric knowledge,
the fatal *pardes* ("paradise") into which, according to legend, four
scholars, all prodigious and original, ventured; only one of them,
Rabbi Akiva, came out alive—perhaps because he more than the
others revered the Law. And "Gilath"? Omitting the vowels, the
root consonants spell out the letters of *galuth*: Hebrew for exile,
displacement.

Gemulah is in exile from her country of charms and talismans
and conjury and divination and necromantic hymn; Jerusalem, the
city of the Law, is inimical to all of these. In her native land,
Gemulah blooms unharnessed, under the mild rule of poetry and
play and random rapture. But in Jerusalem wizards and their
hymns weaken and perish; so Gemulah sickens, and takes to her
bed spiritless and speechless; it is well known that a golem lacks
the capacity for speech. When the moon calls her, she rises up to
meander through Jerusalem, infiltrating her omens and influences
through the city, and then Jerusalem too sickens with the sickness
of exilic ailments: dread and dryness and departure.

But as soon as Gemulah is destroyed, disordered and discon-
solate Jerusalem comes to healthy life again: the water begins to
flow freely in the pipes, the exiles stream home, *yeridah* gives way
to *aliyah*—the narrator's family returns, the Greifenbachs hurry
back from abroad, nothing more is heard of housebreakers, squatters, marauders, or separated couples. The First Religion is routed,
and Jerusalem is restored.

How is it, though, that Gemulah's husband, Gamzu, escapes death? Like Ginath, who is punished for flying after the enticements of the languages of exile, Gamzu has been an enamored soul possessed by the music of the First Religion; and yet Gamzu lives. Like Akiva, he survives the penetration into *pardes*. Gamzu is safe—ultimately he can keep his eye, his only eye, on Jerusalem's principle of Law; he wears his yarmulke, and has the power to stop up Gemulah's mouth, so that she will not lose herself in the song of the deadly bird of beauty. Only in the regions beyond Jerusalem is he powerless before savage beauty.

The principle of Jerusalem versus the principle of exile; *aliyah* versus *yeridah*; redemption versus illusion; seeking to be "safe" versus finding oneself swallowed up by the forces of obliteration. A fugue of antagonisms. Nevertheless one cannot be sure of Agnon's definitive passion, whether he is finally on the side of lyrical sorcery or of Torah. Near the close of *Edo and Enam*, the narrator learns that Dr. Ginath has burned all his papers, among them the record of Gemulah's inchoate utterances. Jerusalem, it would seem, has won over the wilderness. But in the very last sentences of the tale, the Enamite Hymns are lauded for their "grace and beauty," and Dr. Ginath is celebrated for saving them for the world: is this jubilant praise rendered in the narrator's voice or in Agnon's own? And in the end how do we know whether Jerusalem itself is really safe, even after the destruction of the enchantress Gemulah? Heine's Lorelei, after all, now sings in the Holy Tongue, the better to sabotage the citizens of Jerusalem.

Bialik's Hint

What is the question?

GERTRUDE STEIN, dying

I once had a theory about Jewish language. I began by renaming English; I called it "New Yiddish." Since the majority of Jews alive today are native English speakers, I reasoned, English was in the way of becoming a Jewish language for nearly universal Diaspora employment, much as Old Yiddish (or Ladino, its Sephardic counterpart) used to be before its murderous weakening by the mappers of *Lebensraum*. I posited a variety of literary forms for New Yiddish, and imagined for it a liturgical spirit that would nevertheless not contravene what it is nowadays fashionable to call postmodern modes.

Before that, I held some notions, clearly not very original, about the creation of a literature of *midrash*, or fictive commentary. Jewish writing, I thought, whether or not developed by Jews (I cited George Eliot and Thomas Mann), was that literature which dared to introduce into the purely imaginative the elements of judgment and interpretation. Literature, I declared, was not simply an enterprise of essence ("A poem should not mean / But be"), but must

Published in *Commentary*, February 1983

be charged with the power to sift through the light and the dark. Story should not only be but mean. And to back this up, I quoted from Judah Halevi, who accused Hellenism of producing "flowers without fruit," in contrast to the Jewish spirit, which bears the ripe fruit of responsibility and judgment.

In addition, I had a theory about the more local and partial conditions of American Jewish writing. Bellow, Roth, Paley, Malamud, I privately argued, had taken the post-immigration experience as far as it could go. Anyone who hoped to push forward in that same direction of portraiture and sensibility was bound to end up as an imitator. For new work, the aftermath of emigration was played out and offered nothing but repetition and desiccation—or something worse: ventriloquism, fakery, nostalgia, sentimentalism, cardboard romanticism. The solution, it seemed to me, was to escape the descent into "ethnicity"—debased and debasing sociologists' misnomer—and to drive toward the matrix of the Jewish Idea.

The Jewish Idea, I believed, was characterized by two momentous standards. The first, the standard of anti-idolatry, led to the second, the standard of distinction-making*—the understanding that the properties of one proposition are not the properties of another proposition. Together, these two ideals, in the form of urgencies, had created Jewish history. The future of a Jewish literature was to derive from an insight into what a Jew is—not partially, locally, sociologically, "ethnically," but in principle. To be a Jew is to be old in history, but not only that; to be a Jew is to be a member of a distinct civilization expressed through an oceanic culture in possession of a group of essential concepts and a multitude of texts and attitudes elucidating those concepts. Next to the density of such a condition—or possibility—how gossamer are the stories of those writers "of Jewish extraction" whose characters are pale indifferent echoes of whatever lies to hand: this or that popular impingement.

Lately I have been thinking hard about the cultural destiny of

---

*Dr. Avi Erlich's succinct formulation.

those very writers. What comes to me now is far less than "theory"; a mere meditation; a mooning, say, over the effects of the Enlightenment and its concomitant issue, Jewish Emancipation.

Gershom Scholem has revealed, with miraculous intellectual daring, how Sabbatai Zevi, the seventeenth-century false messiah, was the precursor of Jewish Enlightenment fervor as well as of Reform Judaism. The electrifying wand that unites these seemingly dissimilar strands—an irrational mass delusion giving rise to rational skepticism—is the purposeful relinquishment of the "yoke of the Law," Sabbatai Zevi's deliberate snapping of the chain of commitment to the central root-system of historical Jewish expression. A manic-depressive, the false messiah was a performer of "strange acts," kabbalistically inspired religious ceremonies without precedent; and once freedom from the Jewish mainstream was fostered, Scholem claimed, Jewish ideation could and did follow many paths formerly unthinkable. The variety of nineteenth-century currents in which Jews were active, socialism and secularism among them, had their origins in the volcanic pseudo-theological events of the seventeenth. Sabbatai Zevi, hoping to lead a liberated Jewish people triumphantly back to Jerusalem, repudiated the constraints and hatreds of Europe and proclaimed his own immediately serviceable messianic Emancipation; the rules, he showed, could be broken, society and politics need not stand in the way, nothing imaginable was preposterous. That he concluded his own career in the posture of a forced convert to Islam may itself have seemed preposterous; but he had already demonstrated to a rigidly structured and restricted community that anything can happen.

If Sabbatai Zevi, promising extravagant new possibilities, opened the way to internal Jewish liberalization (or deviation), the external route was still barred. Not until the actual Emancipation did Jews experience any choice more subtle or flexible than conversion, and the effects of post-Enlightenment choice have been shaking Jewish life ever since. It is true that Europe canceled both the Enlightenment and the Emancipation for a dozen cataclysmic years in the heart of our own century, the long-range influence of which will perhaps remain unresolved for another hundred years. Or, rather, from another point of view it might be said that Hitler carried the Enlightenment to its inevitable resolution, bringing *liberté* to its highest romantic pitch: the liberty, with no brake of tradition or continuity, to imagine everything, hence to do anything. And Zionism, in one interpretation, is itself a late-blooming version of Jewish Emancipation.

But the object of these speculations is the fact of choice itself. Emancipation threw open the path of entry into all the complex and abundant allure of Gentile culture. On the face of things, the old restrictions fell away, and it was possible to be, as the famous phrase had it, "a man abroad and a Jew at home"; but the very formulation of that notion split off "man" from "Jew," and Jew from humanity, so that "Jew," no longer an instance of humanity, as the rabbinic tradition held, came rather to represent a difference from humanity, eventually an opposition to it, precisely as the advocates of Christian triumphalism had always maintained. And on the Jewish side, to accept the formulation was already to reject the Jewish way, which claimed wholeness of person. Hence the locution "just Jewish." "These matters are not just Jewish," we hear the Jewish heirs of the Enlightenment explain. "They should interest everyone," as if Jews are automatically excluded from the compass of "everyone." As, in the medieval scheme, they were.

Yet we are all of us—all of us, insofar as we live in the world —children of the Enlightenment. It is a condition that was prepared for us generations ago—even in the enclosed chambers of the East European shtetl, when it began to be infiltrated by the Haskalah movement, with its sense of holiness-as-literature and truth-as-art replacing Torah-from-Sinai. For the Sephardim, a kind of foretaste of Enlightenment occurred three centuries early, in the freely intermingling dual culture of the Spanish era; and the same was true of Jews in Renaissance Italy. But Golden Age Spain and Renaissance Italy were idiosyncratic moments, and, so to speak, meteoric flashes; they came as bright patches, erratic and unpredictable, unlike the Enlightenment's singular and steady Grand Principle. It is the Grand Principle that confers on us its

legacy. Especially as writers we may not repudiate the gifts of the
Enlightenment, because freedom of the imagination—the freedom
to imagine alternative lives, on which poets feed—is what the
Enlightenment offered, delectably, in contrast to the traditional
mold of an immovable condition.

Two hundred years post-Enlightenment, our choice is not
whether to accept cultural liberation and variety—we were, after
all, *born* into the Grand Principle—but whether to fuse that freedom with the Sinaitic challenge of distinctive restraint and responsibility that the rabbis held out. The democratic and
egalitarian Grand Principle, seductive to the liberated and broth-
erly mind, celebrated not uniqueness but multiplicity, not *religio*,
a binding together, but proliferation. Nothing could be more natural than that the eighteenth century's Grand Principle should give
birth to the nineteenth century's wayward Romanticism. Yet the
rabbis' contrary call was by no means a cry against imagination; inventive rather than conservative thinkers, the assembly of dispu-
tants who comprise the rabbinic way were nevertheless wary of the
fancifulness of enchanting alternatives and branching roads with no
promise of arrival. The rabbis' call to imagination, by contrast, was
a call to imagine arrival: homecoming, deliverance, fruition, resolution, an idealism of character, right conduct, just determina-
tions, communal well-being. In short, the messianic impulse.

It is plain that the Enlightenment too, though it turned away
from Christianity, was all the same formed in the fertilization dish
of Jewish and Christian messianism. But Liberty, Fraternity, and
Equality tend (more than intend) to break down distinctions, and
right conduct can emerge only out of the stringent will toward
distinction-making. The rabbinic way is to refuse blur, to see how
one thing is not another thing, how the road is not the arrival, the
wish not the deed, the design not the designer, man not God. The
true ship is the shipbuilder, Emerson said, in a single phrase that
sums up all of Romanticism; but the rabbis would not allow for
the ship until it was *there*—not out of literal-mindedness, but
because it is spiritually necessary to make ultimate distinctions;
otherwise Creator becomes confused with creation, leading

to the multiform versions of antinomianism from which Jewish monotheism characteristically, and uniquely, turns away its purified face.

Chaim Nachman Bialik, the great fountain of Hebrew modernism, in a magisterial essay comparing Aggadah to Halachah—the formless to the structured, the imaginatively wanderlusting to the imagination of arrival—remarks that the "whole justification" for "literature" and "creation" is the sense of duty. A stunning conclusion. "Modern Hebrew literature," Bialik wrote in 1916, "on the intellectual side . . . has nothing to say; its only approach to life is through the narrow wicket-gate of a dubious aestheticism." "The value of Aggadah," he asserts, "is that it issues in Halachah. Aggadah that does not bring Halachah in its train is ineffective." If we pause to translate Aggadah as tale and lore, and Halachah as consensus and law, or Aggadah as the realm of the fancy, and Halachah as the court of duty, then what Bialik proposes next is astonishing. Contrariwise, he says, Halachah can bring Aggadah in *its* train. Restraint the begetter of poetry? "Is she not"—and now Bialik is speaking of the Sabbath—"a source of life and holiness to a whole nation, and a fountain of inspiration to its singers and poets?" Yet the Tractates that touch on the Sabbath consist, in their hundreds of pages, "of discussions and decisions on the minutiae of the thirty-nine kinds of work and their branches, and on the limits within which it is permissible to carry on the Sabbath. What the Sabbath candles are to be made of, what a beast may be loaded with; how the limits may be jointly fixed—such are the questions discussed. What weariness of the flesh! What waste of good wits on every trifling point!" Weariness of flesh the begetter of inspiration? Waste of good wits bringing rapture in its train? These hairsplitters deciding on the minutiae of the thirty-nine kinds of work, Bialik determines, "are in very truth artists of life in the throes of creation," and the perfection of their work, "antlike and giantlike at once," is the "sacred and sublime . . . Queen Sabbath . . . endowed with wondrous and dazzling beauty."

In all this Bialik shows us that he is addressing his matter with a post-Enlightenment mentality. His view of the Halachic thinkers is tinged with secularity, anthropology, ambiguity: these rabbis, despite or because of their attention to "trifling points," are "artists," their work is "creation." Not for one moment does Bialik contend that the Sabbath is from Sinai, that the Sabbath is a divine gift. In short, Bialik is engaged in a modernist literary contemplation, and he has, moreover, seized on a post-Enlightenment choice: the choice of the fusion of secular aesthetic culture with Jewish sensibility. Aggadah, pre-European, pre-Christian, is, in its lightning and mercurial way, a prefiguration of the European Christian Enlightenment—i.e., an ideal of imaginative freedom that is nevertheless more compassionate than any purely Hellenic ancestry would allow. The ideal of Fraternity, for instance, inevitably suggests humanitarianism more than aestheticism; and Greek democracy, it should be recalled, though it might be fraternal among patricians, was not humanitarian, lying as it did across the backs of slaves and barbarians.

So it might be argued that the Enlightenment "Judaized" Europe when it granted equality to Jews and agreed to offer them citizenship. On the one hand, it was redolent of Jewishly cherished ideals of messianism. On the other, it was a welcoming, humane, and compassionate act of brotherhood toward real and living Jews. But the Jews, in accepting Emancipation (rather, in rushing fervently toward it), agreed on their side to de-Judaize themselves. To be enthralled by Bach, it is necessary to suspend disbelief in, or at least distrust of, Christianity—one must enter the music with an opening of the heart to Bach's exaltations: and Bach's exaltations belong to Christendom. The cathedrals and all the splendors of European art exacted from Jews a degree of self-negation. But this self-negation in the face of the majority culture—the price of participation in it—was trivial compared to the larger cost implied in the formulation of "a man abroad and a Jew at home." What this meant was the privatization of the Jewish mind, a shrinking of its compass. In political terms, the price of citizenship was the loss of corporate self-government, the relinquishment of the sovereign rights and privileges of internal autonomy. All this was concrete and measurable, the product of a bargain sealed by Napoleon's amazing call for the renewal of the Sanhedrin, which delivered itself up wholly to Napoleonic control, and finished off Jewish life as a self-reliant force, however otherwise restricted. From that moment forward, the idea of the kind of cultural realm in which a Jew is situated began to diminish: the opportunities of citizenship were desperately valued and welcomed, but in mind and in humanistic scope, the physically and socially delimited closet of the ghetto was broader than national citizenship, which critically reduced Jewish self-definition. From an abundant and spacious theory of civilization embracing the whole range of human culture, post-Enlightenment Jewish intellectual territory withdrew to the narrow claims of "religion," "persuasion," "faith." The Enlightenment and the Emancipation, in their offer of breadth, reduced and cramped Jewish creative space.

For some, that space narrowed and darkened so radically that it vanished. Such Jews chose to live entirely within the acreage of Enlightenment. Some made that decision immediately upon Emancipation, and their progeny have not been Jews for two centuries. Others have taken longer, or are just beginning the journey toward radical Jewish abandonment.* But for all Jews everywhere, the idea of what it meant to be a Jew was crucially altered. Jewish meaning, from its origins in the widest understanding of civilization, withered to an "ism." Judaism: the mere denominational

---

*A journey undertaken often in extraordinary ignorance of its starting point. "Chicken soup and Yiddish jokes may tarry awhile. But the history of the Jews from now on will be one with the history of everybody else," the novelist Herbert Gold has written, with a clear sense of Enlightenment destination. Allen Guttman, in a study of assimilation in Jewish-American literature (*The Jewish Writer in America*), astutely comments: "How did chicken soup come to be understood as almost synonymous with Jewishness? How did it happen that Americans often assume that the folkways of *Mitteleuropa* or of the Russian *shtetl* are really the essentials of Jewishness? To answer such questions fully is to tell the story of the American Jews, but this much is certain: a minority that adopted many of the traits of its European neighbors is now distinguished in the eyes of its American neighbors by these adopted characteristics rather than by the fundamental differences that originally accounted for the minority status."

(from which, in an atmosphere of nearly universal Western secularism, it is not only easy but logical to fall away). The effects of this "ism-ization," and its even more one-dimensional American issue, "ethnicity," have been an irritation ever since. In consequence of the reduction of Jewish intellectual authority to a "persuasion," the sense of a Jewish national civilization has been denigrated as "tribal," and the re-establishment of a sovereign and autonomous Israel has been seen as an affront to the Napoleonic bargain that demanded the surrender of autonomy. The idea of a wider Jewish heritage, moreover, is regarded as a betrayal of the Jewish promise of "good behavior": the promise to turn culture itself into the mere marginal sliver of an "ism," hanging, so to speak, from the synagogue lintel. "Be a man in the street and a Jew in your tent, / Be a brother to your countryman and a servant to your king," Judah Leib Gordon sang, not in the France of Voltaire, but in the Russia of 1863.

Everywhere in the Diaspora today this promise is still being meticulously kept, held in place by the ongoing vestige of Napoleon's threat against what—in pluralist and ethnic America!—is designated, in acerbic tones, as "dual loyalty." Recently a post-Enlightenment American citizen of the Jewish persuasion wrote a letter to the editor of *The New York Times*, complaining that Israel is a Jewish country with Jewish institutions, including the effrontery of a Jewish army—a "ghetto," in fact, for Jews only. (Just as, presumably, the Indian subcontinent, with its multiple Indian institutions, including its Indian army, is a ghetto for Indians only.) The revolutionary is taken for the stereotyped; the larger daring and the wider culture are judged to be the smaller and the narrower. Much of Europe's growing fury at the State of Israel, we may be sure, is the frustrated post-Enlightenment realization that the Jews have after all reneged on the Napoleonic bargain, and have dared to move boldly out from being a sometimes tolerated "persuasion" to becoming once again an amply developed concentration of varied human behavior. Europe "humanely" welcomed the State of Israel as long as it was misconstrued to be simply a "haven" for the broken survivors of Europe's own abattoir; but once it begins to be recognized that a more fundamental program is in hand, and that what the founding of Israel represents is, rather, a declaration of the renewal of an entire civilization, uncontained by the self-confining politesse of the Napoleonic bargain, the heirs of Napoleon detect insolence. The Jews are escaping from their normal condition and place into the transcendence of full national expression—a privilege owed to all peoples but the Jews.

Paradoxically, however, Zionism as an Emancipation movement was itself cradled in the Enlightenment, and only provides a new arena for the problem of Jewish cultural allegiance. For the last two hundred years—the period since the promulgation of the Grand Principle—each Jewish intellectual generation, wherever it has lived (and this of course includes Jerusalem and Tel Aviv), has had to make the decision anew: whether or not to pass wholly into the majority civilization and to cut the Jewish tie; or the alternative.

What is the alternative? Remember that we are speaking of Jewish writers and intellectuals. Only for a very tiny minority has the alternative been to remain within what nowadays we think of as the "Jewish world." And let us remind ourselves once again that it was the Enlightenment itself that was responsible for the narrowing of that Jewish world in the mind of modern Jews. Before the Emancipation, Jews might live politically enclosed in a segregated society—but the content of the Jewish mind, through the all-inclusive reach and memory of Talmud, hardly felt itself to be separated from the whole range of human experience, and daily took the pulse of every human concern, from ethics to hygiene to adjudication. If I hammer too much at this, if I pull at your sleeve too decisively in emphasizing all this, it is because such a reminder cannot be urged too often—and because the idea of Talmud as a civilizing and spacious force is not only unpopular with many post-Enlightenment Jewish intellectuals, but repellent to some, and remote from nearly all. An understanding of the unique *content* of Jewish genius has been forfeited by the great majority of modern Jews. It is the Enlightenment that has made us forfeit the understanding and forget the content.

And it was the Enlightenment, in letting Jews "in," that defined them as having been "out." Of course they *were* out, from the point of view of the nations they inhabited. In a Europe of farmers Jews alone could not work the land; Jews were not permitted to own land. In daily occupation Jews alone were bitterly restricted: in some regions Jews were confined to the sale of old clothes and nothing else. Looking for a loophole in a still-feudal economy that was closed to them, an enterprising fraction, eschewing ragpicking and inventing capitalism, became moneylenders, and were hounded and castigated for having developed the rudiments of banking, which the Church called "usury"—though only until the rise of the Christian bankers. Given a thousand strangling restrictions, enthusiastic popular pogroms, steady persecution, and unending general revilement, it is an absolute fact that the Jews were out. But what European historians overlook, or perhaps do not know, what the bigots of the Enlightenment (and the radiant Voltaire was such a bigot, deeply contemptuous of Jews, whom he viewed as obscurantist) deliberately shut themselves off from, was what the inner life of the Jewish community consisted in. In an illiterate Europe, ordinary Jews were not simply literate but text-obsessed. In an idolatrous Europe, ordinary Jews were resolutely monotheist. Jewish history as a record of oppression is only a quarter history. "History is about the positive and not the negative," Benedetto Croce puts it. "Man's action combats obstructing beliefs and tendencies, conquers them, overcomes them, reduces them to mere stuff for his handling; and on this man rears himself up." And: "Creativeness, and it alone, is the true and sole subject of history."

Jewish history is overwhelmingly an instance of Croce's dictum; Jewish history is overwhelmingly intellectual history; and the heroes of the Enlightenment, with whom it might be said modern intellectual history began, were cut off from the energetic and brilliant culture that lived side by side with them, in the same towns, in the despised Jew-streets. In releasing the Jews from the crushing grip of the Church's Judas-views, which declared the Jews to be a murderous, traitorous, obsolete, and superfluous vestige, the Enlightenment nevertheless did not abandon the idea that the

Jews were a people without a worthy culture. The thinkers of the Enlightenment believed that in allowing the Jews entry into European culture, they were offering a dazzling gift—and indeed they were. But they could not conceive that there might lurk, in the shadowy possession of the Jew-streets, an alternative culture with a luminousness of its own, residing in a thousand brains; and no one, Gentile or Jew, understood at once that the Enlightenment was the beginning, for Jewish intellectual life, of a new alternative never before possible.

What, let us ask again, is that new alternative? Its premise is, first, the recognition that no contemporary writer, Gentile or Jewish, Israel-bred or Diaspora-born, remains untouched by the Enlightenment—i.e., by the conditions of modernism. Moreover, for a Jew to continue to move toward Enlightenment values exclusively—and politically these include such later structures as socialism and Marxism—is, by now, not to dissent but to conform. By now, to feel oneself an integral member of the great matrix of European-American arts-and-letters is surely to slide down the greasy pole. In literature, the chief post-Enlightenment value is "originality"; but nothing is less original, by now, than, say, Parisian or New York novelists "of Jewish extraction" who write as if they had never heard of a Jewish idea, especially if, as is likely, they never have. "Be a man abroad and a Jew at home" is finally truncated to "Be a man abroad"—and of these there are a hundred thousand and more, all alike, all purged of Jewish understanding. Consequently it becomes increasingly tedious to read about these hopelessly limited and parochial characters in so-called Jewish fiction whose Jewish connections appear solely in the form of neighborhood origin or played-out imitative sentence structure or superannuated exhausted Bolshevik leaning. By now, for writers to throw themselves entirely into the arms of post-Enlightenment culture is no alternative at all. It is a laziness. It is the final shudder of spent thought: out of which no literature, Jewish or otherwise, can hope to spring.

*   *   *

The new alternative, then. Bialik catches hold of the first strand: the transformation of certain cultural elements of the Enlightenment into Jewish substance and substantiality—belles-lettres, for instance, signifying, for Hebrew, an extraordinary innovation and modernization. This is what Bialik means in urging that "the value of Aggadah [belles-lettres] is that it issues in Halachah [Jewish cognitive substance]."

The new alternative—call it Bialik's hint—leads us back to another period when elements of an influential foreign civilization were converted into Jewish substance—a huge and resplendent precedent, as awesome and finally as immanent as a stroke of nature, worthy of conscientious attention but calling—alas—for genius.

Consider: the protagonists of the great tales of Scripture are in most important respects recognizably Jewish. But in one respect —and for us it is indissoluble from what we think of as Jewish temperament, character, or sensibility—they are not: they appear to be unconcerned with Text. They are indifferent to the sublime passion for study.* They may be the subject of a holy text—the People of the Book is Mohammed's inspired ascription—but the people *in* the Book are, it is entirely clear, not a bookish sort. They are not, but latter-day Jews are; for two millennia Jews have known themselves to be text-centered above all. How is it, then, that such a discontinuity of character should arise? We read that Esau went hunting—but what was Jacob doing in his tent? It is a charm-

---

*Even so, one can't help noticing that a prefiguration of study-centeredness—and of "immanence"—occurs as early as Deuteronomy 29–31, wherein Moses repeatedly calls on every member of the community—"your heads, your tribes, your elders, and your officers, even all the men of Israel, your little ones, your wives, the stranger in your camp, from the hewer of wood to the drawer of water"—to give conscientious attention to the text of "this book." And in Nehemiah 8: 1–9, the people are again convened, and this time Ezra the scribe "opened the book in the sight of all the people," and "all the people wept, when they heard the words of the law." In all these instances, however, what we have is a multitude standing democratically assembled, an intent audience listening with concentration and understanding. But the people do not read for themselves; they are read to. Whereas "study" somehow suggests an independent intellectual act.

ing back-construction to imagine that he was probably studying Torah.

The idea of the holiness of study is an idea born of fusion. The
holiness is Jewish; the study—the majestic elevation of study—is
Greek and Platonic. Formal study—a master and his pupil—is
not to be found in Scripture. Scriptural heroes, even the poets
among them, Moses, Deborah, David, and Solomon, are not heroes rooted in the grandeur of intellectual power, no matter how
gifted or ingenious they may be. One of the vastest minds of
Scripture is surely the brilliantly original Joseph, wily dreamer
and inspired dream-interpreter, salvational economist, and, no
doubt, scientist and architect. Surely Joseph is what we mean when
we speak of genius. But when we try to imagine what the heroism
of intellectual power might be, we do not think of Joseph; we think
of Socrates.

What altered Jews and Jewishness forever was, of course, the
destruction of the Temple, the ruin of Jerusalem, the long bitter
fact of Exile; and, simultaneously, the turn to study as substitute
Temple, substitute Jerusalem, substitute flowering homeland.
When Zechariah called for the greater might of spirit, he was
prophesying the turn to the Jewish text. But the source of study-
consciousness, the source of intellect as the paramount tool of right
conduct, is the Socratic, not the biblical, font. It was the gradual
superimposition of the Socratic primacy of intellect upon the Jewish primacy of holiness that produced the familiar, and now completely characteristic, Jewish personality we know. Because the
Jewish mind has wholly assimilated the Platonic emphasis on the
nobility of pedagogy, on study as the route to mastery and illumination, there is no Jew alive today who is not also resonantly
Greek; and the more ideally Jewish one is in one's devotion to
Torah, the more profoundly Greek.

Bialik's hint (and it *is* only a hint, a hunch; an imaginative construct; an invention; a fiction) is this: as with Greece, so with the
Enlightenment.

The new alternative that lies before us now, astonishing in its
daring and seeming insurmountability, is the fusion of the offerings

of the Enlightenment—which, in any case, we cannot avoid, forgo, or escape—with Jewish primacy. If the opportunity is set aside—and for two hundred years it has, by and large, been set aside, or at least not been seized in all its potency and heat—the result will be either loss or triviality. The loss we have already glimpsed: the ennui that follows the swallowing-up by the aftermath of the Enlightenment. It is true enough that many Jewish writers and intellectuals (in whatever language they write, including Hebrew) prefer the swallowing-up and have chosen it. They may prefer it, they may freely choose it; but what they may *not* do is delude themselves that they are choosing largeness over narrowness, dissent over establishmentarianism, originality over tedium. In fact they are choosing precisely the opposite: the trodden path and the greased pole. In the name of the Enlightenment cry of "universalism," they are the herd choosing the herd. And triviality: there is small invitation to distinctiveness in that blending, and smaller opportunity for genius along the greased pole. Heine and Disraeli discovered this, and responded by roughing up the pole with ironic Jewish romanticism.

The other way—the new alternative, the high muse of fusion, Bialik's hint, the dream delivered up in shadowy shapes by the later writers of the Haskalah movement and by the feverish lost tide of Yiddish—opens out to riches: originality, the astonishments of the unexpected, the explosive hope of fresh form. Only genius can conceive it—and it may require several geniuses, or, to put it otherwise, a collective genius developed over generations. It took generations—a handful of centuries—for the Socratic emphasis on pedagogic exertion to infiltrate the Jewish emphasis on divinely inspired communal responsibility. Undoubtedly it will take another handful of centuries—the two hundred that have elapsed so far are plainly not enough—for Enlightenment ideas of skepticism, originality, individuality, and the assertiveness of the free imagination to leach into what we might call the Jewish language of restraint, sobriety, moral seriousness,* collective conscience. Such

---

*The distinguished Israeli critic Dan Miron has argued that the idea of a Jewish

a hugely combining project is the work not only of generations, but of giants. It will require fifty Bialiks, each one resplendent with the force of Halachic reverence for the minutiae of conscientiousness. "But where is *duty*?" Bialik cried into the enchanting face of love and poetry.

Such a project cannot be answered with a proposal to "compose *midrashim*," by which is usually meant a literature of parable. Surely a literature of parable is not to be despised: Kafka is its practitioner, and so is Borges. But dependence on a single form, however majestic or pliant, is no foundation for an entire literature; and what we are confronting, in a time of empty bewilderment, is just that: the need for a literature.

Nor will such a project be answered by any theory of an indispensable language, such as my old fantasy of New Yiddish—i.e., the Judaization of a single language used by large populations of Jews. The enrichment of any existing language is of course not to be despised, and if English is broadened through the introduction of Jewish concepts, mores, sensibility, and terminology (the last the most prevalent and influential and yet the most trivial), that can only be its good fortune. English has already had the historic good luck (derived from historic bad luck—many invasions) to be richer than other languages. English, in fact, is perhaps the luckiest language with regard to "richness," and we English-speakers are, as writer-technicians, probably the luckiest language-inhabitors, simply because English is really two languages, Germanic and Latinic: so that there are at least two strains of nuance for every noun, fact, feeling, or thought, and every notion has a double face.

"moral seriousness" is itself an Enlightenment development, and that traditionally it was beside the point whether one was or was not morally serious; what mattered was that one performed what was religiously requisite in Jewish law. I am persuaded that he is right about the notion of moral seriousness having gained ascendancy post-Enlightenment, as one of the consequences of the diminution of tradition; but this certainly cannot mean that it is not present *at all* in the tradition, beginning with the appearance of the ram in the thicket. Moral seriousness, it seems to me, is endemic in Jewish particularity; and what has brought about its characterization as a wholly Enlightenment idea is precisely its severance from Jewish particularity.

Hebrew is a lucky language in another sense: it was the original vessel for the revolution in human conscience, teaching the other languages what it early and painfully acquired: that textual immanence I have been calling moral seriousness. Because of the power of scriptural ideas, there is hardly a language left on the planet that does not, through the use of its own syllables and vocabulary, "speak Hebrew." All languages have this Hebrew-speaking capacity, as the literatures of the world have somewhat tentatively, yet often honorably, demonstrated. If this is true, it is a proof that Hebrew does not have a unique ability, by divine right, so to say, to carry certain ideas, although the genius of Abraham and Moses and the Prophets runs like mother milk through its lips. Language is the wineskin, thought the wine. All that is required of any language for it to carry a fresh or revolutionary idea (and what, in the history of humankind, is the Jewish recoil from idolatrous celebration, if not always fresh and always revolutionary?)—all that is required is for the language in question to will itself not to be parochial.

So if the hope of a saving midrashic form is not enough, and if the chimera of a New Yiddish is, at bottom, beside the point, what can answer to Bialik's hint? What is the new alternative to *be*, this unimaginable fusion of what we are as the children of the Enlightenment, what we are as the children of Israel, and what we are to become when these learn to commingle? That they *will* learn to commingle is, I believe, an inevitability; just as with the hindsight of two millennia, we can see how inevitable it was for the Greek schools of philosophy to be reborn as the Jewish academies, and for Socratic *pilpul** to serve Jewish moral seriousness.

*Hebrew for "close analysis."

Ruth

For
Muriel Dance, in New York;
Lee Gleichmann, in Stockholm;
Sarah Halevi, in Jerusalem; and
Inger Mirsky, in New York

I. FLOWERS

There were only two pictures on the walls of the house I grew up
in. One was large, and hung from the molding on a golden cord
with a full golden tassel. It was a painting taken from a photo-
graph—all dark, a kind of grayish-brown; it was of my grandfather
Hirshl, my father's father. My grandfather's coat had big foreign-
looking buttons, and he wore a tall stiff square yarmulke that
descended almost to the middle of his forehead. His eyes were
severe, pale, concentrated. There was no way to escape those eyes;
they came after you wherever you were. I had never known this
grandfather: he died in Russia long ago. My father, a taciturn man,
spoke of him only once, when I was already grown: as a boy, my
father said, he had gone with his father on a teaching expedition
to Kiev; he remembered how the mud was deep in the roads. From
my mother I learned a little more. Zeyde Hirshl was frail. His
wife, Bobe Sore-Libe, was the opposite: quick, energetic, hearty,
a skilled *zogerke*—a women's prayer leader in the synagogue—a
whirlwind who kept a dry goods store and had baby after baby,
all on her own, while Zeyde Hirshl spent his days in the study-
house. Sometimes he fainted on his way there. He was pale, he

240

was mild, he was delicate, unworldly; a student, a *melamed*, a fainter. Why, then, those unforgiving stern eyes that would not let you go?

My grandfather's portrait had its permanent place over the secondhand piano. To the right, farther down the wall, hung the other picture. It was framed modestly in a thin black wooden rectangle, and was, in those spare days, all I knew of "art." Was it torn from a magazine, cut from a calendar? A barefoot young woman, her hair bound in a kerchief, grasping a sickle, stands alone and erect in a field. Behind her a red sun is half-swallowed by the horizon. She wears a loose white peasant's blouse and a long dark skirt, deeply blue; her head and shoulders are isolated against a limitless sky. Her head is held poised: she gazes past my gaze into some infinity of loneliness stiller than the sky.

Below the picture was its title: *The Song of the Lark*. There was no lark. It did not come to me that the young woman, with her lifted face, was straining after the note of a bird who might be in a place invisible to the painter. What I saw and heard was something else: a scene older than this French countryside, a woman lonelier even than the woman alone in the calendar meadow. It was, my mother said, Ruth: Ruth gleaning in the fields of Boaz.

For many years afterward—long after *The Song of the Lark* had disappeared from the living room wall—I had the idea that this landscape (a 1930s fixture, it emerged, in scores of American households and Sunday-school classrooms) was the work of Jean-François Millet, the French painter of farm life. "I try not to have things look as if chance had brought them together," Millet wrote, "but as if they had a necessary bond between them. I want the people I represent to look as if they really belonged to their station, so that imagination cannot conceive of their ever being anything else."

Here is my grandfather. Imagination cannot conceive of his ever being anything else: a *melamed* who once ventured with his young son (my blue-eyed father) as far as Kiev, but mainly stayed at home in his own town, sometimes fainting on the way to the study-house. The study-house was his "station." In his portrait he looks as if he really belonged there; and he did. It was how he lived.

And here is Ruth, on the far side of the piano, in Boaz's field, gleaning. Her mouth is remote: it seems somehow damaged; there is a blur behind her eyes. All the sadness of the earth is in her tender neck, all the blur of loss, all the damage of rupture: remote, remote, rent. The child who stands before the woman standing barefoot, sickle forgotten, has fallen through the barrier of an old wooden frame into the picture itself, into the field; into the smell of the field. There is no lark, no birdcall: only the terrible silence of the living room when no one else is there. The grandfather is always there; his eyes keep their vigil. The silence of the field swims up from a time so profoundly lost that it annihilates time. There is the faint weedy smell of thistle: and masses of meadow flowers. In my childhood I recognized violets, lilacs, roses, daisies, dandelions, black-eyed Susans, tiger lilies, pansies (I planted, one summer, a tiny square of pansies, one in each corner, one in the middle), and no more. The lilacs I knew because of the children who brought them to school in springtime: children with German names, Koechling, Behrens, Kuntz.

To annihilate time, to conjure up unfailingly the fragrance in Boaz's field (his field in *The Song of the Lark*), I have the power now to summon what the child peering into the picture could not. "Tolstoy, come to my aid," I could not call then: I had never heard of Tolstoy: my child's Russia was the grandfather's portrait, and stories of fleeing across borders at night, and wolves, and the baba yaga in the fairy tales. But now: "Tolstoy, come to my aid," I can chant at this hour, with my hair turned silver; and lo, the opening of *Hadji Murad* spills out all the flowers in Boaz's field:

> It was midsummer, the hay harvest was over and they were just beginning to reap the rye. At that season of the year there is a delightful variety of flowers—red, white, and pink scented tufty clover; milk-white ox-eye daisies with their bright yellow centers and pleasant spicy smell; yellow honey-scented rape blossoms; tall campanulas with white and lilac bells, tulip-shaped; creeping vetch; yellow, red, and pink scabious; faintly scented, neatly arranged

purple plantains with blossoms slightly tinged with pink; cornflow-
ers, the newly opened blossoms bright blue in the sunshine but
growing paler and redder towards evening or when growing old;
and delicate almond-scented dodder flowers that withered quickly.

Dodder? Vetch? (Flash of Henry James's Fleda Vetch.) Scabious?
Rape and campanula? The names are unaccustomed; my grandfather in the study-house never sees the flowers. In the text
itself—in the Book of Ruth—not a single flower is mentioned.
And the harvest is neither hay nor rye; in Boaz's field outside
Bethlehem they are cutting down barley and wheat. The flowers
are there all the same, even if the text doesn't show them, and we
are obliged to take in their scents, the weaker with the keener, the
grassier with the meatier: without the smell of flowers, we cannot
pass through the frame of history into that long ago, ancientness
behind ancientness, when Ruth the Moabite gleaned. It is as if the
little spurts and shoots of fragrance form a rod, a rail of light,
along which we are carried, drifting, into that time before time
"when the judges ruled."

Two pictures, divided by an old piano—Ruth in *The Song of the
Lark*, my grandfather in his yarmulke. He looks straight out; so
does she. They sight each other across the breadth of the wall. I
stare at both of them. Eventually I will learn that *The Song of the
Lark* was not painted by Millet, not at all; the painter is Jules
Breton—French like Millet, like Millet devoted to rural scenes.
The Song of the Lark hangs in the Art Institute of Chicago; it is
possible I will die without ever having visited there. Good: I never
want to see the original, out of shock at what a reproduction now
discloses: a mistake, everything is turned the other way! On our
living room wall Ruth faced right. In the Art Institute of Chicago
she faces left. A calendar reversal!—but of course it feels to me
that the original is in sullen error. Breton, unlike Millet, lived into
our century—he died in 1906, the year my nine-year-old mother
came through Castle Garden on her way to framing *The Song of
the Lark* two decades later. About my grandfather Hirshl there is
no "eventually"; I will not learn anything new about him. He will

not acquire a different maker. Nothing in his view will be reversed. He will remain a dusty indoor *melamed* with eyes that drill through bone.

Leaving aside the wall, leaving aside the child who haunts and is haunted by the grandfather and the woman with the sickle, what is the connection between this dusty indoor *melamed* and the nymph in the meadow, standing barefoot amid the tall campanula?

Everything, everything. If the woman had not been in the field, my grandfather, three thousand years afterward, would not have been in the study-house. She, the Moabite, is why he, when hope is embittered, murmurs the Psalms of David. The track her naked toes make through spice and sweetness, through dodder, vetch, rape, and scabious, is the very track his forefinger follows across the letter-speckled sacred page.

II. MERCY

When my grandfather reads the Book of Ruth, it is on Shavuot, the Feast of Weeks, with its twin furrows: the text's straight furrow planted with the alphabet; the harvest's furrow, fuzzy with seedlings. The Feast of Weeks, which comes in May, is a reminder of the late spring crops, but only as an aside. The soul of it is the acceptance of the Torah by the Children of Israel. If there is a garland crowning this festival of May, it is the arms of Israel embracing the Covenant. My grandfather will not dart among field flowers after Ruth and her sickle; the field is fenced round by the rabbis, and the rabbis—those insistent interpretive spirits of Commentary whose arguments and counter-arguments, from generation to generation, comprise the Tradition—seem at first to be vexed with the Book of Ruth. If they are not actually or openly vexed, they are suspicious; and if they are not willing to be judged flatly suspicious, then surely they are cautious.

The Book of Ruth is, after all, about exogamy, and not simple exogamy—marriage with a stranger, a member of a foreign culture: Ruth's ancestry is hardly neutral in that sense. She is a Moabite.

She belongs to an enemy people, callous, pitiless; a people who deal in lethal curses. The children of the wild hunter Esau—the Edomites, who will ultimately stand for the imperial oppressors of Rome—cannot be shut out of the family of Israel. Even the descendants of the enslaving Egyptians are welcome to marry and grow into intimacy. "You shall not abhor an Edomite, for he is your kinsman. You shall not abhor an Egyptian, for you were a stranger in his land. Children born to them may be admitted into the congregation of the Lord in the third generation" (Deut. 23: 8–9). But a Moabite, never: "none of their descendants, even in the tenth generation, shall ever be admitted into the congregation of the Lord, because they did not meet you with food and water on your journey after you left Egypt, and because they hired Balaam . . . to curse you" (Deut. 23: 4–5). An abyss of memory and hurt in that: to have passed through the furnace of the desert famished, parched, and to be chased after by a wonder-worker on an ass hurling the king's maledictions, officially designed to wipe out the straggling mob of exhausted refugees! One might in time reconcile with Esau, one might in time reconcile with hard-hearted Egypt. All this was not merely conceivable—through acculturation, conversion, family ties, and new babies, it could be implemented, it *would* be implemented. But Moabite spite had a lasting sting.

What, then, are the sages to do with Ruth the Moabite as in-law? How account for her presence and resonance in Israel's story? How is it possible for a member of the congregation of the Lord to have violated the edict against marriage with a Moabite? The rabbis, reflecting on the pertinent verses, deduce a rule: *Moabite, not Moabitess*. It was customary for men, they conclude, not for women, to succor travelers in the desert, so only the Moabite males were guilty of a failure of humanity. The women were blameless, hence are exempt from the ban on conversion and marriage.

Even with the discovery of this mitigating loophole (with its odd premise that women are descended only from women, and men from men; or else that all the women, or all the men, in a family line are interchangeable with one another, up and down the ladder of the generations, and that guilt and innocence are collective, sex-linked, and heritable), it is hard for the rabbis to swallow a Moabite bride. They are discomfited by every particle of cause-and-effect that brought about such an eventuality. Why should a family with a pair of marriageable sons find itself in pagan Moab in the first place? The rabbis begin by scolding the text—or, rather, the characters and events of the story as they are straightforwardly set out.

Here is how the Book of Ruth begins:

> In the days when the judges ruled, there was a famine in the land; and a man of Bethlehem in Judah, with his wife and two sons, went to reside in the country of Moab. The man's name was Elimelech, his wife's name was Naomi, and his two sons were named Mahlon and Chilion—Ephrathites of Bethlehem in Judah. They came to the country of Moab and remained there.
>
> Elimelech, Naomi's husband, died; and she was left with her two sons. They married Moabite women, one named Orpah and the other Ruth, and they lived there about ten years. Then those two —Mahlon and Chilion—also died; so the woman was left without her two sons and without her husband.

Famine; migration; three deaths in a single household; three widows. Catastrophe after catastrophe, yet the text, plain and sparse, is only matter-of-fact. There is no anger in it, no one is condemned. What happened, happened—though not unaccoutered by echo and reverberation. Earlier biblical families and journeys-toward-sustenance cluster and chatter around Elimelech's decision: "There was a famine in the land, and Abram went down to Egypt to sojourn there, for the famine was severe in the land" (Gen. 12:10). "So ten of Joseph's brothers went down to get rations in Egypt. . . . Thus the sons of Israel were among those who came to procure rations, for the famine extended to the land of Canaan" (Gen. 42: 3,5). What Abraham did, what the sons of Jacob did, Elimelech also feels constrained to do: there is famine, he will go where the food is.

And the rabbis subject him to bitter censure for it. The famine, they say, is retribution for the times—"the days when the judges ruled"—and the times are coarse, cynical, lawless. "In those days there was no king in Israel; everyone did what he pleased" (Judges 17:6). Ironic that the leaders should be deemed "judges," and that under their aegis the rule of law is loosened, each one pursuing "what is right in his own eyes," without standard or conscience. Elimelech, according to the rabbis, is one of these unraveled and atomized souls: a leader who will not lead. They identify him as a man of substance, distinguished, well-off, an eminence; but arrogant and selfish. Even his name suggests self-aggrandizement: *to me shall kingship come.** Elimelech turns his back on the destitute conditions of hungry Bethlehem, picks up his family, and, because he is rich enough to afford the journey, sets out for where the food is. He looks to his own skin and means to get his own grub. The rabbis charge Elimelech with desertion; they accuse him of running away from the importunings of the impoverished, of provoking discouragement and despair; he is miserly, there is no charitableness in him, he is ungenerous. They call him a "dead stump"— he attends only to his immediate kin and shrugs off the community at large. Worse yet, he is heading for Moab, vile Moab! The very man who might have heartened his generation in a period of upheaval and inspired its moral repair leaves his own country, a land sanctified by Divine Covenant, for a historically repugnant region inhabited by idolators—and only to fill his own belly, and his own wife's, and his own sons'.

Elimelech in Moab will die in his prime. His widow will suffer radical denigration—a drop in status commonly enough observed even among independent women of our era—and, more seriously, a loss of protection. The rabbis will compare Naomi in her widowhood with "the remnants of the meal offerings"—i.e., with detritus and ash. Elimelech's sons—children of a father whose

---

*Latter-day scholarship avers that Elimelech is a run-of-the-mill name in pre-Israelite Canaan, "and is the one name in the Ruth story that seems incapable of being explained as having a symbolic meaning pertinent to the narrative" (Edward F. Campbell, Jr., *Ruth*, The Anchor Bible, p. 52). The rabbis, however, are above all metaphor-seekers and symbolists.

example is abandonment of community and of conscience—will die too soon. Already grown men after the death of Elimelech, they have themselves earned retribution. Instead of returning with their unhappy mother to their own people in the land dedicated to monotheism, they settle down to stay, and marry Moabite women. "One transgression leads to another," chide the rabbis, and argue over whether the brides of Mahlon and Chilion were or were not ritually converted before their weddings. In any case, a decade after those weddings, nothing has flowered for these husbands and wives, fertility eludes them, there will be no blossoming branches: the two young husbands are dead—dead stumps—and the two young widows are childless.

This is the rabbis' view. They are symbolists and metaphor-seekers; it goes without saying they are moralists. Punishment is truthful; punishment is the consequence of reality, it instructs in what happens. It is not that the rabbis are severe; they are just the opposite of severe. What they are after is simple mercy: where is the standard of mercy and humanity in a time when careless men and women follow the whim of their own greedy and expedient eyes? It is not merciful to abandon chaos and neediness; chaos and neediness call out for reclamation. It is not merciful to forsake one's devastated countrymen; opportunism is despicable; desertion is despicable; derogation of responsibility is despicable; it is not merciful to think solely of one's own family: if I am only for myself, what am I? And what of the hallowed land, that sacral ground consecrated to the unity of the Creator and the teaching of mercy, while the babble and garble of polymyth pullulate all around? The man who throws away the country of aspiration, especially in a lamentable hour when failure overruns it—the man who promotes egotism, elevates the material, and deprives his children of idealism—this fellow, this Elimelech, vexes the rabbis and afflicts them with shame.

Of course there is not a grain of any of this in the text itself—not a word about Elimelech's character or motives or even his position in Bethlehem. The rabbis' commentary is all extrapolation, embroidery, plausible invention. What is plausible in it is firmly plausible: it stands to reason that only a wealthy family, traveling together *as* a family, would be able to contemplate emigration to another country with which they have no economic or kinship ties. And it follows also that a wealthy householder is likely to be an established figure in his home town. The rabbis' storytelling faculty is not capricious or fantastic: it is rooted in the way the world actually works, then and now.

But the rabbis are even more interested in the way the world *ought* to work. Their parallel text hardly emerges ex nihilo. They are not oblivious to what-is: they can, in fact, construct a remarkably particularized social density from a handful of skeletal data. Yet, shrewd sociologists though they are, it is not sociology that stirs them. What stirs them is the aura of judgment—or call it ethical interpretation—that rises out of even the most comprehensively imagined social particularity. The rabbis are driven by a struggle to uncover a moral immanence in every human being. It signifies, such a struggle, hopefulness to the point of pathos, and the texture and pliability of this deeply embedded matrix of optimism is more pressing for the rabbis than any other kind of speculation or cultural improvisation. Callousness and egotism are an affront to their expectations. What are their expectations in the Book of Ruth? That an established community figure has an obligation not to demoralize his constituency by walking out on it. And that the Holy Land is to be passionately embraced, clung to, blessed, and defended as the ripening center and historic promise of the covenanted life. Like the Covenant that engendered its sanctifying purpose, Israel cannot be "marginalized." One place is not the same as another place. The rabbis are not cultural relativists.

From the rabbis' vantage, it is not that their commentary is "implicit" in the plain text under their noses; what they see is not implicit so much as it is fully intrinsic. It is there already, like invisible ink gradually made to appear. A system of values produces a story. A system of values? Never mind such Aristotelian language. The rabbis said, and meant, the quality of mercy: human feeling.

III. NORMALITY

I have been diligent in opening the first five verses of the Book of
Ruth to the rabbis' voices, and though I am unwilling to leave
their voices behind—they painstakingly accompany the story inch
by inch, breath for breath—I mean for the rest of my sojourn in
the text (perforce spotty and selective, a point here, a point there)
to go on more or less without them. I say "more or less" because
it is impossible, really, to go on without them. They are (to use
an unsuitable image) the Muses of exegesis: not the current sort
of exegesis that ushers insights out of a tale by scattering a thousand
brilliant fragments, but rather the kind that ushers things *toward*:
a guide toward principle. The Book of Ruth presents two principles. The first is what is normal. The second is what is singular.

Until Elimelech's death, Naomi has been an exemplum of the
normal. She has followed her husband and made no decisions or
choices of her own. What we nowadays call feminism is of course
as old as the oldest society imaginable; there have always been
feminists: women (including the unsung) who will allow no element
of themselves—gift, capacity, natural authority—to go unex-
pressed, whatever the weight of the mores. Naomi has not been
one of these. Until the death of her husband we know nothing of
her but her compliance, and it would be foolish to suppose that
in Naomi's world a wife's obedience is not a fundamental social
virtue. But once Naomi's husband and sons have been tragically
cleared from the stage, Naomi moves from the merely passive
virtue of an honorable dependent to risks and contingencies well
beyond the reach of comfortable common virtue. Stripped of every
social support,* isolated in a foreign land, pitifully unprotected,
her anomalous position apparently wholly ignored by Moabite
practices, responsible for the lives of a pair of foreign daughters-

---

*The rabbis' notion of Elimelech as a man of substance is no help to his widow.
She has not been provided for; we see her as helpless and impoverished.

in-law (themselves isolated and unprotected under her roof), Naomi is transformed overnight. Under the crush of mourning and defenselessness, she becomes, without warning or preparation, a woman of valor.

She is only a village woman, after all. The Book of Ruth, from beginning to end, is played out in village scenes. The history of valor will not find in Naomi what it found in another village woman: she will not arm herself like a man or ride a horse or lead a military expedition. She will never cross over to another style of being. The new ways of her valor will not annul the old ways of her virtue.

And yet—overnight!—she will set out on a program of autonomy. Her first act is a decision: she will return to Bethlehem, "for in the country of Moab she had heard that the Lord had taken note of His people and given them food." After so many years, the famine in Bethlehem is spent—but since Naomi is cognizant of this as the work of the Lord, there is a hint that she would have gone back to Bethlehem in Judah in any event, even if that place were still troubled by hunger. It is no ordinary place for her: the Lord hovers over Judah and its people, and Naomi in returning makes restitution for Elimelech's abandonment. Simply in her determination to go back, she rights an old wrong.

But she does not go back alone. Now, willy-nilly, she is herself the head of a household bound to her by obedience. "Accompanied by her two daughters-in-law, she left the place where she had been living; and they set out on the road back to the land of Judah." On the road, Naomi reflects. What she reflects on—only connect! she is herself an exile—is the ache of exile and the consolations of normality.

> Naomi said to her two daughters-in-law, "Turn back, each of you to her mother's house. May the Lord deal kindly with you, as you have dealt with the dead and with me! May the Lord grant that each of you find security in the house of a husband!" And she kissed them farewell. They broke into weeping and said to her, "No, we will return with you to your people."
>
> But Naomi replied, "Turn back, my daughters! Why should you

go with me? Have I any more sons in my body who might be husbands for you? Turn back, my daughters, for I am too old to be married. Even if I thought there was hope for me, even if I were married tonight and I also bore sons, should you wait for them to grow up? Should you on their account debar yourselves from marriage? Oh no, my daughters!"

In a moment or so we will hear Ruth's incandescent reply spiraling down to us through the ardors of three thousand years; but here let us check the tale, fashion a hiatus, and allow normality to flow in: let young stricken Orpah not be overlooked. She is always overlooked; she is the daughter-in-law who, given the chance, chose not to follow Naomi. She is no one's heroine. Her mark is erased from history; there is no Book of Orpah. And yet Orpah *is* history. Or, rather, she is history's great backdrop. She is the majority of humankind living out its usualness on home ground. These young women—both of them—are cherished by Naomi; she cannot speak to them without flooding them in her fellow feeling. She *knows* what it is to be Orpah and Ruth. They have all suffered and sorrowed together, and in ten years of living in one household much of the superficial cultural strangeness has worn off. She pities them because they are childless, and she honors them because they have "dealt kindly" with their husbands and with their mother-in-law. She calls them—the word as she releases it is accustomed, familiar, close, ripe with dearness—*b'notai*, "my daughters," whereas the voice of the narrative is careful to identify them precisely, though neutrally, as *khalotekha*, "her daughters-in-law."

Orpah is a loving young woman of clear goodness; she has kisses and tears for the loss of Naomi. "They broke into weeping again, and Orpah kissed her mother-in-law farewell." Her sensibility is ungrudging, and she is not in the least narrow-minded. Her upbringing may well have been liberal. Would a narrow-minded Moabite father have given over one of his daughters to the only foreign family in town? Such a surrender goes against the grain of the ordinary. Exogamy is never ordinary. So Orpah has already been stamped with the "abnormal"; she is already a little more daring than most, already somewhat offbeat—she is one of only two young Moabite women to marry Hebrews, and Hebrews have never been congenial to Moabites. If the Hebrews can remember how the Moabites treated them long ago, so can the Moabites: traditions of enmity work in both directions. The mean-spirited have a habit of resenting their victims quite as much as the other way around. Orpah has cut through all this bad blood to plain humanity; it would be unfair to consider her inferior to any other kindhearted young woman who ever lived in the world before or since. She is in fact superior; she has thrown off prejudice, and she has had to endure more than most young women of her class, including the less spunky and the less amiable: an early widowhood and no babies. And what else is there for a good girl like Orpah, in her epoch, and often enough in ours, but family happiness?

Her prototype abounds. She has fine impulses, but she is not an iconoclast. She can push against convention to a generous degree, but it is out of the generosity of her temperament, not out of some large metaphysical idea. Who will demand of Orpah—think of the hugeness of the demand!—that she admit monotheism to the concentration and trials of her mind? Offer monotheism to almost anyone—offer it as something to take seriously—and ninety-nine times out of a hundred it will be declined, even by professing "monotheists." A Lord of History whose intent is felt, whose Commandments stand with immediacy, whose Covenant summons perpetual self-scrutiny and a continual Turning toward moral renewal, and yet *cannot, may not, be physically imagined*? A Creator neither remote and abstract like the God of the philosophers, nor palpable like the "normal" divinities, both ancient and contemporary, both East and West? Give us (cries the nature of our race) our gods and goddesses, give us the little fertility icons with their welcoming breasts and elongated beckoning laps, give us the resplendent Virgin with her suffering brow and her arms outstretched in blessing, give us the Man on the Cross through whom to learn pity and love, and sometimes brutal exclusivity! Only give us what our eyes can see and our understanding understand: who can imagine the unimaginable? That may be for the philosophers; *they* can do it; but then they lack the imagination of the Covenant. The philosophers leave the world naked and blind and deaf and mute and relentlessly indifferent, and the village folk—who refuse a lonely cosmos without consolation—fill it and fill it and fill it with stone and wood and birds and mammals and miraculous potions and holy babes and animate carcasses and magically divine women and magically divine men: images, sights, and swallowings comprehensible to the hand, to the eye, to plain experience. For the nature of our race, God is one of the visual arts.

Is Orpah typical of these plain village folk? She is certainly not a philosopher, but neither is she, after ten years with Naomi, an ordinary Moabite. Not that she has altogether absorbed the Hebrew vision—if she had absorbed it, would she have been tempted to relinquish it so readily? She is somewhere in between, perhaps. In this we may suppose her to be one of us: a modern, no longer a full-fledged member of the pagan world, but always with one foot warming in the seductive bath of those colorful, comfortable, often beautiful old lies (they can console, but because they are lies they can also hurt and kill); not yet given over to the Covenant and its determination to train us away from lies, however warm, colorful, beautiful, and consoling.

Naomi, who is no metaphysician herself, who is, rather, heir to a tradition, imposes no monotheistic claim on either one of her daughters-in-law. She is right not to do this. In the first place, she is not a proselytizer or polemicist or preacher or even a teacher. She is none of those things: she is a bereaved woman far from home, and when she looks at her bereaved daughters-in-law, it is home she is thinking of, for herself and for them. Like the rabbis who will arrive two millennia after her, she is not a cultural relativist: God is God, and God is One. But in her own way, the way of empathy—three millennia before the concept of a democratic pluralist polity—she is a kind of pluralist. She does not require that Orpah accept what it is not natural for her, in the light of how she was reared, to accept. She speaks of Orpah's return not merely to her people but to her gods. Naomi is the opposite of coercive or punitive. One cannot dream of Inquisition

or jihad emerging from her loins. She may not admire the usages
of Orpah's people—they do not concern themselves with the
widow and the destitute; no one in Moab comes forward to care
for Naomi—but she knows that Orpah has a mother, and may
yet have a new husband, and will be secure where she is. It will
not occur to Naomi to initiate a metaphysical discussion with
Orpah! She sends her as a lost child back to her mother's hearth.
(Will there be idols on her mother's hearth? Well, yes. But this
sour comment is mine, not Naomi's.)

So Orpah goes home; or, more to the point, she goes nowhere.
She stays home. She is never, never, never to be blamed for it. If
she is not extraordinary, she is also normal. The extraordinary is
what is not normal, and it is no fault of the normal that it does
not, or cannot, aspire to the extraordinary. What Orpah gains by
staying home with her own people is what she always deserved:
family happiness. She is young and fertile; soon she will marry a
Moabite husband and have a Moabite child.

What Orpah loses is the last three thousand years of being present in history. Israel continues; Moab is not. Still, for Orpah,
historic longevity—the longevity of an Idea to which a people
attaches itself—may not be a loss at all. It is only an absence, and
absence is not felt as loss. Orpah has her husband, her cradle, her
little time. That her gods are false is of no moment to her; she
believes they are true. That her social system does not provide for
the widow and the destitute is of no moment to her; she is no
longer a widow, and as a wife she will not be destitute; as for
looking over her shoulder to see how others fare, there is nothing
in Moab to require it of her. She once loved her oddly foreign
mother-in-law. And why shouldn't openhearted Orpah, in her
little time, also love her Moabite mother-in-law, who is as like her
as her own mother, and will also call her "my daughter"? Does it
matter to Orpah that her great-great-great-grandchildren have
tumbled out of history, and that there is no Book of Orpah, and
that she slips from the Book of Ruth in only its fourteenth verse?

Normality is not visionary. Normality's appetite stops at
satisfaction.

IV. SINGULARITY

No, Naomi makes no metaphysical declaration to Orpah. It falls
to Ruth, who has heard the same compassionate discourse as her
sister-in-law, who has heard her mother-in-law three times call out
"Daughter, turn back"—it falls to Ruth to throw out exactly such
a declaration to Naomi.

Her words have set thirty centuries to trembling: "Your God
shall be my God," uttered in what might be named visionary
language. Does it merely "fall" to Ruth that she speaks possessed
by the visionary? What is at work in her? Is it capacity, seizure,
or the force of intent and the clarity of will? Set this inquiry aside
for now, and—apart from what the story tells us she really did
say—ask instead what Ruth might have replied in the more avail-
able language of pragmatism, answering Naomi's sensible "Turn
back" exigency for exigency. What "natural" reasons might such
a young woman have for leaving her birthplace? Surely there is
nothing advantageous in Ruth's clinging to Naomi. Everything
socially rational is on the side of Ruth's remaining in her own
country: what is true for Orpah is equally true for Ruth. But even
if Ruth happened to think beyond exigency—even if she were
exceptional in reaching past common sense toward ideal conduct
—she need not have thought in the framework of the largest cosmic
questions. Are we to expect of Ruth that she be a prophet? Why
should she, any more than any other village woman, think beyond
personal relations?

In the language of personal relations, in the language of pragmatism and exigency, here is what Ruth might have replied:

> Mother-in-law, I am used to living in your household, and have
> become accustomed to the ways of your family. I would no longer
> feel at home if I resumed the ways of my own people. After all,
> during the ten years or so I was married to your son, haven't I
> flourished under your influence? I was so young when I came into

your family that it was you who completed my upbringing. It isn't for nothing that you call me daughter. So let me go with you.

Or, higher on the spectrum of ideal conduct (rather, the conduct of idealism), but still within the range of reasonable altruism, she might have said:

Mother-in-law, you are heavier in years than I and alone in a strange place, whereas I am stalwart and not likely to be alone for long. Surely I will have a second chance, just as you predict, but you— how helpless you are, how unprotected! If I stayed home in Moab, I would be looking after my own interests, as you recommend, but do you think I can all of a sudden stop feeling for you, just like that? No, don't expect me to abandon you—who knows what can happen to a woman of your years all by herself on the road? And what prospects can there be for you, after all this long time away, in Bethlehem? It's true I'll seem a little odd in your country, but I'd much rather endure a little oddness in Bethlehem than lose you forever, not knowing what's to become of you. Let me go and watch over you.

There is no God in any of that. If these are thoughts Ruth did not speak out, they are all implicit in what has been recorded. Limited though they are by pragmatism, exigency, and personal relations, they are already anomalous. They address extraordinary alterations—of self, of worldly expectation. For Ruth to cling to Naomi as a daughter to her own mother is uncommon enough; a universe of folklore confirms that a daughter-in-law is not a daughter. But for Ruth to become the instrument of Naomi's restoration to safekeeping within her own community—and to prosperity and honor as well—is a thing of magnitude. And, in fact, all these praiseworthy circumstances do come to pass: though circumscribed by pragmatism, exigency, and personal relations. And without the visionary. Ideal conduct—or the conduct of idealism—is possible even in the absence of the language of the visionary. Observe:

They broke into weeping again, and Orpah kissed her mother-in-law farewell. But Ruth clung to her. So she said, "See, your sister-in-law has returned to her people. Go follow your sister-in-law."

But Ruth replied: "Do not urge me to leave you, to turn back and not follow you. For wherever you go, I will go; wherever you lodge, I will lodge; your people shall be my people. Where you die, I will die, and there I will be buried. Only death will part me from you." When Naomi saw how determined she was to go with her, she ceased to argue with her, and the two went on until they reached Bethlehem.

Of course this lovely passage is not the story of the Book of Ruth (any more than my unpoetic made-up monologues are), though it might easily have been Ruth's story. In transcribing from the text, I have left out what Ruth passionately put in: God. And still Ruth's speech, even with God left out, and however particularized by the personal, is a stupendous expression of loyalty and love.

But now, in a sort of conflagration of seeing, the cosmic sweep of a single phrase transforms these spare syllables from the touching language of family feeling to the unearthly tongue of the visionary:

"See, your sister-in-law has returned to her people and her gods. Go and follow your sister-in-law." But Ruth replied, "Do not urge me to leave you, to turn back and not follow you. For wherever you go, I will go; wherever you lodge, I will lodge; your people shall be my people, and your God my God. Where you die, I will die, and there I will be buried. Thus and more may the Lord do to me if anything but death parts me from you."

Your God shall be my God: Ruth's story is kindled into the Book of Ruth by the presence of God on Ruth's lips, and her act is far, far more than a ringing embrace of Naomi, and far, far more than the simple acculturation it resembles. Ruth leaves Moab because she intends to leave childish ideas behind. She is drawn to Israel because Israel is the inheritor of the One Universal Creator.

Has Ruth "learned" this insight from Naomi and from Naomi's son? It may be; the likelihood is almost as pressing as evidence: how, without assimilation into the life of an Israelite family, would Ruth ever have penetrated into the great monotheistic cognition? On the other hand: Orpah too encounters that cognition, and slips

back into Moab to lose it again. Inculcation is not insight, and
what Orpah owns is only that: inculcation without insight.
Abraham—the first Hebrew to catch insight—caught it as genius
does, autonomously, out of the blue, without any inculcating tradition. Ruth is in possession of both inculcation *and* insight.

And yet, so intense is her insight, one can almost imagine her
as a kind of Abraham. Suppose Elimelech had never emigrated to
Moab; suppose Ruth had never married a Hebrew. The fire of
cognition might still have come upon her as it came upon
Abraham—autonomously, out of the blue, without any inculcating
tradition. Abraham's cognition turned into a civilization. Might
Ruth have transmuted Moab? Ruth as a second Abraham! We see
in her that clear power; that power of consummate clarity. But
whether Moab might, through Ruth, have entered the history of
monotheism, like Israel, is a question stalled by the more modest
history of kinship entanglement. In Ruth's story, insight is inexorably accompanied by, fused with, inculcation; how can we sort
out one from the other? If Ruth had not been married to one of
Naomi's sons, perhaps we would have heard no more of her than
we will hear henceforth of Orpah. Or: Moab might have ascended,
like Abraham's seed, from the gods to God. Moab cleansed and
reborn through Ruth! The story as it is given is perforce inflexible,
not amenable to experiment. We cannot have Ruth without Naomi;
nor would we welcome the loss of such loving-kindness. All the
same, Ruth may not count as a second Abraham because her tale
is enfolded in a way Abraham's is not: she has had her saturation
in Abraham's seed. The ingredient of inculcation cannot be ex-
punged: there it is.

Nevertheless it seems insufficient—it seems askew—to leave it
at that. Ruth marries into Israel, yes; but her mind is vaster than
the private or social facts of marriage and inculcation; vaster than
the merely familial. Insight, cognition, intuition, religious genius
—how to name it? It is not simply because of Ruth's love for
Naomi—a love unarguably resplendent—that Naomi's God becomes Ruth's God. To stop at love and loyalty is to have arrived
at much, but not all; to stop at love and loyalty is to stop too soon.

Ruth claims the God of Israel out of her own ontological understanding. She knows—she knows directly, prophetically—that the Creator of the Universe is One.

V. UNFOLDING

The greater part of Ruth's tale is yet to occur—the greater, that is, in length and episode. The central setting of the Book of Ruth is hardly Moab; it is Bethlehem in Judah. But by the time the two destitute widows, the older and the younger, reach Bethlehem, the volcanic heart of the Book of Ruth—the majesty of Ruth's declaration—has already happened. All the rest is an unfolding.

Let it unfold, then, without us. We have witnessed normality and we have witnessed singularity. We will, if we linger, witness these again in Bethlehem; but let the next events flash by without our lingering. Let Naomi come with Ruth to Bethlehem; let Naomi in her distress name herself Mara, meaning bitter, "for the Lord has made my lot very bitter"; let Ruth set out to feed them both by gleaning in the field of Elimelech's kinsman, Boaz—fortuitous, God-given, that she should blunder onto Boaz's property! He is an elderly landowner, an affluent farmer who, like Levin in *Anna Karenina*, works side by side with his laborers. He is at once aware that there is a stranger in his field, and is at once solicitous. He is the sort of man who, in the heat of the harvest, greets the reapers with courteous devoutness: "The Lord be with you!" A benign convention, perhaps, but when he addresses Ruth it is no ordinary invocation: "I have been told of all that you did for your mother-in-law after the death of her husband, how you left your father and mother and the land of your birth and came to a people you had not known before. May the Lord reward your deeds. May you have a full recompense from the Lord, the God of Israel, under whose wings you have sought refuge!" Like Naomi, he calls Ruth "daughter," and he speaks an old-fashioned Hebrew; he and Naomi are of the same generation.*

---

*"Boaz and Naomi talk like older people. Their speeches contain archaic morphology and syntax. Perhaps the most delightful indication of this is the one

But remember that we are hurrying along now; so let Naomi, taking charge behind the scenes, send Ruth to sleep at Boaz's feet on the threshing floor in order to invite his special notice—a contrivance to make known to Boaz that he is eligible for Ruth's salvation within the frame of the levirate code. And let the humane and flexible system of the levirate code work itself out, so that Boaz can marry Ruth, who will become the mother of Obed, who is the father of Jesse, who is the father of King David, author of the Psalms.

The levirate law in Israel—like the rule for gleaners—is designed to redeem the destitute. The reapers may not sweep up every stalk in the meadow; some of the harvest must be left behind for bread for the needy. And if a woman is widowed, the circle of her husband's kin must open their homes to her; in a time when the sole protective provision for a woman is marriage, she must have a new husband from her dead husband's family—the relative closest to the husband, a brother if possible. Otherwise what will become of her? Dust and cinders. She will be like the remnants of the meal offerings.

Boaz in his tenderness (we have hurried past even this, which more than almost anything else merits our hanging back; but there it is on the page, enchanting the centuries—a tenderness sweetly discriminating, morally meticulous, wide-hearted and ripe)—Boaz is touched by Ruth's appeal to become her husband-protector. It is a fatherly tenderness, not an erotic one—though such a scene might, in some other tale, burst with the erotic: a young woman, perfumed, lying at the feet of an old man at night in a barn. The old man is not indifferent to the pulsing of Eros in the young: "Be blessed of the Lord, daughter! Your latest deed of loyalty is greater than the first, in that you have not turned to younger men." The remark may carry a pang of wistfulness, but Boaz in undertaking to marry Ruth is not animated by the lubricious. He is no December panting after May. A forlorn young widow, homeless in every sense, has asked for his guardianship, and he responds under

instance when an archaic form is put into Ruth's mouth, at 2:21—where she is quoting Boaz!" (Edward F. Campbell, Jr., *Ruth*, The Anchor Bible, p. 17)

the merciful levirate proviso with all the dignity and responsibility of his character, including an ethical scruple: "While it is true that I am a redeeming kinsman, there is another redeemer closer than I"—someone more closely related to Elimelech than Boaz, and therefore first in line to assume the right, and burden, of kinship protection.

In this closer relative we have a sudden pale reminder of Orpah. Though she has long vanished from the story, normality has not. Who conforms more vividly to the type of Average Man than that practical head of a household we call John Doe? And now John Doe (the exact Hebrew equivalent is Ploni Almoni) briefly enters the narrative and quickly jumps out of it; averageness leaves no reputation, except for averageness. John Doe, a.k.a. Ploni Almoni, is the closer relative Boaz has in mind, and he appears at a meeting of town elders convened to sort out the levirate succession in Naomi's case. The hearing happens also to include some business about a piece of land that Elimelech owned; if sold, it will bring a little money for Naomi. Naomi may not have known of the existence of this property—or else why would she be reduced to living on Ruth's gleaning? But Boaz is informed of it, and immediately arranges for a transaction aimed at relieving both Naomi and Ruth. The sale of Elimelech's property, though secondary to the issue of marital guardianship for Naomi's young daughter-in-law, is legally attached to it: whoever acquires the land acquires Ruth. The closer relative, Ploni Almoni (curious how the text refuses him a real name of his own, as if it couldn't be bothered, as if it were all at once impatient with averageness), is willing enough to buy the land: John Doe always understands money and property. But he is not at all willing to accept Ruth. The moment he learns he is also being asked to take on the care of a widow— one young enough to bear children, when very likely he already has a family to support—he changes his mind. He worries, he explains, that he will impair his estate. An entirely reasonable, even a dutiful, worry, and who can blame him? If he has missed his chance to become the great-grandfather of the Psalmist, he is probably, like Ploni Almoni everywhere, a philistine scorner of poetry anyhow.

And we are glad to see him go. In this he is no reminder of Orpah; Orpah, a loving young woman, is regretted. But like Orpah he has only the usual order of courage. He avoids risk, the unexpected, the lightning move into imagination. He thinks of what he has, not of what he might do: he recoils from the conduct of idealism. He is perfectly conventional, and wants to stick with what is familiar. Then let him go in peace—he is too ordinary to be the husband of Ruth. We have not heard him make a single inquiry about her. He has not troubled over any gesture of interest or sympathy. Ruth is no more to him than an object of acquisition offered for sale. He declines to buy; he has his own life to get on with, and no intention of altering it, levirate code or no levirate code. "You do it," he tells Boaz.

Boaz does it. At every step he has given more than full measure, whether of barley or benevolence. We have watched him load Ruth's sack with extra grain to take back to Naomi. He has instructed the reapers to scatter extra stalks for her to scoop up. He has summoned her to his own table for lunch in the field. He is generous, he is kindly, he is old, and in spite of his years he opens his remaining strength to the imagination of the future: he enters on a new life inconceivable to him on the day a penniless young foreigner wandered over his field behind the harvest workers. *Mercy, pity, peace, and love*: these Blakean words lead, in our pastoral, to a beginning.

The beginning is of course a baby, and when Naomi cradles her grandchild in her bosom, the village women cry: "A son is born to Naomi!" And they cry: "Blessed be the Lord, who hath not withheld a redeemer from you today! May his name be perpetuated in Israel! He will renew your life and sustain your old age; for he is born of your daughter-in-law, who loves you and is better to you than seven sons."

Only eighty-five verses tell Ruth's and Naomi's story. To talk of it takes much longer. Not that the greatest stories are the shortest—not at all. But a short story has a stalk—or shoot—through which its life rushes, and out of which the flowery head erupts. The Book of Ruth—wherein goodness grows out of goodness, and the extraordinary is found here, and here, and here—is

sown in desertion, bereavement, barrenness, death, loss, displacement, destitution. What can sprout from such ash? Then Ruth
sees into the nature of Covenant, and the life of the story streams
in. Out of this stalk mercy and redemption unfold; flowers flood
Ruth's feet; and my grandfather goes on following her track until
the coming of Messiah from the shoot of David, in the line of Ruth
and Naomi.

Metaphor and Memory

Not long ago I was invited to read some tale of mine before an assembly of physicians. I was invited not because I knew anything about disease or medicine or physiology, but precisely because I knew nothing at all. And the doctors, on their side, were not much concerned with tales or their tellers, unless the writer were to come to them with an interesting complaint. But a writer standing there in dull good health, reading aloud from a page, with not so much as a toothache or a common cold or even a mild rash, with no visible malady other than word-besottedness, could hardly serve. To the lives of doctors, given over as they are to the hard sad heavy push against mortality—what salve or balm or use might a word-besotted scribbler be? For a writer to turn up among doctors without a rash was rash indeed.

These doctors, however, had a visionary captain, or viceroy, or prince, who had read his Emerson. Emerson in "The American Scholar" noted what he called the "amputation" of society, each trade and profession "ridden by the routine of . . . craft": "The

The Phi Beta Kappa Oration, Harvard University, Spring 1985. Published as "The Moral Life of Metaphor," *Harper's*, January 1986

priest becomes a form; the attorney a statute-book; the mechanic a machine; the sailor a rope of the ship." And the doctor a CAT scan.

In response, the captain of the doctors formulates an Emersonian idea: an idea of interpenetration: of cutting through the dividing membrane: of peopling one cell with two temperaments. He will set the writer down among the doctors, the fabulist among the healers. The purpose of the experiment will be to increase the doctors' capacity to imagine. The doctors, explains their captain, too often do not presume a connection of vulnerability between the catastrophe that besets the patient and the susceptibility of the doctors' own flesh: the doctors do not conceive of themselves as equally mortal, equally open to fortune's disasters. The writer, an imaginer by trade, will suggest a course of connecting, of entering into the tremulous spirit of the helpless, the fearful, the apart. In short, the writer will demonstrate the contagion of passion and compassion that is known in medicine as "empathy," and in art as insight.

This, then, is the plan. The writer, though ignorant of every scientific punctilio, will command the leap into the Other.* That is how tales are made.

Yet the writer is cautious, even frightened. Here among the doctors, the redemptive ardor of literature begins to take on a vanity. How frivolous it seems, how trivial—vanity of vanities! The doctors are absorbed by blood and bone; each one, alone in his judgment, walks the fragile bridge between the salvation into life and the morbid slide toward death. The writer is as innocent as a privileged child before all this, a sybarite of libraries, a voluptuary of print. The doctors, by contrast, are soaked in the disinfectant fetor of hospitals, where the broken and the moribund swarm in their cold white beds. What gall, to suppose that a dreamer of tales can bring news of the human predicament to the doctors on their dread rounds!

All the same, I had my obligation; I had been summoned to

---

*A term now grown severely stale, but I have been unable to discover a substitute.

tell the doctors a story, to speak out of the enlarging lung of chronicle. And so, not suspecting what would come of it, I began to read out a narrative about a sexually active faraway planet where the birth of children is no longer welcome, and finally, for prurient technological reasons, no longer possible. The most refined intellectuals on that planet are those least willing to bear children—not only because children interfere with the *tidiness* of any planet, but also because the intellectuals have discovered that children interrupt: they interrupt careers, journeys, vacations, appointments, games, erotic attachments, telephone calls, self-development, education, meditation, and other enlightened, useful, and joyous pursuits. A number of children manage to get born in any case, illicitly and improbably, and I wish I could tell you how these children turned out, and what happened to that sophisticated though unlucky planet afterward; my intent, however, is not to disclose the destiny of the children, but rather the behavior of the doctors. Perhaps it is enough to mention that in my story everything ended in barbarism and savagery.

Now you can hear even from this truncated, raw, bare-bones, tablet-sized account that the story I had chosen to present to the doctors was part parable, part satire, outfitted in drollery and ribaldry, in deepest imitative tertiary debt to the history of literary forms—Kafka, Swift, Chaucer; drenched, above all, in metaphor. The tale of a lascivious planet too earnestly self-important to tolerate children could only have been directed against artifice and malice, sophistry and self-indulgence; it could only have pressed for fruitfulness and health, sanity and generosity, bloom and—especially—continuity. My story, I thought, was a contrivance that declared itself on the side of life; and therefore, presumably, on the side of the doctors themselves. In the lovely lists of parable, how light the lance, how economical, how sudden! To be able to unfold artifice and malice and self-indulgence, fruitfulness, health, sanity, generosity, bloom, continuity—and never once the need to drag these blatant carcasses of heavy nouns across the greensward! The power and charm of fable are in the force of its automatic metaphorical engine, and in bringing metaphor to the doctors, surely I was obeying their captain, and opening the inmost valve of the imagining heart?

But among the doctors something was rumbling just then— a stirring, a murmuring, an angry collective hiss. The doctors, their captain included, were not simply discontent; they were all at once ranked before me as a white-coated captious tribe, excited, resentful, bewildered, belligerent. They accused me of obscurantism, of having mean-spiritedly resolved to perplex. They wanted—they demanded—the principles of ordinary telling. They wanted—*this* is what they wanted—plain speech. They were appalled by metaphor (the shock of metaphor), by fable, image, echo, irony, satire, obliqueness, double meaning, the call to interpret, the call to penetrate, the call to comment and diagnose. They were stung by what they instantly named "ambiguity." They protested, they repudiated, the writer's instruments and devices as arcane, specialist, oracular, technical. Before the use of the metaphor they felt themselves stripped and defenseless: they complained that the examining tables had been turned on them; that their reasoning authority had fallen away; that they stood before the parable as a naked laity; that I had sickened them.

And so I had. I had sickened the doctors—or at least the intrusion of metaphorical thinking had.

Now the argument may be urged that physicians are themselves abundantly given to metaphorical speech and thought; that they live every hour under the raucous wing of the Angel of Death and Crippling, whose devastating imagery they cannot deny, and whose symbols they read cell by cell, X-ray by X-ray; that ambiguity and interpretation are ineluctably in the grain of their tasks; that all medical literature, however hidden in obscure vocabularies in abstruse journals, is, case after case, a literature of redemption through parable: new cases remember past cases. And, finally, that no cast of mind is more surrendered to the figurative than the namers of organs: the color-bearing circular diaphragm of the eye, that flower of the mind's eye called *iris* after the rainbow goddess; the palisades cells and the goblet cells; the pancreatic islets of Langerhans, the imagination's archipelago.

But dismiss all this. Say that the doctors have rejected metaphor as not of their realm—as inimical to their gravity. They do it because they have one certainty: they know that, whatever else they may be, they are serious men and women. They may be too frail, as their captain proposed, to enter into psychological twinship with the even frailer souls of the sick; but the struggle to heal, the will to repair the shattered, the will to redeem and make whole— this is what we mean when we speak of lives lived under the conscientious pressure of our moral nature. And metaphor, what is metaphor? Frivolity. Triviality. Lightness of mind. Irrational immateriality. Baubles. To talk in metaphor to serious men and women, indeed to talk *of* metaphor to serious men and women, is to disengage oneself from the great necessary bond of community: it is to disengage oneself from the capacity to put humanity before pleasure, clear judgment before sensation, useful acts before the allure of words. It is to cut oneself off from the heat of human pity—and all for the sake of a figure of speech.

If the doctors think this way—if a great many other serious men and women think this way—it may be, first, because they associate metaphor with writers and artists of every sort, and, second, because they associate writers and artists with what we always call "inspiration." It isn't only that doctors like to keep away from inspiration on grounds of science and empiricism and predictability. Nor is it, for serious people, mainly a matter of valuing stability over spontaneity, or responsibility over elation. Something there is in inspiration that hints of wildness—a wildness even beyond the quick unearned streak of "knowing" that brings resolution without warning. Serious people are used to feeling an at-homeness in their minds. Inspiration is an intruder, a kidnapper of reason, a burglar who shoots the watchdogs dead. Inspiration chases off sentries and censors and monitors. Inspiration instigates reckless cliff-walking; it sweeps its quarry to the edge of unfamiliar abysses. Inspiration is the secret sharer who flies out of pandemonium.

All these characteristics do suggest that inspiration is allied to the stuff of metaphor. Isn't metaphor the poetry-making faculty itself? And where does the poetry-making faculty derive from, if not from inspiration? It is in fact a truism to equate poetry and inspiration, metaphor and inspiration. Though truisms are sometimes at least partly true, my purpose is to tell something else about metaphor. I mean to persuade the doctors that metaphor belongs less to inspiration than it does to memory and pity. I want to argue that metaphor is one of the chief agents of our moral nature, and that the more serious we are in life, the less we can do without it.

Begin, then, with the history of inspiration. Inspiration is one of those ideas that can, without objection, claim a clear history; but never the history of poetry. Its genesis is in natural religion, or, rather, in the religion of nature. To come to Emerson again: in an essay rather unsuitably called "History"—it might more accurately have been named "Anti-History," since it annihilates the distinction between Then and Now—Emerson recounts a picturesque conversation with "a lady with whom I was riding in a forest [who] said to me that the woods always seemed to her *to wait*, as if the genii who inhabit them suspended their deeds until the wayfarer had passed onward; a thought which poetry has celebrated in the dance of the fairies, which breaks off on the approach of human feet." Now that is a very pretty story, but only because in Emerson's day the woods around Concord were safe, and the civilization of genii and fairies long finished. Inspiration may end in daydream or fancy, but it sets out in terror. For us Pan is all poetry, a charming faun with a flute; among the Greeks he caused panic. Fairies and all the other spirits of natural religion were once malevolent powers profoundly feared. Devout Athenians on the third day of the important Anthesterion festival took the ceremony of frightening away the spirits as a somber religious duty. Emerson, reading history as benign nature, reads natural religion as a sublime illumination—"The idiot, the Indian, the child and the unschooled farmer's boy," he announces, "stand nearer to the light by which nature is to be read, than the dissector or the antiquary"—whereas for its historical adherents, its flesh-and-blood congregants, the religion of nature was mainly panic, dread, and desperate appeasement of the uncanny. Poetry, including Emersonian poetizing, seeps in only after two millennia have exhausted and silenced the fairies; only after the great god Pan is indisputably, unexaggeratedly, dead. In natural religion there are no metaphors; the genii are *there*; the poetry is not yet born.

The genii are there, potent and ubiquitous. They are in the birds and in the beasts, in the brooks, in the muttering oaks—the majestic Zeus himself got his start as a god who spoke out of the oak tree. Divinity lives even in a notched stick. In natural religion, there is nothing that is not an organ of omen, divination, enthusiasm. But when we reflect on this "enthusiasm"—a Greek locution, *én theos*, the god within—there is one instance of it so celebrated that it comes to mind before all others. The syllables themselves have turned into the full sweetness of poetry: the Oracle at Delphi; the sound of it is as beautiful as "nightingale." The cult of the Eleusinian Mysteries remains a secret, a speculation, to this day; we know only that there was immersion in a river, that sacred cakes were eaten, a sacred potion drunk, and the birth of a holy infant proclaimed. The exalting ritual performed by the initiates, shrouded all through antiquity, had no public scribe or record-keeper. The events at Eleusis continue inscrutable. But about what went on at the shrine of Apollo at Delphi almost everything has been disclosed. We can still follow its process, and there is nothing metaphoric in any of it.

Apollo was a latecomer to Delphi. Earthquake-prone, the place had once belonged to Gaea, the earth-goddess, and the shrine was built over a gorge, or pit; a sort of saucer in the ground, within sight of the mountains of Parnassus. Excavations have uncovered no crack or opening of any kind in the floor of the saucer, but a certain gas was said to issue from a hole in the earth: the narcotic stench of decomposition—below lay the carcass of the terrible python Apollo slew. An underground stream flowed there, prophetic waters called Kassotis; these too had narcotic properties. The agent of divination—the enthusiast, the sibyl possessed by the god—was at first, apparently, a young virgin. Then the rules were changed, no one seems to know why, and now the votary had to be a respectable, often married, woman of at least fifty—

she was, however, required to dress up as a maiden. This was the Pythoness, or Pythia, Apollo's oracle, the incarnation of everything we mean, in our own civilization and language, by inspiration.

Her method was to induce frenzy. She chewed the leaves of a narcotic plant, drank from the narcotic spring, breathed in the narcotic vapor. A number of attending priests, called the Holy Ones, members of important local families, waited until she seemed on the brink of seizure, and then led her to a tripod, the seat of the god's speaking. These notables already had in hand the question the god was to treat. The answer came, in the moment of possession, from the mouth of the sibyl either as howls or as murmurs—cascades of gibberish flooded the shrine. Here is how the Swedish novelist Pär Lagerkvist imagines the moment of possession:

> It was he! He! It was he who filled me, I felt it, I knew it! He was filling me, he was annihilating me and filling me utterly with himself, with his happiness, his joy, his rapture. Ah, it was wonderful to feel his spirit, his inspiration coming upon me—to be his, his alone, to be possessed by god. . . .
>
> But the feeling mounted and mounted; it was still full of delight and joy but it was too violent, too overpowering, it broke all bounds—it broke me, hurt me, it was immeasurable, demented— and I felt my body beginning to writhe, to writhe in agony and torment; being tossed to and fro and strangled, as if I were to be suffocated. But I was not suffocated, and instead I began to hiss forth dreadful, anguished sounds, utterly strange to me, and my lips moved without my will; it was not I who was doing this. And I heard shrieks, loud shrieks; I didn't understand them, they were quite unintelligible, yet it was I who uttered them. They issued from my gaping mouth, though they were not mine. It was not myself at all, I was no longer I, I was his, his alone; it was terrible, terrible and nothing else!
>
> How long it went on I don't know. I had no sense of time while it was happening. Nor do I know how I afterwards got out of the holy of holies or what happened next; who helped me and took care of me. I awoke in the house next to the temple where I lived during this time, and they said I had lain in a deep sleep of utter exhaustion. And they told me that the priests were much pleased with me.

That, of course, is the drama of fiction. The priestly role was more intellectual, and certainly political, and lends itself less to theatrical reconstruction. When the Pythia's vatic fit was over, the priests had to take up the task of interpretation. It is conceivable that their interpretations were composed in advance, since the questioner's predicament had been submitted in advance, and often in writing. Being both human and bureaucratic, the priests now and then accepted a bribe in exchange for a politically favorable interpretation. Still, they were without doubt men of no small gifts; they were in fact devoted to their ingenious versifying, and would sometimes set their interpretations in the meter of Homer or Hesiod, or else in succinctly ambiguous prose that, no matter what the future brought, was always on the mark. The replies of the oracle were famously broad, ranging from family-court matters to statecraft. The priests, like most priests everywhere, were conservative: when much of Greece seemed ready to give up the practice of human sacrifice, the Delphic Oracle had nothing to say against it, and the priests continued to approve it.* There were

---

*But current anthropology, I am told, has it that human sacrifice was, in fact, never practiced in Greece at all. This view diverges sharply from the scholarship of, say, sixty years ago. The thirteenth edition of the *Encyclopaedia Britannica*, for instance, describes the Thargelia festival, an agricultural celebration, as "a purifying and expiatory ceremony. While the people offered the first-fruits of the earth to the god in token of thankfulness, it was at the same time necessary to propitiate him. . . . Two men, . . . the ugliest that could be found, were chosen to die, one for the men, the other (according to some, a woman) for the women. On the day of the sacrifice they were led round with strings of figs on their necks, and whipped on the genitals with rods of figwood and squills. When they reached the place of sacrifice on the shore, they were stoned to death, their bodies burnt, and the ashes thrown into the sea (or over the land, to act as a fertilizing influence). The whipping with squills and figwood was intended to stimulate the reproductive energies of the [sacrificial victim], who represented the god of vegetation, annually slain to be born again. It is agreed that an actual human sacrifice took place on this occasion, replaced in later times by a milder form of expiation."

Apparently it is no longer agreed, and the claim is as dated as an old encyclopaedia article tends to become. But whether human sacrifice was actually or only symbolically practiced in Greece, the issue—the concept as applying to the imagination of a civilization—is still very much to the point. In the history of comparative culture, what counts is whether the idea of human sacrifice is present at all, in any embodiment, even that of legend, and what this might portend (since both pity and pitilessness require teaching) in the necessary nurturing of pity. Consider the nature of the internalization of the same idea at the dawn of

some liberal decisions nonetheless: the occasional manumission of slaves, for instance. Delphi, the fount of inspiration, was in essence the seat of pragmatism. Santayana, recalling that Plato too identifies madness with inspiration, and acknowledging that the "aboriginal madness" of the oracle could produce "faith, humility, courage, conformity," yet marvels that "the most intelligent and temperate of nations submitted, in the most crucial matters, to the inspiration of idiots."

All this does not mean to insinuate—it would be an untruth—that because the oracle's infusion of the god-spirit at Delphi had nothing to do with our idea of religion as conscience, Greece was a society that paid no attention to the moral life. We know otherwise, from Socrates, Plato, and Aristotle preëminently; we know otherwise from Greek drama, Greek poetry, Greek history, Greek speculation. What else is the story of Antigone if not a story of conscience? What else is tragedy if not moral seriousness? And beyond these, the mind of science, the mind of art, are Greek. There is not one Greece, but a hundred: heroes side by side with slaves, reason side by side with magic, the self-restraint of Epictetus side by side with sensuousness. It is the Greeks, W. H. Auden reminds us, "who have taught us, not to think—that all human beings have always done—but to think about our thinking." If one nation can be measured as more intelligent than all other nations that ever were, or were to be, that is how we can measure the Greeks. And the priestly interpretations at Delphi were them-

---

Judaism, in its earliest hour: Judaism's first social task, so to speak. The story of Abraham and Isaac announces, in the voice of divinity itself, the end of human sacrifice forever afterward. The binding of Isaac both represents and introduces the supreme scriptural valuation of innocent life. The sacrifice of Isaac never occurred and was not permitted to occur—the image and the possibility are wiped out once and for all. A heavenly instruction directs Abraham to the ram in the thicket—after which the idea of human sacrifice in the service of the divine is never again broached in the line of Jewish thinking (and without a moment's regression in a people well known for backsliding).

The ram in the thicket is the herald of metaphor—a way station to the ultimate means of God-encounter, which will more and more distance itself from the altar (a literal-minded device that will finally vanish) to become purely verbal and textual. And metaphor, as I hope to show, is the herald of human pity.

selves grounded in an immensity of human understanding: ambiguity is psychology; ambiguity is how we sort things out, how we decide. "Nothing in excess" is a Delphic inscription.

Yet what was missing in the glory that was Greece was metaphor. Perhaps this statement shocks with its instant absurdity. You will want to say, What? A nation of myth, and you claim it has no metaphor? Aren't myths the greatest metaphors of all? And surely the most blatant? Or you will want to listen again to the priestly interpretations at Delphi: aren't these, in their fertility of implication, exactly what we mean by metaphoric language?

The answer in both instances, I think, is no. Remember that mythology took on the inwardness of poetry only when the gods were no longer efficacious, only after they had ascended out of the reality of their belief-system into the misted charms of enchantment. And even now, when we read that Apollo slew the python, what do we learn? We learn that snakes are dangerous and that the gods are brave and strong. For Apollo's constituents, the aversion to snakes—and also their strange sacredness—was confirmed; so was the reverence for Apollo. If there is a lesson, it is either that the bravery of the gods ought to be emulated; or else that it is hubris to suppose the bravery of the gods can be emulated. But why, you will say, why speak of "learning," of "lessons"? Do we go to the gods for schooling, or for self-revelation? Look, you will say, how humanly resplendent: each god represents an aspect of human passion. Here is beauty, here is lust, here is wisdom, here is chance, here is courage, here is mendacity, here is war, and so on and so on. Isn't that metaphoric enough for you?

Observe: there is no god or goddess who stands for the still small voice of conscience.

As for the Delphic riddles: they were recipes, not standards. They were directions, not principles. Nor was there any consistent social compassion inherent in their readings. The oracle remembered nothing. The voice of conscience did not speak through the god at Delphi, or through any of the gods. Moral seriousness could be found again and again in Greece, especially among the geniuses; it could be found almost anywhere, except in religion, among the people. The reason is plain. Inspiration has no memory. Inspiration is spontaneity; its opposite is memory, which is history as judgment. When conscience flashed out of Greece, as it did again and again, it did so idiosyncratically, individually, without a base in a community model or a collective history. There was no heritage of a common historical experience to universalize ethical feeling. To put it otherwise: there was no will to create a universal moral parable; there was no will to enter and harness metaphor for the sake of a universal conscience.

By turning their religious life into poetry, we have long since universalized the Greeks. They are our psychology. But that is our doing, not theirs. The Greeks, with all their astonishments, and in spite of the serenity of "Nothing in excess," were brutally parochial. This ravishingly civilized people kept slaves. Greeks enslaved foreigners and other Greeks. Anyone captured in war was dragged back as a slave, even if he was a Greek of a neighboring polis. In Athens, slaves, especially women, were often domestic servants, but of one hundred and fifty thousand adult male slaves, twenty thousand were set to work in the silver mines, in ten-hour shifts, in tunnels three feet high, shackled and lashed; the forehead of a retrieved runaway was branded with a hot iron. Aristotle called slaves "animate tools," forever indispensable, he thought, unless you were a utopian who believed in some future invention of automatic machinery. In Athens it was understood that the most efficient administrator of many slaves was someone who had himself been born into slavery and then freed; such a man would know, out of his own oppressive experience with severity, how to bear down hard. A foreigner who was not enslaved lived under prejudice and restriction. Demosthenes tells about the humiliation of a certain Euxitheus, a prosperous Athenian whose citizenship suddenly came under a cloud because his father happened to be overheard speaking with an un-Athenian accent. Euxitheus had to prove that his father had in fact been Athenian-born, or his own status would drop to that of resident alien, stripping him of his property and his rights, and endangering his freedom. That the Greeks called all foreigners "barbarians" is notorious enough; but it was not so much a category as a jeer. It imputed to all foreign languages the animal sound of a grunt or a bark: bar-bar, bar-bar.

So there is much irony in our having universalized Greece through poetizing it. The Greeks were not only not universalists; they scorned the idea. They were proud of despising the stranger. They had no pity for the stranger. They were proud of hating their enemies. As a society they never undertook to imagine what it was to be the Other; the outsider; the alien; the slave; the oppressed; the sufferer; the outcast; the opponent; the barbarian who owns feelings and deserves rights. And that is because they did not, as a society, cultivate memory, or search out any historical metaphor to contain memory.

We come now to a jump. A short jump across the Mediterranean; a long jump to the experience of another people, less lucky than the Greeks, and—perhaps because less lucky—collectively obsessed with the imagination of pity; or call it the imagination of reciprocity. The Jews—they were named Hebrews then—were driven to a preoccupation with history and with memory almost at the start of their hard-pressed desert voyage into civilization. The distinguished Greeks had their complex polity, their stunning cities; in these great cities they nurtured unrivaled sophistications. The Jews began as primitives and nomads, naive shepherds as remote from scientific thinking as any other primitives; in their own culture, when at length they established their simple towns, they had no art or theater or athletics, and never would have. A good case can be made—though not a watertight one—that the Jews did not become students and scholars until they learned how from the Greeks—surely the classroom is a Greek innovation. And, finally, the Jews carried the memory of four hundred years of torment. Unlike the citizen-Greeks, their history did not introduce civics; it introduced bricks without straw, and the Jews who escaped from Rameses' Egypt were a rough slave rabble, a mixed multitude, a rowdy discontented rebellious ragtag mob. A nation of slaves is different from a nation of philosophers.

Out of that slavery a new thing was made. It should not be

called a "philosophy," because philosophy was Greek, and this
was an envisioning the Greeks had always avoided, or else had
never wished to invent, or else had been unable to invent. I have
all along been calling this new thing "metaphor." It came about
because thirty generations of slavery in Egypt were never
forgotten—though not as a form of grudge-holding. A distinction
should be drawn between grudge-holding and memory; they are
never the same. As for grudge-holding, it was forbidden to the ex-
slave rabble. The helping hand, says Exodus, reaches out to your
enemy. If you meet your enemy's donkey or ox going astray, you
must bring it back to him. If you happen on your enemy's donkey
collapsed under its burden, you may not pass by; you must help
your enemy relieve the animal. The Egyptians were cruel enemies
and crueler oppressors; the ex-slaves will not forget—not out of
spite for the wrongdoers, but as a means to understand what it is
to be an outcast, a foreigner, an alien of any kind. By turning the
concrete memory of slavery into a universalizing metaphor of reciprocity, the ex-slaves discover a way to convert imagination into
a serious moral instrument.

Now a fair representation of the Delphic Oracle is not the work
of a minute; this we have seen, and it is a paradox. Inspiration,
which is as sudden and as transient as an electrical trajectory, takes
a long time to delineate, possibly because latency (a hidden prior
knowing) and unintelligibility (the mysterious grace that surpasseth
understanding) are in its nature. It is in the nature of metaphor to
be succinct. Four hundred years of bondage in Egypt, rendered
as metaphoric memory, can be spoken in a moment; in a single
sentence. What this sentence is, we know; we have built every
idea of moral civilization on it. It is a sentence that conceivably
sums up at the start every revelation that came afterward. It has
given birth and tongue to saints and prophets, early and late. Its
first dreamers are not its exclusive owners and operators; it belongs
to everyone. That is the point of its having been dreamed into
existence at all.

The sentence is easily identified. It follows sixteen verses behind
"Love thy neighbor as thyself," but majestic as that is, it is not
the most majestic, because its subject is not the most recalcitrant.

Our neighbor is usually of our own tribe, and looks like us and talks like us. Our neighbor is usually familiar; our neighbor is usually not foreign, or of another race. "Love thy neighbor as thyself" is a glorious, civilizing, unifying sentence, an exhortation of consummate moral beauty, difficult of performance, difficult *in* performance. And it reveals at once the little seed of parable: the phrase "as thyself." "Thyself"—that universe of feeling—is the model. "*As* thyself" becomes the commanding metaphor. But we are still, with our neighbor, in Our Town. We are still, with the self, in psychology. We have not yet penetrated to history and memory. The more compelling sentence carries us there—Leviticus 19, verse 34, and you will hear in it history as metaphor, memory raised to parable:

> The stranger that sojourneth with you shall be unto you as the home-born among you, and you shall love him as yourself; because you were strangers in the land of Egypt.

Leviticus 24, verse 22, insists further: "You shall have one manner of law, the same for the stranger as for the home-born." A similar injunction appears in Exodus, and again in Deuteronomy, and again in Numbers. Altogether, this precept of loving the stranger, and treating the stranger as an equal both in emotion and under law, appears thirty-six times in the Pentateuch. It is there because a moral connection has been made with the memory of bondage. Leviticus 24, verse 22, demands memory, and then converts memory into metaphor: "Because you were strangers in the land of Egypt." Bondage becomes a metaphor of pity for the outsider; Egypt becomes the great metaphor of reciprocity. "And a stranger shall you not oppress," says Exodus 23, verse 8, "for you know the heart of a stranger, seeing you were strangers in the land of Egypt." There stands the parable; there stands the sacred metaphor of belonging, one heart to another. Without the metaphor of memory and history, we cannot imagine the life of the Other. We cannot imagine what it is to be someone else. Metaphor is the reciprocal agent, the universalizing force: it makes possible the power to envision the stranger's heart.

In the absence of this metaphoric capability, what are the consequences? The Romans originally had a single word, *hostis*, to signify both enemy and stranger. Nowhere beyond the reach of the Pentateuch did the alien and the home-born live under the same code; in early Roman law, every alien was classed as an enemy, devoid of rights. In Germanic law the alien was *rechtsunfähig*, a pariah with no access to justice. The Greeks made slaves of the stranger and then taunted him with barks. There have been, and still are, religio-political systems that have incorporated the teaching of contempt, turning the closest neighbors into the most despised strangers—a loathing expressed in words like "untouchable," "dhimmi," "deicide." In our own country, slavery thrived under the wing of a freedom-proclaiming Constitution until the middle of the last century. And in 1945, a British camera on a single day in a single German death camp just liberated photographed a bulldozer sweeping into five pits five thousand starved and abused human corpses at a time, a thousand to a pit, all of them having been judged unfit for the right to live.

By now you will have noticed that I have been quoting Scripture—a temptation that is always perilous, not only because it is a famously devilish pastime, but also because it induces the sermonizing tone, which for some reason always seems to settle in the nasal cavities. For this I apologize. My intended subject, after all, has not been national character or ethics or religion or history; it has not even, appearances to the contrary, been Matthew Arnold's fertile delta: Hebraism and Hellenism. What I have been thinking of is *language*—explicitly the work of metaphor.

And it is time now to ask what metaphor *is*. One way to begin is to recognize that metaphor is what inspiration is not. Inspiration is ad hoc and has no history. Metaphor relies on what has been experienced before; it transforms the strange into the familiar. This is the rule even of the simplest metaphor—Homer's wine-dark sea, for example. If you know wine, says the image, you will know the sea; the sea is for sailors, but wine is what we learn at home. Inspiration calls for possession and increases strangeness. Metaphor uses what we already possess and reduces strangeness. Inspiration belongs to riddle and oracle. Metaphor belongs to clarification and humane conduct. This is the meaning of the contrast between the Oracle at Delphi and the parable of servitude in Egypt. Inspiration attaches to the mysterious temples of anti-language. Metaphor overwhelmingly attaches to the house of language.

Should it, then, seem perplexing that both the oracle and the parable are identically dedicated to interpretation? The chief business of the priests at Delphi is practical interpretation. The incessant allusion to Egyptian bondage is again for the purpose of usable interpretation. And still the differences are total. Because the Delphic priests must begin each time with a fresh-hatched inspiration, with the annihilation of experience, they cannot arrive at any universal principle or precept. Principles and precepts derive from an accumulation of old event. Delphi never has old event; every event in that place is singular; the cry from the tripod is blazingly individual, particular, peculiar unto itself. From the tripod rises the curse of nepenthe; amnesia; forgetting; nor is it the voice of the race of humanity and its continuities we hear. The tragedy of the Delphic priests is not that their interpretations are obliged to start from gibberish. After all, what goes in as raw gibberish comes out as subject to rational decision, and it is more than conceivable that social principles might be extracted from a body of such decisions. But the priests think consciously only of their own moment. Their system is not organized toward the universalizing formulation. The tragedy of the priests is that, cut off from the uses of history, experience, and memory, they are helpless to make the future. They may, in a manner of speaking, "prophesy," with whatever luck such prophets have,*

---

*A parenthetical bemusement. Nowadays much of American literature is included in this Delphic fix. Certain novelists claim that fiction must express a pure autonomy—must become a self-sufficient language-machine—in order to be innovative; others strip language bare of any nuance. These aestheticians and reductionists, seeming opposites, both end inevitably at the gates of nihilism. A certain style of poetry is so far committed to the exquisitely self-contained that it has long since given up on that incandescent dream we call criticism of life. Abandoning attachments, annihilating society, the airless verse of self-scrutiny ends, paradoxically, in loss of the self. A certain style of criticism becomes a series

but they cannot construct a heritage. They have nothing to pass on. They cannot give birth to metaphor; one thing does not suggest another thing; in a place where each heart is meant to rave on in its uniqueness, there is no means for the grief of one heart to implicate the understanding of another heart. In the end, inspiration and its devices turn away from the hope of regeneration.

Metaphor, though never to be found at Delphi, is also a priest of interpretation; but what it interprets is memory. Metaphor is compelled to press hard on language and storytelling; it inhabits language at its most concrete. As the shocking extension of the unknown into our most intimate, most feeling, most private selves, metaphor is the enemy of abstraction. Irony is of course implicit. Think how ironic it would be, declares the parable of Egypt, if you did *not* take the memory of slavery as your exemplar! Think how ironic your life would be if you passed through it without the power of connection! Novels, those vessels of irony and connection, are nothing if not metaphors. The great novels transform experience into idea because it is the way of metaphor to transform memory into a principle of continuity. By "continuity" I mean nothing less than literary seriousness, which is unquestionably a branch of life-seriousness.

Now if all this has persisted in sounding more like a lecture in morals than the meditation on language it professes to be, it may be worth turning to that astonishing comment in T. S. Eliot's indispensable essay on what he terms "concentration" of experience. "Someone said," says Eliot in "Tradition and the Individual Talent," " 'The dead writers are remote from us because we *know* so much more than they did.' Precisely, and they are that which we know." He is speaking of the transforming effect of memory. The dead writers have turned metaphoric; they contain our experience, and they alter both our being and our becoming. Here

---

of overlapping solipsisms—consider those types of "deconstruction" that end only in formulae. Insofar as these incommunicado literary movements are interested in interpretation at all, they have their ear at the Pythian tripod.

we have an exact counterpart of biblical memory: *because you were strangers in Egypt*. Through metaphor, the past has the capacity to imagine us, and we it. Through metaphorical concentration, doctors can imagine what it is to be their patients. Those who have no pain can imagine those who suffer. Those at the center can imagine what it is to be outside. The strong can imagine the weak. Illuminated lives can imagine the dark. Poets in their twilight can imagine the borders of stellar fire. We strangers can imagine the familiar hearts of strangers.

PERMISSIONS ACKNOWLEDGMENTS

A NOTE ON THE TYPE

This book was set in a digitized version of Janson, a redrawing of type cast from matrices long thought to have been made by the Dutchman Anton Janson, who was a practicing type founder in Leipzig during the years 1668–87. However, it has been conclusively demonstrated that these types are actually the work of Nicholas Kis (1650–1702), a Hungarian, who most probably learned his trade from the master Dutch type founder Dirk Voskens. The type is an excellent example of the influential and sturdy Dutch types that prevailed in England up to the time William Caslon developed his own incomparable designs from them.

Composed by Crane Typesetting Service,
Barnstable, Massachusetts

Printed and bound by The Haddon Craftsmen,
Scranton, Pennsylvania

Typography and binding design by
Dorothy Schmiderer Baker